P9-EDS-934

THE STOCK OPTIONS MANUAL

THE
STOCK OPTIONS
MANUAL

GARY L. GASTINEAU

McGRAW-HILL BOOK COMPANY
New York   St. Louis   San Francisco   Auckland
Düsseldorf   Johannesburg   Kuala Lumpur   London
Mexico   Montreal   New Delhi   Panama   Paris
São Paulo   Singapore   Sydney   Tokyo   Toronto

Library of Congress Cataloging in Publication Data:

Gastineau, Gary L
  The stock options manual.

  Bibliography: p.
  1. Put and call options.   2. Hedging (Finance)–
Mathematical models.   I. Title.
HG6041.G38   332.6'45   75-16229

ISBN 0-07-022969-4

Copyright © 1975 by McGraw-Hill, Inc. All rights reserved.
Printed in the United States of America. No part of this publication
may be reproduced, stored in a retrieval system, or transmitted, in any
form or by any means, electronic, mechanical, photocopying, recording, or
otherwise, without the prior written permission of the publisher.

  3 4 5 6 7 8 9 0   MUBP   7 8 3 2 1 0 9 8 7 6

The author is not engaged in rendering legal, tax, accounting, or
similar professional services. While legal, tax, and accounting
issues covered in this book have been checked with sources
believed to be reliable, some questions–particularly in the area of
taxes–have not been resolved by the Internal Revenue Service or
the courts, and the accuracy and completeness of such information
and the opinions based thereon are not guaranteed. If legal,
accounting, tax, investment, or other expert advice is required,
the services of a competent practitioner should be obtained.

  The investment strategies outlined in this book are not suitable
for every investor, and no specific investment recommendations
are intended. Readers should satisfy themselves by a careful reading
of the Options Clearing Corporation prospectus and by seeking
competent investment advice that they thoroughly understand the
risks as well as the potential rewards of trading in options.

The editors for this book were W. Hodson Mogan and Ruth L. Weine,
the designer was Elliot Epstein, and the production
supervisor was Teresa F. Leaden. It was set in VIP Palatino
by Monotype Composition Co., Inc.

It was printed by The Murray Printing Company
and bound by The Book Press.

CONTENTS

FOREWORD

The success of The Chicago Board Options Exchange has both modified and strengthened the fundamental tenets of capital market theory. For 30 years most economists and students of portfolio theory have agreed that the buyer of common stocks faces two kinds of risk. One type of risk is a function of the fortunes of a particular corporation and that firm's relative valuation in the securities markets. If an investor diversifies his portfolio he can eliminate most of the risk associated with his particular choice of corporation for investment.

A second kind of risk cannot be diversified away by purchasing the securities of a number of companies. It is the systematic or market risk that stems from the tendency of stocks to move up or down together. Some hedge funds and sophisticated individual investors have tried to reduce their exposure to this market risk by offsetting long positions in one security with short positions in another. The average investor has never really had the wherewithal to participate in these hedging activities. As a result, the theorist's argument that the buyer of common stocks cannot avoid market risk has been borne out in practice.

The Chicago Board Options Exchange not only provides a way to hedge the market risk of a large stock portfolio; it also enables the small investor to hedge his positions. With other securities exchanges now joining the CBOE in trading listed stock options, every investor can adjust the market risk of his portfolio to suit his personal preferences. The recognition of the functional relation between risk and rate of return is a cornerstone of modern portfolio theory. Stock options increase an investor's range of risk-return choices.

Popular investment publications usually portray stock options as instruments of speculation. Only recently have writers for some leading periodicals begun to explore the implications of stock options for the conservative investor. This new emphasis on the conservative uses of stock options is not without hazards. Reading many articles on options, one is left with the impression that an option buyer is a speculator and an option writer is a conservative investor. The real world is not so simple, as the reader of this book will soon learn.

The controversial aspects of options have been of limited interest and concern to most investors because option trading has been a small, obscure sector of the securities business. The recent bear market and the surprising success of the CBOE have expanded public interest in options and awakened renewed criticism of option trading. Neither the widespread interest nor the criticism has been based on a full understanding of what options can and cannot do. This book should prove helpful to the investor or portfolio manager who wants to expand his understanding of options. It should also focus any criticism of option trading on the few real regulatory problems rather than on some widespread but false impressions of the nature and place of options in the securities markets.

Albert Madansky
University of Chicago
April 1975

PREFACE

I am fully aware that there are many women actively playing all kinds of roles in the stock market. Unfortunately, our language can become stilted and unmanageable when he/she or she/he is constantly repeated. For this reason, the pronoun "he" is used quite frequently as a generic term, and no offense is intended.

A number of people made important contributions to my understanding of key points discussed in the text and to the preparation of the manuscript itself. While it is impossible to remember the source of each suggestion, a number of individuals were conspicuously helpful. I am particularly indebted to Dr. Albert Madansky, not only for his useful comments, but for his crucial role in the development of the option evaluation model discussed in Chapter 7. Meyer Berman played the vital role of *shadchan* in bringing us together.

Other individuals who provided significant information or made important comments on the manuscript include Martin Askowitz, Jayusia P. Bernstein, Samuel M. Feder, Robert Kunzelman, Martin L. Leibowitz, Andrew A. Levy, Harry Markowitz, and Seymour Suskin. Finally, I wish to acknowledge the assistance of Mary Beth Minton, Catherine A. Swartz, and my wife, Nancy, for their help in preparing the manuscript. Many other contributions from my wife and other members of my family, while perhaps less tangible, were no less important.

Gary L. Gastineau

1 INTRODUCTION

The decision to write this book evolved from the author's strong and growing conviction that there is a major deficiency in the literature on put and call options. A large number of books on options and related topics have been published or reprinted since the Chicago Board Options Exchange (CBOE) began listed trading of call options in April 1973; so the deficiency is certainly not quantitative. The problem with most of these books is that they are either too elementary or too technical for the intelligent investor who is looking for a comprehensive discussion of the investment characteristics of stock options, but who lacks the mathematical background to tackle the specialized literature on capital market and portfolio theory. The advisory services are not much more helpful to the serious investor who wants to *understand* options.

In fairness, most of the basic option books and services do an excellent job of explaining the mechanics of the option market and the procedures for option trading to the beginning investor. On the other hand, the material available to the average investor rarely provides any really helpful insights into the evaluation of an option contract or into the impact of options on the risk-return characteristics of a portfolio. When specific option recommendations are provided, they are usually based on a discussion of the leverage features of the option contract and on a technical forecast of the direction of stock price movement. Occasionally a recommendation will be based on the relationship between present and historic option premiums.

In the author's judgment, the popular literature on options spends too much time translating a specific stock price forecast into the most leveraged way to play the expected move, and far too little time evaluating the risk-reward relationship of an option contract to its underlying stock. Leverage calculations and stock price forecasts have their place. Unless the forecast is unprecedentedly accurate, however, the option buyer who consistently pays more than a fair price for the options bought and the option writer who accepts inadequate premiums are virtually certain to experience substandard performance.

In contrast to the popular literature on options, a wealth of excellent material has been written by some of the finest minds in the academic community. Among the well-known economists who have done important work on options are Nobel laureate Paul Samuelson of M.I.T. and Burton Malkiel of Princeton, author of the recent bestseller, *A Random Walk Down Wall Street*. Other authors who have recently written key articles on options but who are not so well known outside the academic community are Robert Merton of M.I.T. and Fischer Black and Myron Scholes of the University of Chicago. Unfortunately, most of this academic literature is available only in specialized publications rarely found in neighborhood libraries. Furthermore, these articles are difficult to understand if the reader is not well versed in mathematics.

One of the principal purposes of this book is to make the significant findings of the academic community understandable and, it is hoped, useful to the intelligent investor. No attempt is made to explain the fine points of puts and calls to the investor who barely comprehends the difference between a common stock and a bond. On the other hand, most investors intelligent enough to use options can understand the investment characteristics and tax treatment of options and the principles behind the rational evaluation of an option contract. Investors who have a few years of experience with stocks and bonds should be able to use options rationally and effectively in investment programs.

The key concept which the investor must understand to make intelligent use of options is the *fair value* of an option contract. Option evaluation is the focus of most academic option literature but is rarely discussed in depth in books and articles prepared for broad distribution. Probably option evaluation is neglected by authors of most basic books on options for one or more of the following reasons:

1. The author does not understand option evaluation.

2. The fair value of an option is not the easiest concept to explain to the average reader.

3. It is easier to base option recommendations on stock price predictions than to worry about whether the option itself might be overpriced or underpriced.

4. Actually calculating the fair value of an option is even more difficult than explaining the concept.

Because of the importance of determining the fair value of an option contract before taking an option investment position, the significance of fair value will be briefly explained in this Introduction. If the reader finds this explanation difficult to understand, it is expanded on in Chapter 7, Section A. If the reader has no difficulty with the explanation of fair value, everything else in the book should be readily understandable.

Fair value   Assuming a call is not exercised or sold prior to its expiration date, its ultimate value will depend on the price of the underlying stock on the expiration date. Any price at which the call might be bought or sold during its life will reflect the buyer's and seller's respective estimates of the option's probable terminal value.

If the price of the stock is below the striking price of the call on the expiration date, the option is worthless to the buyer. The option writer, under these circumstances, will get to keep the entire call premium. If the price of the stock rises above the striking price as the expiration date approaches, the value of the buyer's position will climb point-for-point with the stock price while the writer's position will deteriorate point-for-point.

Figure 1-1 depicts the gain and loss positions of a call buyer and an uncovered writer in a hypothetical call option transaction. In this example, which for illustrative purposes neglects the effect of commissions, the buyer has purchased and the writer has sold a call option with a striking price of $100 for an option premium of $10. Starting at the left-hand side of the graph, the top line illustrates the uncovered writer's profit and loss position. As long as the price of the stock does not exceed $100 on the day the option expires, the writer keeps the entire $10 option premium. If the price of the stock rises to $120, the writer loses the premium plus another $10 per share. The call buyer's profit and loss position, represented by the line that starts on the lower left-hand side of the graph, exactly mirrors that of the writer. If the stock stays below $100, the buyer loses the entire investment.

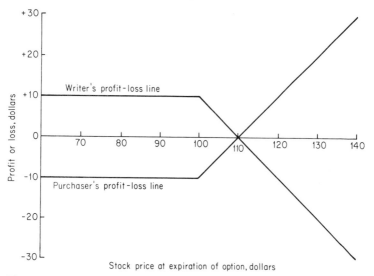

Figure 1-1. Profit-loss positions of the buyer and writer of a call.

If the stock rises to $120, the buyer gets back not only the premium but another $10 as well. If the stock sells at $110 at the end of the option period, neither buyer nor writer is better or worse off than before, except by the amount of commissions.

An important lesson to be learned from this graph is that the buyer's line and the writer's line move toward or away from the zero profit line together. If the option premium paid by the buyer increases by $1, the writer will receive $1 more. At every possible price of the stock on the expiration date, the value of the buyer's position will be reduced by the extra dollar paid for the option. Likewise, the writer's line will move up by $1 at every price because, at each possible price, the writer's position will be improved by the additional dollar received.

In their evaluation of a particular option, both buyer and writer consider, at least implicitly, a probability distribution of expected prices on the underlying stock at the date of expiration. The probability distributions envisioned by buyer and writer, respectively, may have different shapes. Neither of these hypothetical distributions need be objective nor have any direct relationship to past or future distributions of price changes.

It is possible to derive a relatively neutral probability distribution of future prices for any stock. This distribution is based primarily on the present stock price, the past volatility pattern of the stock, and a careful appraisal of factors likely to affect volatility over the life of the option. The curve in Figure 1-2 shows what this probability distribution might look like. This distribution is not strictly objective in that certain of its parameters are based on human judgment. It is, however, approximately neutral with respect to the probable direction of stock price changes. Using this probability distribution, it is possible to estimate the *expected* profit from an option for the buyer or the writer. We need only multiply the profit or loss at each possible stock price by the probability that the stock will sell at that price on the expiration date. The sum of these probability-weighted values will give us

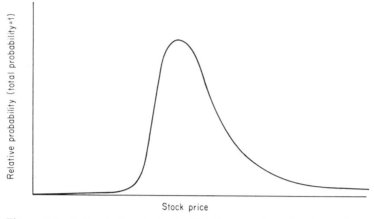

Figure 1-2. Estimated probability distribution of stock prices when option expires.

the expected profit or loss for the investor who takes that position.

If we neglect the effect of commissions, risk, present value adjustments, and other considerations too complex for this brief explanation, it is possible to make the following statement: *For every option there is an option price or premium at which, given the probable distribution of stock prices on the expiration date, the expected profit to both the buyer and the writer is equal to zero. This option price is the fair value of the option.* To phrase this point differently, the fair value of the option is simply the option price at which both the buyer and writer can expect to break even, excluding commissions. They will not break even on each individual transaction. However, over a long period and a large number of such transactions, they should expect no net profit or loss on transactions made at fair value.

Though supply and demand determine option *prices,* the *value* of an option is determined largely by the volatility of the underlying stock. Of course, *price* and *value* will ordinarily be related. If large swings in the stock's price are common, the option buyer will be willing to pay a larger premium for a call because chances of profit from a large upswing are better. Likewise, the option writer will insist on a larger premium because chances of substantial loss are increased.

While more details of this explanation of option value will be given in the chapters on option evaluation, it is important that the reader understand at the outset that options are different from virtually any other asset in a very important respect. Because the option has a limited life and derives its value from the underlying common stock, the *price* of an option does not *necessarily* reflect the *value* of that option to a rational investor at every moment in time. Unless both the buyer and writer use appropriate probability distributions of future stock prices in determining the price they are willing to pay or receive, the option price may differ significantly from fair value. A rational investor must consider whether or not an option is fairly priced *as well as* what he expects the stock price to do. Given the range of error inherent in any stock price prediction, consistently paying too much or receiving too little for an option contract will adversely affect investment results.

Superior investment results using options depend on the investor's ability (1) to buy options selling for less than fair value, (2) to write options selling for more than fair value, or (3) to predict accurately the *direction* in which the stock price will move. As difficult as it may be to determine the fair value of an option, it is probably easier to evaluate an option than to predict accurately and regularly whether a particular stock will rise or fall over the life of an option contract. Whether a technician, a fundamentalist, or an advocate of the random walk hypothesis, the reader can improve the odds by buying only undervalued options and writing only overvalued option contracts, consistent with other features of a personal investment strategy.

Other topics   While our overall focus is on the effect of options on the risk characteristics of a portfolio and on option evaluation, an attempt has been made to include material that will be useful to any option investor, regardless of the technique used to make option decisions. In particular, the chapters on taxes should be useful to investors interested in the implications of recent IRS rulings on the tax treatment of listed options.

The section on investment strategies should help either the beginner or the experienced portfolio manager to understand how one can use options to reduce or eliminate entirely the market risk of holding a diversified equity portfolio. While it is not possible to completely eliminate all types of investment risk with options, a carefully constructed, appropriately diversified portfolio of stock and option positions should give the investor a reasonably stable return on investment that is largely independent of the movement of broad market averages.

To avoid repeating or belaboring material familiar to nearly all option users, it will be assumed that the reader is familiar with The Options Clearing Corporation prospectus and has read one or more of the explanatory booklets distributed by brokerage firms. Several fairly complex equations have been reproduced in the section of the book which discusses option evaluation. However, these formulas are reproduced solely for the convenience of the mathematically inclined reader. No understanding of these equations is necessary to follow the argument of the text. While the reader may find high school algebra helpful, even this level of mathematical sophistication is not essential.

2 INVESTMENT CHARACTERISTICS OF BASIC OPTION CONTRACTS

Before we examine the investment characteristics of puts and calls, it will be helpful to define a few terms:

Option: A negotiable contract in which the writer, for a certain sum of money called the option premium, gives the buyer the right to demand, within a specified time, the purchase or sale by the writer of a specified number of shares of stock at a fixed price called the striking price. Unless otherwise stated, options are written for units of 100 shares. They are ordinarily issued for periods of less than 1 year.

Call option: An option to buy stock from the writer.

Put option: An option to sell stock to the writer.

Combination option: An option consisting of at least one put and one call. The individual option contracts which make up the combination are originally sold as a unit but they may be exercised or resold separately.

Straddle: A combination option consisting of one put and one call with a common striking price and a common expiration date.

Striking price or exercise price: The price at which an option is exercisable; i.e., the price per share the buyer of a call option must pay the writer for the stock or the price the writer must pay the holder of a put option.

Option premium: The price of an option contract. In this book the convention of stating the option premium in terms of dollars per share under option is adopted. If the total premium for a 100 share option is $1,000, the option premium is given as $10.

Expiration date: The date after which an option is void.

Option buyer: The individual or, less frequently, the institutional investor who buys options.

Option writer: The individual or institutional investor who sells or writes options.

This list of definitions is basic and purposely short. Additional definitions of option terms appear in the Glossary. Readers should be certain that they are familiar with these basic terms before they continue reading.

No matter how intricate an option investment strategy the investor may adopt, *the principal result of any option purchase or sale is to modify the risk characteristics of an investor's position.* This feature of options can have an important impact on portfolio structure and on the investor's overall risk exposure. Most investors find themselves at the mercy of trends in the stock and bond markets. If they are not satisfied with a modest return on short-term debt instruments (the high short-term interest rates of the past several years are an exception to the historic pattern), they have been forced to accept the market risks associated with investment in common stocks and bonds. Options can help reduce this market risk.

At times in the past an investor has been able to modify his risk exposure by splitting his portfolio between common stocks and bonds. Stock prices and bond prices have frequently been imperfectly correlated with one another. Whatever past patterns may have been, a variety of factors, such as more volatile interest rates and the broader impact of Federal Reserve Board activities in recent years, seem to have tied bond market and stock market fluctuations together.

As a result of the synchronization of recent bond and stock price movements, the investor who wishes to moderate his exposure to price fluctuations has been forced to reduce his exposure to both of these long-term security markets at the same time. While buying commercial paper and certificates of deposit damps fluctuations in the market value of a portfolio, few investors are willing to count on continuing high, short-term interest rates. Furthermore, the overall effect on a portfolio of swings in the value of the assets still invested in long-term securities may be greater than an investor finds acceptable, even after he switches part of his assets to short-term debt.

Stock options provide the investor with a unique way to modify his exposure to market risk. In particular, options traded on the Chicago Board Options Exchange, the American Stock Exchange, and now the Philadelphia-Baltimore-Washington Exchange are extremely versatile instruments for the modification of risk. This statement appears at odds with the popular view of call options as speculative tools which permit the small investor to obtain superior leverage on a small amount of capital. Options can fulfill much more important functions in an investment portfolio than this popular view suggests. Options can be of substantial aid to investors, large or small, who wish to reduce the exposure of their portfolios to market fluctuations.

Before undertaking a discussion of the complicated option investment strategies which may be required to achieve a particular relationship of risk and reward, we must examine the risk-reward characteristics of the basic put and call contracts as they apply to the option buyer and writer. In contrast to most discussions of the risk-reward characteristics of options which focus on the position either of the buyer or the writer, this chapter stresses the interrelationships between the buying and writing positions. Also, rather than content ourselves with brief written descriptions of the investment characteristics of these option contracts, we will return to the graphic method of illustrating profits and losses used in the Introduction. (These graphs will be discussed in much greater detail in Chapter 4, Section A.)

The graph in Figure 2-1 illustrates the basic investment characteristics of a call option from the respective viewpoints of the buyer and the writer. As most investors who have any

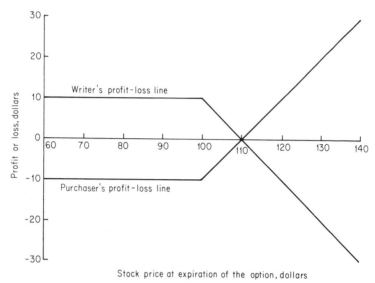

Figure 2-1. Profit-loss positions of the buyer and writer of a call.

familiarity with options are aware, an option buyer can never lose more than the premium paid for the option contract. On the other hand, if the price of the stock rises substantially over the life of the call option, the buyer's potential reward is theoretically unlimited. This position is illustrated by the line which begins in the lower left-hand corner of Figure 2-1.

The uncovered or "naked" call writer's position is, in many respects, the exact opposite of the call buyer's position. As the line which begins in the upper left-hand corner of Figure 2-1 illustrates, the call writer keeps the entire premium unless the stock price rises above the exercise price at the time the option expires or is exercised. In return for the option premium received, the writer of the call agrees to sell the stock at the striking price, no matter how high the stock may go. If the writer does not own the shares covered by the option, the writer's position deteriorates by $1 per share for every point by which the price of the stock exceeds the exercise price.

The essence of the uncovered call writer's position is that he or she can earn no more than the amount of the option premium and can lose a large amount if the price of the underlying stock runs up. In contrast to the call buyer who is fixing the risk at the amount of the premium and accepting the possibility of a widely varying reward, the uncovered writer is fixing the reward at the amount of the premium and accepting a highly variable risk.

Figure 2-2 illustrates the profit and loss positions of the buyer and writer of an uncovered put. In return for a fixed premium, the buyer of a put obtains the right to receive a reward that increases as the price of the underlying stock declines. As in the case of the call, both the buyer and the writer of a put option fix one side of the risk-reward equation and permit the other side to vary.

The offsetting risk-reward features of the buying and writing positions are clarified by these graphs. Any profit to the option buyer is exactly offset by a loss to the writer and vice versa. Neglecting transaction costs, *the net effect of an option transaction is simply a reallocation of risk and reward between buyer and writer.*

It is no accident that the word "premium" is used in both the insurance business and the option business. Option con-

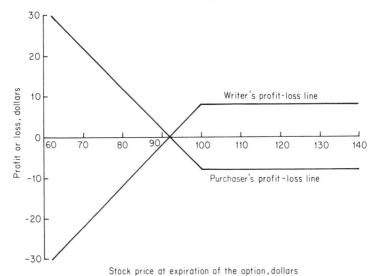

Figure 2-2. Profit-loss positions of the buyer and writer of a put.

tracts, like insurance policies, are used to protect the investor, whether writer or buyer, from unacceptable risk. In these graphs, the option buyer appears to be in a position analogous to that of the owner of an insurance policy. The uncovered option writer is like the insurance underwriter who accepts risk in return for premium income. When options are incorporated in an overall portfolio plan, however, the risks and rewards can change remarkably. For example, the call writer who has a position in the underlying stock will actually be *reducing* the overall volatility or market risk of his portfolio by writing the option because the premium he receives protects his assets in the event of a price decline, while his writer's obligation limits his gain on the upside. Although options do not increase or decrease the total level of risk in the financial system, *both parties to a particular option transaction can reduce their portfolio risk simultaneously through a combination of stock, option, and short-term debt positions.* Chapter 4 will cover the ways in which this unusual and desirable result can be accomplished. The purpose here has been to define and illustrate the risk-reward features of the simplest option positions to help the reader better understand the structure and functions of option markets. These markets will be the subject of the next chapter.

3 THE HISTORY AND STRUCTURE OF OPTION MARKETS

A. A SHORT HISTORY OF OPTIONS

Like any other financial instrument, options can serve either constructive or destructive purposes. The principal constructive feature of options is that they enable an investor to systematically increase or decrease the amount and kind of risk he accepts. Whether the option pertains to real estate or to securities, the seller or grantor of an option typically forgoes the opportunity for further appreciation in the value of an asset he owns in return for the payment of an option premium which reduces his loss in the event the value of the asset drops. The buyer of an option is able to control a larger quantity of assets through the payment of option premiums than he would be able to control if he purchased the assets outright. Though the option buyer benefits from any increase in the value of an asset, his potential loss is limited to the amount of the option premium.

Combinations of purchases and sales of options and related assets permit the astute investor to structure the risk-reward parameters of his investment position within the framework of permissible and available option contracts. The fact that an investor can structure risk and reward in practically any way he desires suggests that options should be a highly regarded financial tool, and that options should be widely used by investors with a variety of attitudes toward risk. In fact, options have not been highly regarded or widely used. Furthermore, the history of options is replete with occasions when unregulated option trading contributed to speculative boom and bust because options were used for questionable purposes.

Though the terms of option contracts have changed over the years, the concept of the option was in use by the ancients. Extensive research might uncover earlier examples, but the following quotation from Aristotle indicates that options were familiar to the ancient Greeks:

There is an anecdote of Thales the Milesian and his financial device, which involves a principle of universal application, but is attributed to him on account of his reputation for wisdom. He was reproached for his poverty, which was supposed to show that philosophy was of no use. According to the story, he knew by his skill in the stars while it was yet winter that there would be a great harvest of olives in the coming year; so, having a little money, he gave deposits for the use of all the olive presses in Chios and Miletus, which he hired at a low price because no one bid against him. When the harvest time came, and many wanted them all at once and of a sudden, he let them out at any rate which he pleased, and made a quantity of money. Thus he showed the world that philosophers can easily be rich if they like. . . .

Aristotle's *Politics*, Book One, Chapter Eleven, Jowett translation

The Greeks had no monopoly on the use of options. The Phoenicians and Romans reportedly granted options on cargos transported by their ships.

The use of options in these earlier civilizations appears to have been at worst harmless and probably constructive on balance. In contrast, the first extensive use of options after the Middle Ages occurred during the Dutch tulip bulb mania of the early seventeenth century. Options have never fully recovered from the tarnish they accumulated by association with this speculative episode.

Tulip bulb options were used in several ways. Dealers in

tulip bulbs would sell bulbs for future delivery based on call options granted them by growers. If they wished, growers could assure themselves of a minimum price on their bulbs by purchasing puts from dealers. All parties found they could adjust their risk exposure to what they considered appropriate levels. Options were particularly useful to growers in reducing their exposure to price fluctuations. Everything could have worked out reasonably well if there had been a regulatory mechanism to assure the option buyers that their contracts would be honored.

The tulip bulb option market was totally undisciplined. There were no financially sound option endorsers to guarantee that writers would fulfill their contracts. There were no margin requirements to keep speculators from ruining themselves and everyone who did business with them.

When the market in tulip bulbs broke in 1636, a number of writers of puts were wiped out. With the losers either unable or unwilling to pay and with no effective precedent to permit dealing with the situation quickly, the authorities called on the Provincial Council at The Hague to devise a solution which would restore credit to the nation. After exhaustive deliberations the Council advised that these contracts should be enforced. This sagacious decision accomplished nothing, it being as difficult to get blood out of a tulip bulb as out of a turnip. The courts refused to enforce the Council's impossible verdict, leaving holders of puts holding the bag. Writers were never required to perform on their contracts.

Neglect of other commerce during this period of tulipomania and delay in resolving the debts and dislocations caused by the collapse had an adverse effect on Holland's economy for many years after the tulip craze was over. The role of options in the excesses of the tulipomania and the fact that specific performance was not enforced on option contracts gave options a bad name throughout Europe. Ironically, the Dutch continued to use options in spite of their experience with tulip bulb contracts. Puts, calls, and straddles on the shares of the Dutch West India Company were traded in Amsterdam only a few years after the tulip bulb debacle.

Organized trading in puts and calls on securities began in

London late in the seventeenth century. In part because of the Dutch experience with tulip bulb options and in part because options were usually associated with speculative activity, considerable opposition soon developed to trading in stock options. Options were declared illegal by Barnard's Act of 1733. This legislation was not effective in stopping option trading, though it was not repealed until 1860. Option dealings continued throughout the period Barnard's Act was on the books. The scale of trading was modest, however, because many of the leading securities firms refused to have anything to do with options.

Puts and calls were traded in London until the financial crisis of 1931, when they were temporarily banned. Options were also banned for a period between World War II and the late 1950s. In 1958 option trading resumed on a small scale. Today the London option market is probably the largest in Europe, though options are also traded in France, West Germany, and Switzerland.

Option trading in America began late in the eighteenth century. While options have never been banned in this country, as in London, options have been associated with some rather questionable practices over the years. For example, Russell Sage, widely credited with development of the modern put and call system, apparently devised the procedure for converting puts into calls to get around the usury laws.

Although the conversion process is described at length in Appendix B, Sage's use of the technique to avoid usury restrictions is worth special mention as an example of the abuses possible with unregulated options. Sage bought the securities which were to serve as loan collateral from the investor who wanted to borrow money at a usurious rate and received a put option permitting him to sell the securities back to the investor at the purchase price. He then sold this investor a call. The premium on the call was calculated to permit Sage to earn the maximum interest rate the traffic would bear. The legal interest rate ceiling for a margin loan did not apply to the implicit interest rate charged for the option conversion. Unlike the typical owner of a call, Sage's customer participated fully in any rise *or fall* in the stock because the put he issued to Sage would be exercised if the stock dropped. If this technique had been widely used to circumvent margin and usury rules, it could have led to violent stock price fluctuations and, ultimately, to the deterioration of the market structure.

The so-called bucket shops (in which Jesse Livermore and many other speculators of the early twentieth century got their start) charged a small premium, typically $1 per share, to carry a speculator's position for a short period of time. If the stock declined, the speculator was, in effect, sold out. The bucket shops had devised an early form of the down-and-out call. Though the association with options is usually forgotten when the expression is used today, the term *bucket shop* retains its unfavorable connotations.

Many of the manipulative schemes of the 1920s were made possible by the practice of granting brokers options on certain stocks in return for an agreement to recommend those stocks to their customers. Stock pool operators and unethical promoters made extensive use of this kind of option. Many small investors were the victims of stock salesmen whose natural enthusiasm was augmented by ownership of these options.

Most large-scale abuses of stock options disappeared with the passage of the securities legislation of the 1930s. The lawmakers directed their attention to specific abuses involving options and established a constructive regulatory framework which dealt effectively with the misuse of options without destroying these useful tools. Occasionally, even today, a manipulative scheme uncovered by the Securities and Exchange Commission (SEC), the National Association of Securities Dealers (NASD), or one of the exchanges will feature grants of stock options to brokers or investment advisers who are expected to promote the stock to their clients. The use of inside information in the purchase of stock options has also surfaced, notably in the Texas Gulf case. On balance, however, abuses involving options have been relatively minor for the past 40 years. When major problems have cropped up, such as recent cases of inadequately margined commodity options, the regulators have dealt with the situation effectively.

The regulatory authorities have learned that the existence of a securities option market can even serve an important regulatory function. Large-scale option transactions that coincide with major events in a corporation's history can provide an important clue to the improper use of inside information.

The present regulatory environment effectively prevents the speculative abuses which led to the collapse of the Dutch economy in the seventeenth century and to the loss of faith in the securities markets during the depression of the 1930s. Option writers are now required to post adequate margin to ensure they will honor their contracts. Granting options to induce a broker or investment adviser to recommend a stock and buying options to take advantage of inside information are prohibited. In short, with rare exceptions, current regulations deal adequately with the historic abuses of the option contract. These regulations may have made it impossible to duplicate the shoestring leverage that was possible in earlier years, but they also ensure the viability of the securities option market under virtually all conditions.

B. STRUCTURE OF THE CONVENTIONAL OR OVER-THE-COUNTER OPTION MARKET

In spite of Wall Street's recent frenetic interest in options, trading volume in the conventional option market is much lower today than it was prior to the inauguration of the Chicago Board Options Exchange. As a result of the CBOE's success and the relative decline in conventional option volume, major structural changes in the conventional option market are likely during the next few years. Because of its declining relative importance and the high probability of structural changes, the conventional option market will not be discussed in great detail. Most books on options stress conventional options, so the reader can easily find further information on topics mentioned only briefly here. The discussion of this market will focus on the role of the specialized put and call broker who is the heart of the over-the-counter option trading system and whose survival is threatened by listed option trading.

A glance at the figures in Table 3-1 suggests that prior to

Table 3-1. Comparison of Option Trading Volume and New York Stock Exchange Volume (All figures in thousands of shares of underlying stock)

Year	Conventional Option Volume	As a Percent of NYSE Volume	CBOE Option Volume	As a Percent of NYSE Volume
1940	1,205	.58		
1945	2,108	.56		
1950	2,631	.50		
1955	6,012	.93		
1960	8,561	1.12		
1965	15,256	.98		
1970	19,681	.67		
1971	29,516	.76		
1972	32,851	.79		
1973	18,920	.47	109,800	2.71
1974	N.A.	N.A.	564,458	16.1

Conventional option volume figures are based on reports from members of the Put and Call Brokers and Dealers Association. These data include only sales of original options by writers and do not include sales by one dealer to another. Certain specialized options not processed by members of the Association such as down-and-out calls and up-and-out puts are also excluded. Data for 1974 have not been compiled.

For 1973, CBOE option volume figures cover only the period the CBOE was open. Share equivalent volume was running about 20 percent of NYSE volume in late 1974.

1973 option trading volume was in a modest upward trend relative to volume on the New York Stock Exchange (NYSE). The decline in conventional option activity in 1973 was directly related to the opening of the Chicago Board Options Exchange.

Until 1973, the membership of the Put and Call Brokers and Dealers Association appeared relatively immune to the revenue shrinkage which has debilitated the rest of the securities business since the end of 1968. The revenues of option firms had risen and declined cyclically with changes in the popularity of options, but there was no reason prior to the CBOE "revolution" to doubt the economic viability of the approximately 30 firms that belonged to the Association. In contrast to the rest of Wall Street, these firms had operated for years with competitively negotiated commission rates. Even these competitive rates, however, were much higher than the CBOE fixed rates on listed options because the conventional option market is a custom market with inherently higher transaction costs than the streamlined, standardized listed option market.

Lower transaction costs are not the only reason behind the overnight success of listed options. The sponsors and management of the CBOE have done an outstanding job of educating registered representatives and the investing public to the virtues of options. Brokerage firms in search of new sources of revenue have emphasized options for the first time. Any reluctance an investor has shown in the past, based on the unknown size of the put and call dealer's spread (the difference between the premium paid by the buyer and the premium received by the writer), has disappeared with the introduction of the auction market and its published prices.

As a result of the outstanding success of listed option trading, several members of the Put and Call Brokers and Dealers Association have been absorbed by NYSE member firms to provide the acquiring firm with in-house option expertise. Other members have simply gone out of business or resigned from the Association for other reasons. The remaining Association members who specialize in conventional options find their revenues greatly reduced as investors abandon the conventional option market for listed options. To understand why the long-term viability of these independent conventional option houses is in doubt, it is necessary to understand the role of the put and call broker in the conventional option market. Examining each aspect of the put and call broker's task is also an excellent way of discovering how the conventional option market works.

A put and call broker's basic function is to bring buyers and writers of conventional options together. Typically, both the buyer and writer are customers of NYSE member firms. Usually the buyer will be a customer of one firm and the writer a customer of another firm. The put and call broker's role is to act as a broker's broker, as an intermediary between the firms representing buyer and writer.

For a variety of reasons most NYSE members have been happy with this arrangement and only a few have joined the Put and Call Brokers and Dealers Association themselves. The put and call broker's spread is a charge which a Stock Exchange member might find difficult to collect from the customer if the brokerage firm performed the option trading function in-house. Also, the put and call broker handles many of the details of an option trade in return for his fee. Because most NYSE members did not do enough option business to justify employing an option specialist prior to the establishment of the CBOE, they had relied heavily on the put and call broker's expertise.

One of the greatest incentives to use an independent option house is that a NYSE member firm ordinarily obtains more stock commission business from an option house than is generated on options bought and sold by the firm's own customers. This commission business is from the stock transactions of retail clients of the put and call house and from the stock trading of the option firm. This business is usually divided among NYSE member firms roughly in proportion to the amount of business they direct to the option house.

In addition to the basic task of bringing buyers and writers of conventional options together, the put and call broker performs a number of other services. Some option firms act as dealers and make markets in options on certain stocks. When a potential buyer or writer is anxious to trade an option on a particular stock and the option firm is unable to find the other side of the transaction, some dealers will buy or write the option for their own account in the expectation that they will be able to find the other side of the contract in the relatively near future. Many of the "special options" advertised in *The New York Times*, *The Wall Street Journal*, and *Barron's* have their origin in the put and call dealer's market-making activity.

Apart from functions related to negotiating the terms of the trade, the put and call broker plays an important role in the mechanical aspects of an option transaction. Specifically, the put and call broker arranges for the conversion of puts into calls and makes certain that the endorsement or performance guarantee by the NYSE member firm representing the option writer is in the proper form. Finally, the Put and Call Brokers and Dealers Association publishes standard option contract forms and sets policies for the adjustment of option striking prices or expiration dates if changes are required.

Conversion is the process of transforming a put into a call or a call into a put. Conversion is frequently necessary because buyers are interested primarily in call options, while option writers often prefer to write straddles. Though the put and call broker arranges for conversions, the actual conversion is done by a small number of NYSE member firms. As the reader will understand after reading Appendix B, conversion is not a complex process. However, conversion is sufficiently esoteric that most participants in the option market are content to leave it to the put and call broker and the NYSE member firm which runs a conversion account.

All options traded through members of the Put and Call Brokers and Dealers Association are endorsed by a NYSE member who guarantees that the option will be honored. The option buyer and writer are usually unknown to one another. To eliminate the need for personal credit checks and to remove most of the credit risk from the transaction, the endorsing firm guarantees that the writer has met NYSE or more stringent requirements for the deposit of collateral to guarantee his performance on the option contract. Even if the writer should fail to perform, the NYSE member firm itself guarantees fulfillment of the option contract. In fact, the contract which the option buyer receives is a contract with the endorsing firm, not with the option writer.

In spite of the failure of numerous firms over the years, all option contracts endorsed by NYSE member firms have been honored. As good as this record is, the conventional option endorsement process is obsolete and will probably be replaced in time by a central clearing and endorsement process like that used for listed options. For the time being, the put and call broker makes the endorsement system work. If a brokerage house is in trouble and the buyer's broker is nervous, the put and call firm can help switch the endorsement to a stronger house, usually without the knowledge of either the option buyer or the option writer.

Standard conventional put and call contracts similar to those published by the Put and Call Brokers and Dealers Association appear in Figure 3-1. These contracts spell out the basic adjustments of the striking price for cash dividends, rights, and

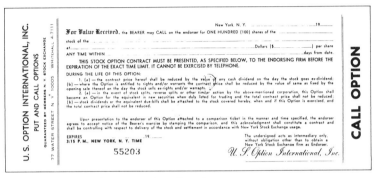

Figure 3-1. Sample conventional option contracts.

warrants (the striking price is reduced by the amount or value of the distribution) and for stock splits, stock dividends, and reverse splits (both the striking price and the number of shares subject to option are changed so that the option buyer's net position is unaffected).

Although the contract form does not spell the procedure out in detail, should a merger occur during the life of the option contract, the buyer has the right to purchase or sell the package of securities issued in exchange for the optioned stock on terms equivalent to those stated in the option contract. For example, if the option contract is a call on 100 shares of stock at $20 per share and the optioned stock is exchanged in a merger for 50 shares of stock in a new corporation, the holder of the option has the right to buy 50 shares of the new corporation's stock at $40 per share.

The Put and Call Brokers and Dealers Association determines how option contracts should be settled when an unexpected event makes the exact terms of the contract impossible to meet. For example, when the NYSE closed on certain days during 1968 to permit brokers to catch up with their paperwork, the Association ruled that options scheduled to expire on those days would not expire until 3:15 P.M. on the next trading day. Perhaps the most difficult problem is caused by a suspension of trading in the stock which is the subject of an option contract. In such cases, the holder of the option must give notice of exercise before the contractual option expiration date; but the actual exercise of the contract is deferred until trading in the stock resumes.

Another notable function of the put and call broker is the repurchase of an option from the investor. If the option is trading in the money, the transaction occurs at intrinsic value net of applicable stock commissions to permit the customer to obtain a long-term capital gain on the option purchase. The NYSE member firm which represents the option buyer will deliver the option and will receive the commissions from the purchase and sale of the underlying stock. If the option holder is a retail customer of the option house, the commission will go to a favored NYSE member. If the owner of an out-of-the-money option wants to avoid letting the loss on that position go long-term, the option dealer will buy it for a nominal sum, usually $1.

In time, most option houses that function as brokers' brokers will probably be eliminated. The only conventional option houses which seem likely to survive as independents are those which have made a fast transition to active trading of listed options. The most successful option houses appear to have adopted two complementary strategies. First, they have continued to act as brokers' brokers for listed options, providing trading and clearing services to other firms. In addition, they have attempted to develop a public customer business of their own. Success of the latter strategy is critical to their long-term survival as independent firms.

The outlook for the independent put and call broker may be bleak, but the conventional option market is by no means dead. Listed trading in standardized options on a limited number of stocks will never satisfy the needs of all option writers and buyers. Several changes are inevitable, however. The days of enormous transaction costs are gone. Work is underway on primary and secondary trading and clearing techniques that will improve the efficiency and lower the operating costs of the conventional option market. The most promising of these trading and clearing systems is one devised by the Option Organization, Inc. In all probability, this system or an adaptation based on it will ultimately be used to "automate" the conventional option market. The vested interests of some option market participants in maintaining high transaction costs have delayed implementation of an efficient central market for conventional options. When low-cost, centralized trading is finally adopted, the volume of conventional option activity will probably be much greater than at any time in the past.

C. THE SIGNIFICANCE OF THE CHICAGO BOARD OPTIONS EXCHANGE

This section focuses on the major innovations introduced by the Chicago Board Options Exchange that have revolutionized option trading. The text focuses on the economic and investment significance of the differences between listed and conventional option markets. Table 3-2 at the end of this section provides an item-by-item comparison of the two markets.

Three of the most important changes instituted by the CBOE and adopted by other exchanges are

1. Standardization of the striking price and the expiration date of the option contract

2. Fungibility or interchangeability of option contracts which eliminates the direct tie between option writer and buyer and facilitates the development of a secondary market in options

3. Sharply lower net transaction costs and an organized secondary market

The importance of standardized option terms in the development of a secondary market in option contracts cannot be overemphasized. Standardization facilitates secondary trading because the number of distinct contracts a buyer or seller must evaluate is reduced. In contrast to the conventional option market where it is possible to buy or write an option with practically any striking price or expiration date, the terms of contracts available on the exchanges are more limited. The striking price of a listed option always ends in $5 or $0 unless a stock dividend or other capital change occurs after trading in the option begins. If American Telephone and Telegraph is selling at $51 a share at the time options for a new expiration month are being listed for trading, the new AT&T option will have a striking price of $50 per share. If the stock price closes above $52.50 for 2 consecutive days, the exchange will add $55 contracts for each expiration date beyond 60 days. Barring stock dividends, splits, or other capital changes, it will be impossible to buy or write an AT&T option on the exchange with a striking price between $50 and $55 per share.

In addition to standardization of striking prices, the exchanges have standardized expiration dates. Listed options may be exercised at any time prior to 10:30 A.M. Chicago time or 11:30 A.M. New York time, on the last Monday of the expiration month. Beginning with options expiring in 1976, the expiration date will be the Saturday after the third Friday in the month. While most options expire in January, April, July, and October, some recently added underlying stocks have options expiring in February, May, August, and November.

Fungibility or interchangeability is a second important characteristic of listed options necessary for the development of an active secondary market. Fungibility means substitutability or equivalence. Each listed option with a common expiration date and striking price is interchangeable with any similar listed option. In contrast, a conventional option is a direct contract between a particular writer (or, rather, his brokerage firm) and a particular buyer. One conventional option contract is not substitutable for another, even if the terms are identical. As a result of the direct tie between buyer and writer, it is frequently difficult for the owner of a conventional option to sell or exchange the option privilege for a price in excess of the intrinsic or exercise value of the option. More importantly, it is impossible for an option writer to terminate his obligation except through direct negotiation with the buyer of the specific contract he wrote.

With listed options, either party can usually close out a position that no longer meets his needs without undue sacrifice. The buyer and writer in a listed option transaction have no direct connection. Each has a contract only with The Options Clearing Corporation which is the issuer of listed options. The option buyer relies on the Clearing Corporation to make good on the contract. The writer's obligation is an obligation to the Clearing Corporation, not to the buyer his broker happens to meet on the exchange floor. Either the option buyer or the writer can close out his position by simply reversing the initial transaction. For a more complete explanation of the relationship between the Clearing Corporation and the other parties to an option contract, the reader should examine the relevant sections of The Options Clearing Corporation prospectus.

A third important characteristic of listed options is their relatively low transaction cost. As will be seen in Section D, the total transaction cost of any listed option trade is substantially lower than the transaction cost of a similar conventional option trade. Lower transaction costs have an important effect on trading volume and market liquidity. As the spread between the premium paid by the buyer and the premium received by the writer grows smaller, the number of transactions will tend to grow larger. If the option premium paid by the buyer is $500 and the amount received by the writer, net of transaction costs, is only $400, a writer who was willing to accept a net premium of $425 and a buyer who was willing to pay a premium of $475 would be excluded from the market. On the other hand, if the spread were narrower, both the buyer and the writer could be accommodated and the total volume of option transactions would increase. Relatively low transaction costs have been a very important factor in the high trading volume of listed options.

In addition to these three major features of listed options, there are a number of other characteristics which have contributed to their success. In contrast to the conventional option market, listed option striking prices are not reduced to compensate for the payment of cash dividends. Less frequent and more significant changes like stock dividends, stock splits, and similar distributions are handled in the same way for conventional and listed options. Apart from simplifying published trading summaries, not reducing the striking price for cash dividends is probably consistent with the preferences of option market participants. Typically, the option buyer does not value a modest reduction of the striking price very highly. The option writer may, however, see his ability to retain the dividend as an important feature of the listed option contract. Though the difference is frequently minor, the method of handling cash dividends affects the relative value of conventional and listed options on the same underlying stock.

Another important feature of listed options is that they are far more flexible instruments than conventional options and can be used in a wider variety of transactions. Because both writer and buyer can close out positions relatively quickly, trading and investment strategies which require the use of options for only a short period of time are feasible. Strategies which depend on an investor's ability to buy or sell additional options as time passes are greatly facilitated by a secondary market.

The prices at which listed option transactions actually take place are published daily. Published prices and known commission rates assure both buyer and writer of a fair market. While we are not aware of any widespread abuse of the relative obscurity of conventional option dealer spreads, the mere fact that daily trading summaries are published in the newspapers removes some of the mystery and, quite frankly, some of the suspicion from the option market.

In an era when the financial soundness of much of the securities industry has been called into question, most option buyers will have more confidence in the endorsement of The Options Clearing Corporation than they would have in the option endorsement of most NYSE member firms. Appropriate or inappropriate though this difference in the investor's level of confidence may be, it is nonetheless a factor in some option transactions. The fact that the actual risk of accepting endorsements is probably small does not prevent reliance on these endorsements from being a potential problem in the over-the-counter option market.

In some respects, one of the most important innovations pioneered by the CBOE is the introduction of certificate-less clearing. Except in unusual cases where an option trader insists on evidence of the transaction in addition to a brokerage firm confirmation slip, The Options Clearing Corporation does not issue an actual option contract or certificate. This feature of listed option trading reduces the amount of paperwork and eliminates the physical movement of securities, in this case option contracts, between brokerage firms. The Options Clearing Corporation has sharply reduced the time required to clear a transaction and, as the brokerage community gains additional experience with certificate-less trading, the cost of clearing a transaction should decline. The CBOE was a pilot project not only for organized trading of option contracts, but also for the introduction of certificate-less trading to the securities markets. Based on results to date, both features of the pilot project are unqualified successes.

Table 3-2. Comparison of Conventional and Listed Options and Markets

	Conventional	Listed
Type of options traded	Calls, puts, combination options	Calls only, puts scheduled for late 1975
Striking price	Any price buyer and writer negotiate	Standardized price ending in $5 or $0
Expiration date	Any date buyer and writer negotiate	Last Monday in the expiration month for 1975; becomes third Friday in month for expirations in 1976
Expiration time	3:15 P.M. eastern time	11:30 A.M. eastern time for 1975; 5:30 P.M. in 1976
Last date and time option can be sold	Same as expiration date and time	2:00 P.M. central time 3:00 P.M. eastern time on the business day immediately prior to the expiration date
Adjustment for cash dividend	Striking price reduced on ex dividend date	No change in striking price
Adjustment for stock dividends, stock splits, and reverse splits	Both striking price and number of shares covered by options are adjusted to reflect the capital change	
Adjustment for rights or warrants issued to common share holders	Striking price reduced by the value of the rights or warrants	
Limitation on purchase of options on one stock	None, but limits have been proposed	500 contracts per stock per expiration date; 1,000 contracts per stock all expiration dates
Limitation on sale of options on one stock	None, but limits have been proposed	500 uncovered contracts per stock per expiration date plus 500 contracts covered by ownership of stock or a long option position with a lower striking price than the option sold. 1,000 contracts per stock all expiration dates
Unit of trading	One contract is an option on 100 shares of the underlying stock before any adjustments	

Table 3-2. Comparison of Conventional and Listed Options and Markets—(Continued)

	Conventional	Listed
Method of option price determination	Buyer and writer negotiate through put and call broker	Central auction market
Secondary market	Limited; special options advertised in newspaper	Very active secondary market
Buyer's recourse to obtain performance on option contract	Primary responsibility for performance belongs to the endorsing broker who may be any member of the New York Stock Exchange	The Options Clearing Corporation is the primary obligor guaranteeing the writer's performance
Evidence of ownership	Bearer certificate	Broker's confirmation slip
Method of closing out transaction when stock sells above striking price	Option may be exercised by buyer or sold to put and call broker who exercises the option and sells the stock	Exercise is rare. Contract is usually closed out in a closing purchase/sale transaction
Transaction costs	High	Moderate
Commission structure	Basic charge is negotiated by put and call broker as a spread between premium paid by buyer and premium paid to writer	Negotiated commission rates since May 1, 1975
Stocks on which options are available	Almost any stock	Only selected stocks
Pricing information	Brokers publish indicated premiums to buyers or writers	Actual transaction prices published daily
Procedure for exercise	Buyer exercises by notifying endorsing broker	Buyer's broker notifies The Options Clearing Corporation which selects writers essentially at random
Extensions	Available if writer agrees	Not available
Tax treatment	Only significant difference is that covered writers of listed options can easily realize ordinary losses and long-term gains if stock price rises. A covered writer of a conventional option may find this tax treatment more difficult to obtain	

Table 3-2. Comparison of Conventional and Listed Options and Markets—(Continued)

	Conventional	Listed
Margin requirement: Call buyer	100% of the option premium	Same
Margin requirement: Covered writer	No margin required beyond that needed to carry stock position	
Margin requirement: Uncovered writer	Minimum requirement is related to price of stock with adjustment for amount of premium received and amount by which option is in or out of the money. Margin requirements should be checked in detail with each brokerage firm. See Appendix A for minimum requirements in detail.	

D. FACTORS AFFECTING THE VOLUME OF OPTION TRADING

For many years, the volume of option trading in the United States has exceeded securities option trading activity in all other countries combined. The birth of listed option trading promises to expand option activity well beyond historic levels.

It is interesting to consider why options have attained this degree of success in the United States. A cynic might argue that the entire securities market in the United States is larger than markets abroad; consequently, we should expect more option trading as well. Although good statistical information is not available, the level of option trading in the United States appears to be several times as great as any proportionate relationship to trading in underlying shares would suggest. There are several explanations, unrelated to size, for the success of option trading in this country. If these explanations are correct, option trading in the United States is just entering its period of greatest growth.

An important historic fact behind the development of the option market is the constructive regulatory environment in the United States. Close scrutiny of option markets by the Securities and Exchange Commission and the National Association of Securities Dealers might suggest a constraint on speculative fervor and, therefore, less interest in options. Actually, close regulation probably encourages option trading.

During a highly speculative period, option activity will be high under virtually any regulatory conditions. When speculative activity wanes, however, options may be written or purchased on something approaching a rational basis. Although some observers would argue that option prices, as opposed to values, are rarely rational, both buyer and writer will be interested in the market structure within which the option is traded. Unless his speculative urges are overwhelming, a buyer wants to feel that he has access to the same sources of information as the option writer, that the market will not be manipulated, and that the writer will honor the option contract. The writer would like similar protection. Both parties take comfort in the fact that the vigilance of the SEC, the NASD, and the major stock exchanges has largely eliminated the illicit market practices that were so prevalent during the first third of this century.

Although the features of the option contract are probably less important than the strength of the regulatory process, the American stock option contract is inherently more attractive than its European counterpart. The European securities option is exercisable only on the date of expiration. The American option is exercisable at any time prior to the expiration date as well. In practice, most American options are exercised within a week of expiration, but the restriction that an option can be exercised on only one day does reduce a buyer's flexibility. The length of the period during which the contract can be exercised and the health of the regulatory environment interact; the European contract increases the option holder's vulnerability to any manipulative activity which might be concentrated on the day his contract expires.

Building on the framework created by the constructive regulatory atmosphere and the variable exercise date, the listed option has added several new dimensions. One of the most important features of exchange trading of options is that it provides a secondary market for contracts which are no longer attractive to the original purchaser or writer. If a listed call has performed as anticipated, the buyer can probably re-sell it at a price which will yield a premium over the intrinsic value of the call. If the option had been purchased over the counter, the buyer might not be able to get more than the option's exercise value. Likewise, the writer can terminate the listed option obligation if it becomes advisable. Writing the call no longer locks the writer in for the life of the contract.

Probably the single most significant contribution of listed option trading to the expansion of the option market is that it sharply reduces the cost of a transaction. Both the writer and the buyer of a call can fare better on an exchange than with a conventional call. If commission and other transaction costs are too large, they act as a deterrent to trading. Commissions on the exchange are low enough that the buyer can consider purchasing options for a relatively small expected move in the stock. The writer has reasonable assurance that the commission cost to close out the transaction will not consume most of the premium. The lower transaction cost leads to more active trading and, consequently, to more liquid markets. The example chosen for Table 3-3 illustrates a typical difference between transaction costs for a listed option and those for a conventional option. The actual difference in a particular case always depends on what happens to the price of the stock and what the parties do to close out their respective sides of the contract.

Nonetheless, examination of the table reveals that the costs of the conventional option transaction are, in this case, more than two and one-half times as high as for the comparable listed option transaction. In fact, the total of commissions and other charges paid by the two parties to the conventional option trade are equal to about two-thirds of the total option premium paid by the buyer. If one assumed the transaction involved *one* call rather than ten, the costs would consume an amount nearly equal to the entire premium. With transaction costs of this magnitude, neither buyer nor writer can realistically expect superior performance unless premiums are grossly out of line with any measure of fair value.

Table 3-3. Comparison of Transaction Costs: Conventional vs. Listed Option Markets

Buyer buys 10 calls at $500 each with a $50 striking price. Stock rises to $60 where buyer sells or exercises calls, receiving $1,000 per contract before costs. Writer initially buys 500 shares of stock or enough to cover one-half of his obligation. All figures are expressed on a per contract basis with commissions calculated on the assumption that the transaction consists of 10 contracts.

	Conventional	Listed
BUYER'S POSITION:		
Premium paid by buyer	$ 500.00	$ 500.00
Commission to buyer's broker	12.50	12.70
Cost to buyer to establish position	$ 512.50	$ 512.70
Gross proceeds from selling call ($60−$50) × 100 shares	$1000.00	$1000.00
Listed option commission		(17.20)
Round-trip stock commission on sale of options	(107.06)	
Transfer taxes	(5.00)	
Cost to establish position	(512.50)	(512.70)
Net profit to buyer	$ 375.44	$ 470.10
WRITER'S POSITION:		
Premium paid by buyer	$ 500.00	$ 500.00
Option commission paid by writer to his broker	12.50	12.70
Put & call broker's spread (est.)	75.00	
Net premium to writer	$ 412.50	$ 487.30
Cost of repurchasing call from buyer	$1000.00	$1000.00
Add: Listed option commission		17.20
Purchase commissions initial stock position	30.13	30.13
Sale commission initial stock position		33.58
Purchase commission additional stock called	33.58	
Sale commission on stock called	50.83	
Transfer taxes	5.00	2.50
Subtract: Net premium received	(412.50)	(487.30)
Profit on stock owned	(500.00)	(500.00)
Net loss to writer	$ 207.04	$ 96.11
Net profit to buyer	$ 375.44	$ 470.10
Subtract: Net loss to writer	(207.04)	(96.11)
Net profit to investors	$ 168.40	$ 373.99
Total transaction costs	$ 331.60	$ 126.01
Less:	(126.01)	
Difference in transaction costs: Conventional vs. listed calls	$ 205.39 per contract	

Table 3-3. Comparison of Transaction Costs: Conventional vs. Listed Option Markets—(*Continued*)

NOTES:

1. If the writer had written conventional straddles instead of two calls against each round lot owned, he would have fared better but the *total* transaction cost would have been even higher. (See Appendix B.)

2. If the stock declines, total transaction costs may drop slightly faster for the conventional option but they are always substantially higher than listed option costs.

3. Transfer taxes are based on New York residence.

4. Commissions are calculated on the basis of an initial position of 10 calls and a stock position of 500 shares bought by the writer. Stock and option commission rates are those in effect prior to May 1, 1975, on the NYSE and CBOE respectively. These commission charges are then stated on a per call basis. The total charges are 10 times the figures listed.

4. USES OF OPTIONS—INVESTMENT POSITIONS AND STRATEGIES

A. GRAPHIC REPRESENTATION OF INVESTMENT POSITIONS

This chapter deals with the analysis of investment positions using a simple graphic method that allows one to illustrate the risk-reward characteristics of any holding. These graphs facilitate a profitability analysis of any position, whether that position consists of cash, of cash and securities, or of cash, securities, and options. The graphic approach also permits relatively easy adjustment for borrowing costs, taxes, and commissions. Using the graphic method, the reader can work out the profitability of any strategy that might be devised under a variety of assumptions about the likely course of stock prices.

Algebraic formulations are difficult for most investors to use, let alone to understand. In contrast, most investors with enough sophistication to use options can use graphs easily and effectively. Also, while it is easy to plug numbers mindlessly into a formula and get worthless results, if a graph is wrong, it frequently looks wrong.

To avoid dealing with stocks and options in the abstract, a specific set of stock and option terms and prices has been selected. Apart from the fact that this approach makes the examples comparable and, it is hoped, somewhat more meaningful, it permits the reader to combine two or more strategies. The particular option characteristics illustrated should help bridge the gap between conventional options and listed options.

Traditional discussions of option strategies and their risk-reward characteristics focus on the conventional option market where most options are written with the striking price equal to the market price. For listed options, the market price of the stock generally differs (sometimes substantially) from the striking price of the option. In the graphs, a listed-type option with differing market and striking prices is used, but the method of making commission, dividend, and interest adjustments for both listed and conventional options is discussed. The purpose throughout the presentation is to develop an approach which the investor can use as the basis for a rational analysis of any conceivable option strategy.

To simplify the discussion, the following basic assumptions have been adopted:

1. The investor can obtain interest at a 7 percent annual rate on any monies he wishes to lend or invest in short-term debt instruments.

2. The investor will pay interest at a 9 percent rate for any borrowing from his broker or from a bank.

3. The common stock the investor purchases or sells short or which underlies any options he may buy or write is selling at $95 a share.

4. There is available a listed call option with approximately 6 months remaining until expiration. It has a striking price of $100 and the current price of this call is $10 ($1,000 per 100-share contract).

5. It is possible to buy or sell a put analogous to the listed call with a striking price of $100 and ready marketability. These puts are selling at $11 ($1,100 per 100-share contract).

Except where indicated, the profit-loss lines on the graphs have not been adjusted for dividends, commissions, taxes, interest, or opportunity costs. Though option writing generates a cash balance which can be invested by the writer, an interest credit is not added. With the exception of taxes, the nature and direction of the adjustments as they apply to the simpler investment strategies are discussed. A complex strategy can usually be adjusted by dealing separately with each component part. In later chapters on option spreads and taxes, tax-adjusted illustrations are provided and adjustments for the tax effects of an investment are discussed at length. The basic explanation of the graphic approach does not require a detailed understanding of these adjustments. Many investors will conclude that adjustments are not worth the bother. If one excepts some adjustments for the tax impact of an investment and adjustments for commission costs related to spreads and conventional options, this attitude is probably correct for most purposes.

There are several reasons behind the use of the 6-month time horizon. Because 6 months and 1 day is the holding period required for long-term, capital-gain tax treatment, most investors are used to thinking in terms of this time horizon in evaluating investment positions. Also, one expects that the incentive of long-term, capital-gain tax treatment will eventually lead to greater activity in longer-term listed options.

The investment positions chosen for illustration are, for the most part, those discussed by Malkiel and Quandt in *Strategies and Rational Decisions in the Securities Options Market.* The author has added several positions not used by Malkiel and Quandt because readily marketable listed options, not available when their book was written, increase the range of possible positions.

Each investment position or strategy is depicted on a standardized graph. The profit-loss line on the graph shows the dollar profit or loss the investor will experience at each possible stock price approximately 6 months after the position is initiated. In the case of strategies involving options, one assumes that the options will expire in 6 months, so the price 6 months out is also the price of the stock when the option expires. Any two strategies can be compared at any stock price by transferring the profit-loss line from one graph to the other or by preparing a new graph and imposing both strategies on that graph.

The reader may be tempted to skip over the earlier and

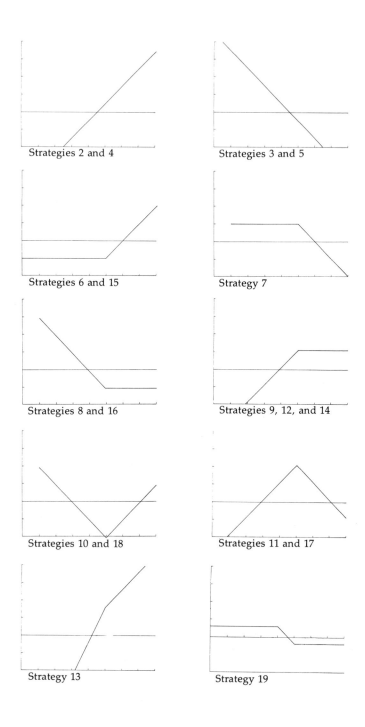

Strategies 2 and 4

Strategies 3 and 5

Strategies 6 and 15

Strategy 7

Strategies 8 and 16

Strategies 9, 12, and 14

Strategies 10 and 18

Strategies 11 and 17

Strategy 13

Strategy 19

simpler investment strategies and go directly to the particular option-related strategy which seems most interesting. The author urges at least a casual reading of the simpler strategies, since the graphic display method selected will be of most use if its application is thoroughly understood in a variety of cases.

One of the major advantages of options is that they permit an investor to adjust his investment position to virtually any degree of bullishness, bearishness, uncertainty, or neutrality he may feel toward the market or an individual stock. The diagrams in Figure 4-1 illustrate the "shape" of a few of the simpler strategies an investor can follow to express his opinion on a stock. Under the diagrams are listed the numbers of strategies with profit-loss lines of that approximate shape. The general "shapes" can be adjusted to reflect subtly different attitudes toward a stock or the market.

Strategy 1: Cash (Purchase Short-Term Debt Securities)

This first simple graph (Figure 4-2) is important primarily because it helps explain the use of the graphic technique. The vertical axis on the chart measures the dollar profit which the investor will realize by following this strategy. The horizontal axis lists possible prices for the hypothetical stock 6 months from the day the investment is initiated.

In the example illustrated here, the investor places money in a short-term debt instrument paying, under our assumptions, 7 percent annually or $3\frac{1}{2}$ percent over the 6-month period. On a $95 investment, the interest income for 6 months is $3\frac{1}{2}\% \times \$95$ or $3.33. As indicated by the horizontal profit-loss line, this income is totally independent of the price of any security. Though modest, the interest income is always positive.

Figure 4-1. (Opposite) Each of these graphs has a shape characteristic of one or more specific strategies. The vertical axis on each graph represents profit or loss at a particular stock price. The straight horizontal line signifies zero profit. The horizontal axis measures the stock price, with the price rising from left to right. Detailed graphs will be found later in the chapter.

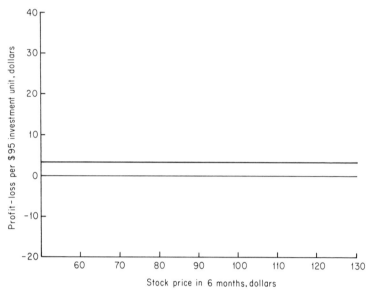

Figure 4-2. Strategy 1: Cash (purchase short-term debt securities).

The fact that the 7 percent interest has to be divided in half because one is dealing with a 6-month period illustrates a feature the reader should keep in mind when interpreting other graphs. To annualize profit or loss, we multiply the gain or loss at a given stock price by two. Of course, if the period covered by the graph is not 6 months, the multiplier will be different.

Adjustment of the interest income for taxes or any transaction costs would lower the line by the amount of the adjustment.

Strategy 2: Purchase Stock

In this example (Figure 4-3) the investor purchases 100 shares of common stock at a price of $95 per share. The profit or loss is strictly a function of the price of the stock 6 months in the future. If the price of the stock falls to $70, the investor suffers a loss of $25 per share over the 6-month period. If the price of the stock rises to $110, the investor earns $15. The significant risk-reward feature of this strategy, as every stockholder

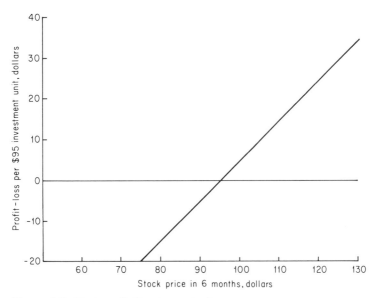

Figure 4-3. Strategy 2: Purchase stock.

knows, is that the investor's profit or loss bears a direct linear relationship to the price of the stock on the date the determination of return is made. If an investor is optimistic about the probable course of stock prices in general and this stock price in particular, he will favor this position. If he is not unreservedly optimistic, an unhedged long position in the stock is probably inappropriate. Habit, convention, and, perhaps, ignorance appear to be the principal reasons many investors accept this position without questioning its suitability to their risk preferences.

There are several adjustments necessary to calculate the precise profit or loss from this strategy. To adjust for dividends, the profit line is simply raised by the rate of the dividend payments. If, for example, dividend payments over the life of the investment aggregated $1.90, the profit-loss line would be higher by $1.90 at every possible stock price. In a similar manner, we can adjust for commissions on the purchase and/or sale of the shares. The purchase commission would reduce the line equally at every share price because the purchase commission is calculated at a share price of $95. Alternatively, a sale commission would often increase or decrease with the price of the stock. If the investor is not seriously considering sale of the shares at the end of the 6-month interval, it would probably be inappropriate to adjust for a sale commission. Adjustments for stock splits, stock dividends, and other capital changes are best made either by redrawing the graph or relabeling the horizontal axis. These changes do not affect the dollar profit.

Strategy 3: Sell Stock Short

The graph (Figure 4-4) depicting the short seller's position is the converse of the stock buyer's graph illustrated in Figure 4-3. For every point the stock rises, the buyer gains $1 per share and the short seller loses $1 per share. If the stock declines, the short seller profits to exactly the extent that the buyer loses.

Adjustments to the short seller's profit-loss line for dividends can be important. Whereas dividends increase the stock buyer's return, the short seller must pay out dividends to the

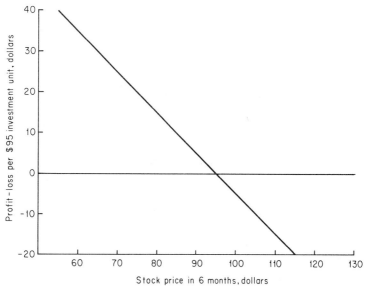

Figure 4-4. Strategy 3: Sell stock short.

owner of the stock; therefore dividends reduce the short seller's return. Commission and other adjustments are similar for both the short seller and the buyer.

Strategy 4: Purchase Stock on Margin

The principal effect of buying a stock on margin is to increase the slope of the profit-loss line so that both gain and loss, as a percent of the investor's equity, increase more rapidly as the price moves away from the original purchase price. With current initial margin requirements set at 50 percent, the approximate effect of margin transactions is to double the amount of stock an investor can carry by borrowing against his equity. Consequently, margin transactions based on this 50 percent rate will approximately double an investor's profit or loss (before interest cost) as the stock price moves away from the purchase price.

Once the investor begins to buy on margin, the adjustments he might wish to make to his profit-loss line become more complicated. The graph in Figure 4-5 assumes that the

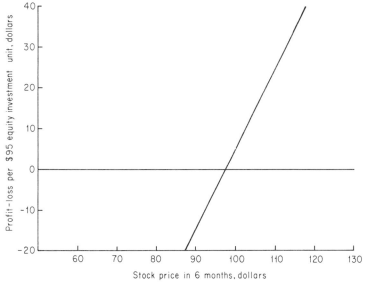

Figure 4-5. Strategy 4: Purchase stock on margin.

investor uses the 50 percent margin rules to carry two shares of stock instead of one with each $95 of equity. The graph has also been adjusted to reflect the cost of the money borrowed to carry half of the stock position. To make this adjustment, the entire profit-loss line is lowered by the cost of the borrowed money. In this case, the investor borrows $47.50 per share owned at a 9 percent interest rate for 6 months. This borrowing reduces his profit or increases his loss for the 6 months by $4.28 for each pair of shares owned, regardless of the price at which the stock sells on the day the transaction is closed out. A further complicating feature of margin transactions is that if the price of the stock drops much below $70, the investor may receive a margin call. At that time, he will have to invest more equity or allow his broker to liquidate the position for failure to meet margin requirements.

Adjustment for dividends, commissions, and capital changes such as stock splits are slightly complicated by the margin transactions, but if these adjustments are approached one at a time, there is no insurmountable difficulty in making them.

Strategy 5: Sell Stock Short on Margin

Selling stock short on margin is not quite the converse of buying stock on margin. The slope of the profit-loss line (Figure 4-6) for the doubled stock position is increased from the basic short-selling case as it is when stock is bought on margin, but there is usually no interest charge for borrowing money to carry part of the position. The margin required for a short sale serves only to guarantee that the short seller will meet his obligation if the stock rises. Money does not have to be borrowed to meet this requirement.*

---

* Investors are sometimes puzzled that a broker charges interest when a margin account shows a credit balance as a result of a combination of margin purchases and short sales. The reason for the interest charge is that the owner of the shares which the investor borrowed to sell short is entitled to the use of the money generated by the sale. Thus, though the investor's account shows a credit balance, the proceeds of the short sale usually do not offset his debit balance.

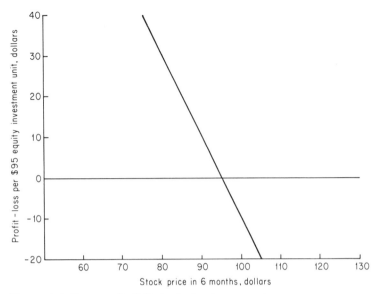

Figure 4-6. Strategy 5: Sell stock short on margin.

On 50 percent margin, dividend and other adjustments are double the magnitude of the 100 percent equity short selling case.

Strategy 6: Purchase a Call

When the investor purchases a call, the profit-loss line is no longer a straight line passing through the price of the stock on the day the purchase was made. In the case illustrated (purchase of a $10 call with a striking price of $100) the investor loses the entire investment if the call expires with the stock selling below the striking price of $100 per share. Furthermore, the investor does not even begin to make money until the price of the stock exceeds the striking price *plus* the option premium paid for the call. In this case, $100 (striking price) plus $10 (option premium) equals $110 (break-even point). If the price of the stock on the expiration date rises to $120 per share, the buyer of a call will have approximately doubled his initial investment. If the stock price rises ten more points to $130 per share, the call buyer will have tripled his investment.

The principal advantages and disadvantages of owning a call option should be clarified by the diagram (Figure 4-7). Although he loses his entire investment if the stock sells below the striking price when the option expires, the investor's maximum risk exposure is limited to the amount of the option premium. This is true regardless of how low the price of the stock may drop. On the positive side, the call buyer participates in any advance in the price of the stock above the striking price. His profit increases point-for-point, no matter how high the price of the stock may rise over the life of the option.

Possible adjustments to the graph can be either quite simple or very complicated. For example, the commission adjustment on a listed call is relatively easy to make. The call purchase commission simply lowers the line by a constant amount at every possible price. If the call expires worthless, there is no sale or exercise commission, but if the option has value at the time the transaction is closed out, the sale commission increases as the value of the call increases. Commission adjustments for conventional options are more complex. Purchase commissions will ordinarily be nominal, and there will be no

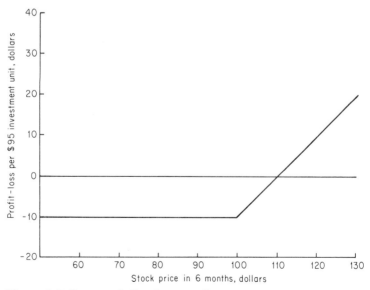

Figure 4-7. Strategy 6: Purchase a call.

sale commission if the option expires worthless. If the conventional option has value, the call buyer will ordinarily have to pay a round-trip stock commission when he sells the call or exercises it and sells the stock. One side of this round-trip commission will be based on the $100 striking price of the call, and the other side will be based on the market value of the stock at the time the call is exercised or sold.

Just as the commission adjustment is different, a dividend is treated differently with conventional and listed options. In the case of listed options, there is no adjustment to the striking price for cash dividends. With conventional options, the striking price of the option is reduced on the ex dividend date by the amount of any dividend paid. This has the effect of moving the diagonal line on the graph to the left by the amount of the dividend. If the dividend is, as we assumed before, $1.90 over the life of the option, the striking price of a conventional call will be reduced to $98.10. Thus, the call, neglecting for a moment the effect of commissions, would have value at any stock price above $98.10, and the profit would be increased (or the loss reduced) by $1.90 at every price above the adjusted exercise price.

If a stock dividend is paid or a stock split declared, both the striking price and the number of shares are adjusted, but the dollar profit or loss is unchanged. These adjustments are similar for listed and conventional options.

Strategy 7: Sell or Write a Call

The graph in Figure 4-8 illustrates the position of the "naked" or uncovered call option writer. The uncovered writer gets to keep all of the call premium if the buyer of the option does not exercise it. The "naked" writing position will be profitable as long as the price of the stock does not rise above the writer's break-even point: $100 (striking price) plus $10 (call premium) equals $110 (break-even point).

Most adjustments are similar to those made by the call buyer. In the case of a conventional or over-the-counter option, the writer will have to pay a round-trip commission equal to a purchase commission based on the price of the

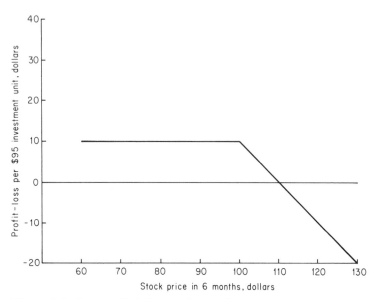

Figure 4-8. Strategy 7: Sell or write a call.

stock at the time the call is exercised plus a sale commission based on the striking price. If the call is listed, the commission adjustment is much more modest, since the uncovered writer can close out his obligation by repurchasing the option contract on the exchange. The commission is based on the price of the call at the time the repurchase transaction occurs.

Any dividend adjustment will depend on the rules of the market in which the call is traded. In the conventional option market the striking price would be reduced by the amount of any dividend. The striking price of a listed call is unaffected by a cash dividend. As indicated earlier, both the striking price and the number of shares subject to option are adjusted for stock dividends and splits.

The premium received by the option writer is available to him as soon as the transaction clears. He can invest it in Treasury bills or use it to reduce the debit balance in his margin account. At the interest rates we have assumed, the $10 premium from the uncovered call would save the investor with a debit balance about $0.45 in interest charges over the life of the call (9 percent interest on a $10 reduction in borrowing for 6 months). Adjusting for this interest credit would improve the writer's profit by $0.45 at every stock price.

The risk position of the "naked" call writer is unique. He can never gain more than the amount of the call premium, yet his possible loss in the event of a runaway stock is enormous. The loss could easily be four or five times the amount of the option premium. In spite of this risk, "naked" writing can be an extremely effective strategy when used intelligently. If an investor feels strongly that a particular stock is going to decline, yet does not anticipate that the decline will be of such magnitude that a short sale will be conspicuously profitable, he might elect to write "naked" calls. As long as his commitment to this strategy is not substantial relative to his resources, the profitability can be excellent, and the "naked" writing position can actually reduce the overall level of risk (or variability of return) in the portfolio. The way in which this apparently high-risk strategy can reduce risk will be clear when we examine Strategy 17, which deals with the option hedge.

Strategy 8: Purchase a Put

In some respects, purchase of a put is the reverse of buying a call. Unless the put buyer is able to sell or exercise his put at a time when the price of the stock is *below* the striking price, he can lose his entire investment. To the extent that the price of the stock drops precipitately, the buyer of a put participates point-for-point in any *decline* below the striking price. In the example illustrated in the graph (Figure 4-9), the put is profitable at any price below $89 (the striking price minus the option premium), neglecting the effect of commissions.

Adjustments are analogous to the adjustments discussed for the buyer of a call. If a put has value at the time it is sold or exercised, the put buyer will have to pay a round-trip commission. One side of this double commission will be based on the striking price, the other side on the market price of the stock at the time the put is closed out. As in the case of a conventional call, the striking price on a conventional put will be

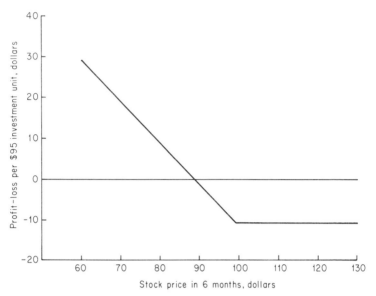

Figure 4-9. Strategy 8: Purchase a put.

reduced by the amount of any cash dividend paid on the stock. While the reader would be well advised to check this point carefully before engaging in a transaction, the striking price of a put written for conversion into a listed call or created by reversal of a listed call would probably not be reduced by the amount of a dividend. Some adjustment for any dividend would probably be made, however.

Strategy 9: Sell or Write a Put

Just as the writer of "naked" calls receives 100 percent of the premium if the stock is selling below the striking price when the call expires, the seller of "naked" puts receives 100 percent of the put premium if the stock is selling above the striking price when the put expires. The "naked" put seller's reward declines as the price of the stock falls below the striking price. In the example illustrated in Figure 4-10, the seller of the "naked" put actually begins to lose money when the stock price falls below $89.

The motivation of the writer of "naked" puts is usually dif-

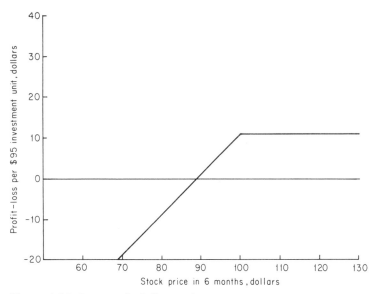

Figure 4-10. Strategy 9: Sell or write a put.

ferent from that of the writer of "naked" calls. In general, the writer of "naked" calls sees this strategy as an alternative to short selling. A "naked" put writer is usually a potential investor in the underlying stock who would like the price of the stock to decline so that he can buy it more cheaply. He is not trying to profit from the option premium itself. The writer's goal is to buy the stock at a lower net price. If the put is exercised, his cost on the stock is reduced by the amount of the put premium. The option premium is his consolation in the event that he does not get an opportunity to buy the stock.

The adjustment of a conventional "naked" put contract is similar to the adjustment of a conventional "naked" call contract. The net proceeds to the seller of the option are decreased by round-trip commissions if the put is exercised. If, however, a "naked" put writer is writing the put in an attempt to lower the effective purchase price, it may be appropriate to disregard the commission adjustment on grounds that the relevant alternative would be to buy the stock outright at the market price. The striking price of a put is reduced by the amount of any cash dividend. However, if the writer of the "naked" put is selling the option to a converter for conversion into a listed call, the commission and dividend adjustments may be materially different, and should be checked carefully. All other adjustments are analogous to the adjustments on calls, including any interest credit for the use of the premium.

Strategy 10: Purchase a Straddle

As illustrated by the graph in Figure 4-11, the buyer of a straddle is in a unique position. Like other option buyers, he can lose no more than 100 percent of the amount he invests in the straddle; but he can lose that much only if the price of the stock on the expiration date of the options is exactly equal to the striking price, or so close to it that sale or exercise of at least one side of the straddle does not justify the outlay of round-trip stock commissions.

Just as it is hard to lose the entire premium paid for a straddle, it can also be hard to make a profit. In spite of the fact that the investor has paid substantial option premiums for both the put and call sides of the straddle, at least one of them is

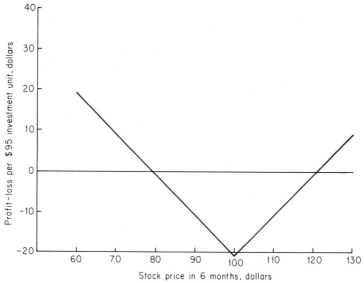

Figure 4-11. Strategy 10: Purchase a straddle.

nearly certain to expire worthless. Consequently, the stock has to move substantially, either up or down, before the straddle buyer recovers his investment, let alone makes a profit. In the graph the break-even point on the upside is $100 (striking price) plus $11 (put premium) plus $10 (call premium) or $121 (break-even point). On the down side the break-even calculation is similar: $100 (striking price) minus $11 (put premium) minus $10 (call premium) equals $79 (break-even point).

Purchase of a straddle makes sense when the investor is convinced that a stock will make a dramatic move but is uncertain whether the move will be up or down. Once the stock price passes the break-even point in either direction, the investor participates point-for-point in any further advance or decline in the price of the stock.

The adjustments to the graph portraying a straddle are similar to the adjustments for a call and a put. The important point is that *both* the appropriate adjustments for a put *and* for a call must be made because the straddle *is* a put and a call.

Strategy 11: Sell a Straddle

Writing "naked" straddles is not a common strategy, though when used with care it can be very effective. Ordinarily the writer of a "naked" put or call has some thoughts about the direction a stock is likely to move during the life of the option. The seller of a "naked" straddle, on the other hand, is making a bet on the magnitude of the move. His point of maximum profitability is the striking price of the options which make up the straddle. At that price neither side of the option will be exercised. As the price of the stock on the expiration date moves away from the striking price, the profit to the writer of the uncovered straddle declines. In the example illustrated on the graph (Figure 4-12) the seller of the straddle will earn a profit over a $42 range of stock prices from $79 on the low side to $121 on the high side. In writing the straddle he is betting that on the day the option expires, the stock will be selling within this range, hopefully close to the center of it.

The adjustments necessary to make this graph represent the actual cash flows are simply the adjustments necessary for the

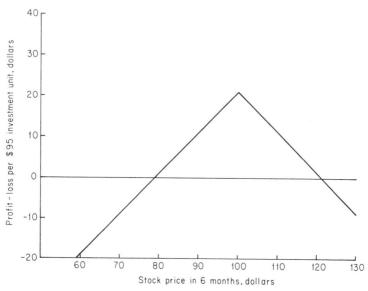

Figure 4-12. Strategy 11: Sell a straddle.

two components of the straddle, the put and the call. If the options are conventional, any dividend paid over the life of the options moves the whole triangular shaped formation to the left by the amount of the dividend because the striking prices on both the put and the call are adjusted downward. Since both sides of the straddle are rarely exercised, each leg of the triangle must be adjusted downward by round-trip commission charges based on the commission requirements of the option that will be exercised.

Selling a "naked" straddle can be a sensible strategy when the investor feels strongly that the underlying stock will not move significantly in either direction over the life of the option. A more common strategy with many similar investment characteristics is the option hedge, usually constructed using listed options. The option hedge is discussed as Strategy 17.

Strategy 12: Purchase the Stock and Sell a Call

This strategy, illustrated by the solid line in the graph (Figure 4-13), is the classic posture of the covered call writer. The

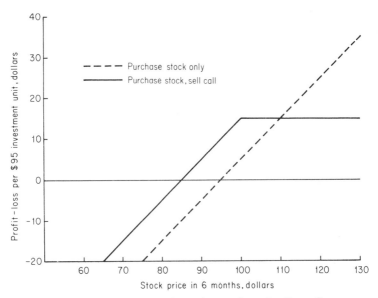

Figure 4-13. Strategy 12: Purchase the stock and sell a call.

covered call writer buys 100 shares of the underlying stock and writes one call contract using the stock position as collateral. The call premium provides a degree of protection should the underlying stock decline during the life of the option. In return for this downside protection, the covered writer's profit is limited, in this case to $15 per share over 6 months, no matter how high the stock price rises. At any stock price in excess of $110 per share the writer would have been better off not to have written the call, as indicated by the intersection of the solid line and the dashed line which represents Strategy 2, owning the stock without writing a call.

The commission and dividend adjustments are a combination of the adjustments necessary to analyze the basic stock ownership position (Strategy 2) and those necessary to analyze the uncovered call writer's position (Strategy 7). When these strategies are combined, certain adjustments cancel out. For example, if the call is a conventional call, no dividend adjustment will be necessary if the call is exercised because the adjustment in the striking price exactly offsets the dividend received by the writer as owner of the stock.

The motivations of covered writers are diverse. An investor may own a long-term position in the underlying stock which, for tax reasons, he is reluctant to sell even though he is not optimistic about the near-term price action of the stock. Rather than incur a large tax liability, he writes options to partially insulate himself from what he feels is a significant downside risk. In the event that this investor's appraisal of the stock proves incorrect and it rises over the life of the option, he does not have to deliver his long-term low-cost stock. If the call was written on an exchange, he can repurchase the option, terminating his writer's obligation and realizing an ordinary loss on the option. If a conventional option is exercised, the writer can purchase new shares in the open market and deliver them against the call, keeping his long-term position in the stock intact. Any investor who buys stock in this manner to deliver in lieu of his long-term, low-basis position should try to structure the transaction to avoid making a "wash sale" which will prevent him from deducting the loss on the transaction. The "wash sale" rules are discussed in some detail in Chapter 5, Section A.

In contrast to the writer who uses long-term, low-basis stock as collateral, some writers write calls only on stocks they like and are willing to hold. This approach may seem peculiar because by writing the option, these investors are precluded from obtaining more than a limited profit if the stock rises as they anticipate. If the stock rises above the striking price, these writers are sure to earn the option premium. When earned consistently, option premiums can provide a highly satisfactory return. The major risk in adopting this strategy is that the premium may limit the return when the stock rises by substantially more than it reduces the loss when the stock declines.

A third group of writers will write covered options only when they feel the option premium is high relative to the fair value of the option. This group is usually relatively neutral toward the stock, yet can have a strong opinion that the option is overpriced. The merits of this approach will be clearer after we have examined the evaluation of option contracts in more detail.

Strategy 13: Purchase the Stock and Sell a Put

The investor who sells a put on a stock he already owns will participate fully in any upside move due to his long position in the stock. (See Figure 4-14.) In addition, he will receive the amount of the premium paid by the buyer of the put. On the other hand, he doubles his leverage on the downside. For every point that the stock drops below the striking price, the value of this investor's position will drop by two points, one point from the decline in value of the stock he owns long and one point from the decline in value of the stock that will be sold to him by the holder of the put.

The adjustments for this combined strategy are simply the sum of the adjustments which the owner of the stock and the "uncovered" seller of a put would make, a combination of Strategies 2 and 9.

The motivations of an investor adopting this strategy may seem somewhat obscure. Usually, this investor has a very constructive attitude toward the underlying stock. In fact, by selling the put he is expressing a willingness to double his

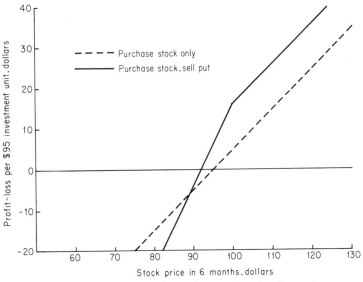

Figure 4-14. Strategy 13: Purchase the stock and sell a put.

position. By selling a put rather than simply purchasing the stock outright, the investor is trying to have the best of all possible worlds. If the stock rises as expected, he will participate in the rise through the increase in the value of his stock holding. The put will not be exercised, and the premium will be pure profit. If the price of the stock declines, he will find himself the proud owner of twice as much stock as he owned before. Thanks to the premium received for writing the put, his effective cost on the additional stock purchased will be $89 per share, a saving of $6 over the $95 market price at the time the transaction is initiated.

On the negative side, this strategy can be dangerous if an investor's resources are limited. The collateral value of his stock position will be declining at the time he is called upon to buy additional shares. Unless an investor's feelings on a stock are particularly strong, or he wishes to engage in a program of compulsory averaging down, writing puts against a long position in the stock is probably not a sound strategy.

Strategy 14: Purchase the Stock and Sell a Straddle

This position illustrates a strategy frequently adopted by writers of conventional options. The demand for options is primarily a demand for calls, but because the premium income is larger and because of certain tax benefits, which will be discussed later, option writers often prefer to write straddles. The put side of the straddle is usually converted into a second call.

The apparent attraction of writing straddles collateralized by a long position in the underlying stock should be clear from the diagram which shows this strategy imposed upon the graph of buying the stock alone. (See Figure 4-15.) Over a price range of some $42, $21 on each side of the striking price, the investor is better off adopting this strategy than owning the stock alone. He will show a profit at any stock price above $87 per share. Should the stock sell above the striking price, his profit will be a substantial $26 per underlying share for the 6-month period, or double that amount when annualized.

The only significant weakness in this strategy is apparent if

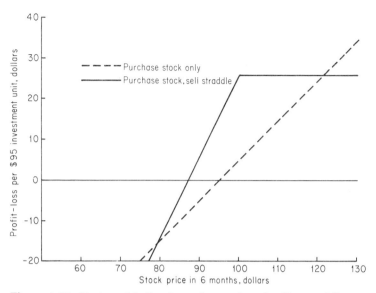

Figure 4-15. Strategy 14: Purchase the stock and sell a straddle.

the price of the stock declines sharply. For every point that the stock declines below the striking price, the covered straddle writer is in essentially the same position as the writer of a put who also owns the underlying stock. The value of his position decreases by one point on the stock he owns and one point on the stock that will be sold to him by the owner of the put side of his straddle. If it were not for the tax features of selling straddles, it is doubtful that most option writers would consciously put themselves in this risk position. From a risk viewpoint, both the option hedge and the "naked" or uncovered straddle are usually preferable to the covered straddle writing position.

Strategy 15: Purchase the Stock and Purchase a Put

This is usually considered to be an insurance or risk-reduction strategy. When he buys the put, the investor is insuring that his loss can be no more than the amount of the premium on the put less the amount by which the put is selling in the money. On the upside, once the price of the stock passes the striking price, the investor who adopts this strategy will participate point-for-point in any increase in the price of the stock. (See Figure 4-16.)

Adjustments to this position can be made by combining the appropriate adjustments for being long the stock (Strategy 2) with the adjustments for owning the put (Strategy 8).

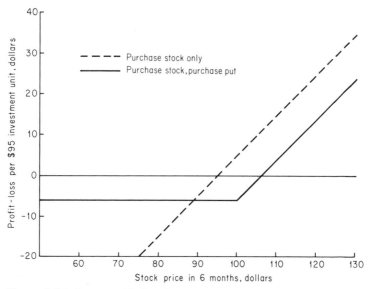

Figure 4-16. Strategy 15: Purchase the stock and purchase a put.

The investment rationale for this strategy is virtually identical to the rationale used to justify the purchase of a call; in fact, the shapes of the profit-loss lines are identical. The downside risk is limited; yet, after deduction of the put premium, the upside potential is unlimited. Though tax factors may complicate the decision slightly, this strategy will usually be less attractive than the alternative of investing most of an individual's cash in high-yielding debt securities and buying a call to give the same upside exposure.

Strategy 16: Sell the Stock Short and Purchase a Call

As in the case of Strategy 15, the option serves as an insurance policy, limiting the investor's risk. Here the call protects the investor from a major upward move in the price of the stock

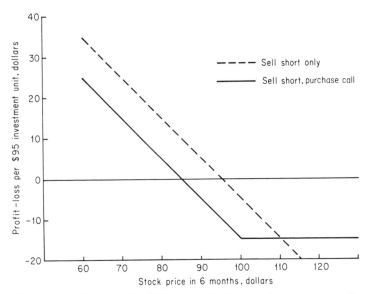

Figure 4-17. Strategy 16: Sell the stock short and purchase a call.

(Figure 4-17). If this configuration of possible gains and losses appeals to him, the investor should look into the possibility of buying a put and keeping any unused cash in short-term debt instruments. Buying the put will always be a cheaper way of achieving this risk-reward relationship, and it can also provide a tax advantage. If the investor is correct in anticipating a decline in the stock, owning a long-term put can give him a long-term capital gain.

For a variety of reasons, most importantly the high transaction costs of conventional options, Strategies 17, 18, and 19 are practical only with listed options. If any of the proposals to lower the transaction costs of conventional options and create a secondary market are adopted, the applicability of these strategies would expand.

Strategy 17: Set Up an Option Hedge

The investment posture illustrated here consists of a long position in the underlying stock used as collateral for writing two calls. The number of calls written in an option hedge is less important than the fact that the calls cover more shares than the investor owns and that the profit-loss line on the graph peaks at the striking price and begins to decline as the stock rises further (Figure 4-18).

The reader will recognize in this diagram the shape of the graph developed for Strategy 11, the sale of an uncovered straddle. As in the cases of previous strategies, the investor can achieve comparable results by writing a "naked" straddle against collateral consisting of short-term debt securities. Unlike our earlier examples, the option hedge may be preferable to writing a straddle. The investor will probably find the option hedge easier to "unwind" than the "naked" straddle. Also, he may enjoy lower net transaction costs if he retains the position in the underlying stock and continues to write options against it. In addition, he can defer any long-term capital gain on the stock position by continuing to write options against the stock as his present option positions expire or are closed out. Finally, the writer of an option hedge can obtain a long-term capital gain on his stock position. The straddle writer can only get a short-term gain on the unexer-

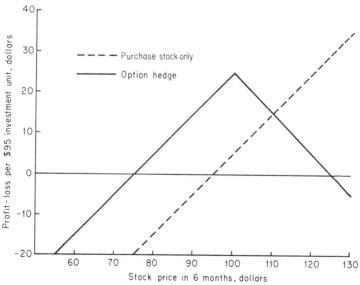

Figure 4-18. Strategy 17: Set up an option hedge.

cised side of the straddle. On the other hand, if an investor has excess capital losses or has no intention of holding the stock beyond the expiration date of the options, he will find writing straddles more attractive.

The most important feature of the option hedge and the straddle is that peak profitability is achieved at the striking price of the option and the striking price is usually close to the present stock price. To the extent that the future stock price is likely to be close to the present price (or the striking price), the most profitable point is also one of the most probable. The option hedge is one of very few investment positions that provides a respectable profit if the stock stands still. This feature makes it useful in reducing the investor's exposure to market risk.

Strategy 18: Set Up a Reverse Option Hedge

Figure 4-19 illustrates a reverse option hedge consisting of a short position in the common stock, offset by a long position in two calls on that stock. As in the case of the option hedge,

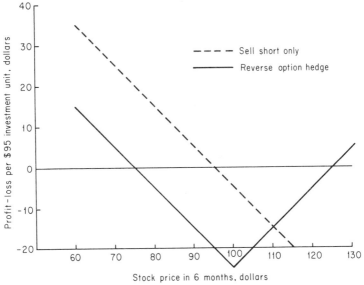

Figure 4-19. Strategy 18: Set up a reverse option hedge.

the number of calls purchased will depend on the risk-reward preferences of the investor. In contrast to the option hedge, which is based on the expectation that the stock price will be stable, the reverse option hedge will be profitable only if the stock moves dramatically in either direction. In the same way that an option hedge is comparable to writing a straddle, a reverse option hedge is comparable in terms of its risk-reward characteristics to buying a straddle.

Whereas it was argued that the option hedge was frequently preferable to writing a "naked" straddle collateralized by short-term debt securities, transaction costs and tax considerations ordinarily make purchase of a straddle preferable to the reverse option hedge, if listed calls can be reversed to create puts on reasonable terms. (For a comprehensive discussion of the conversion of puts into calls and the reversal of calls to create puts, see Appendix B.) When listed trading in puts begins, buying a straddle will be preferable for most investors.

The buyer can get a long-term gain on either side of a long-term straddle. He can only get a long-term gain on the call side of a reverse option hedge. More importantly, he has to pay out the proceeds of the short sale to the lender of the stock. While creation of the straddle through reversal of a call will involve a short sale by the conversion house, payment of the proceeds of the short sale to the stock lender will probably be only partially reflected in the price of the put side of the straddle. Only when conversion/reversal terms are onerous will the reverse option hedge be an appropriate strategy.

Strategy 19: Set Up a Listed Call Spread

The listed call spread is a hedged strategy consisting of a long position in one option and an offsetting short position in another option. Ordinarily both options will be listed options, though some spreads have been done using a conventional option as one side of the spread. The possible variety of spreads is so great that Section D of this chapter will be devoted to this investment phenomenon.

The spread illustrated in Figure 4-20 is a type normally set up to take advantage of the tax features of listed options.

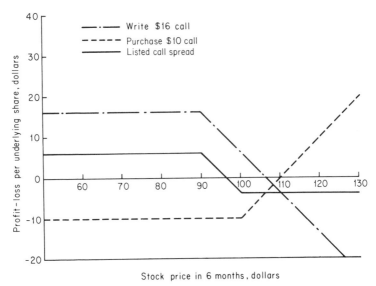

Figure 4-20. Strategy 19: Set up a listed call spread.

Specifically, this spread assumes that the investor buys the $10 option with the $100 striking price used in the previous graphs. To set up the spread, the investor writes an option having the same expiration date but a striking price of $90, that is selling for $16; that is, $1,600 per 100-share contract. Although the investment characteristics of this spread will be discussed in more detail in the chapter on spreads, the unadjusted profit-loss line shows a fair profit if the stock declines and a loss if the stock rises. As we shall see, after adjustment for taxes and commissions, this spread can be highly profitable no matter which way the stock moves, so long as it moves far enough.

In addition to the long-term spread illustrated here, some investors find very short-term spreads in expiring options attractive; others attempt to set up arbitrage spreads to take advantage of temporary price disparities; and still others set up bullish spreads that are most attractive when the stock rises. Each of these spreads has different investment characteristics which will be discussed in detail in Section D of this chapter.

By this time, it should be clear that with options an investor can structure the risk-reward characteristics of an individual investment position or his entire portfolio in virtually any way he chooses. In fact, by combining long and short positions in stocks and options, it is possible to almost completely eliminate market risk from a diversified portfolio. To understand one of the many ways in which this can be done, the reader need only visualize half of his portfolio in option hedges and the other half in reverse option hedges or straddles. If he has sufficiently diversified his stock positions, *his rate of return will be independent of the direction of stock price movement.* By setting up diversified hedged positions, the portfolio manager can use options to *virtually eliminate market risk.*

Obviously, protection from risk is only half the answer. To make these machinations worthwhile, the investor needs to obtain a superior return on investment as well as reduce his risk exposure. The key to a superior return, as noted in the Introduction, is option evaluation. With option hedges, the investor must write overpriced options. Straddles or reverse option hedges must be based on purchases of underpriced options. The key, then, to consistently superior performance with minimum risk is effective use of properly evaluated option contracts. This point will arise frequently in subsequent chapters.

B. WHY INVESTORS USE OPTIONS

As the various investment positions were examined closely in Section A, some of the motives that might lead an investor to adopt a particular strategy became apparent. The purpose here is to expand upon and evaluate the reasoning used by investors to justify their various uses of options. While most strategies make sense under certain assumptions or circumstances, the rationale leading investors to adopt a particular strategy might be incomplete or erroneous.

Most option buyers say that they purchase puts and calls to increase their leverage when they expect a significant move in the stock. Because the purchase of options permits investors to control more shares of stock than they could possibly con-

trol under any realistic set of common stock margin requirements, options can provide more return on the investor's
dollar than any other method of investing in securities. The
100 percent cash requirement applied to the purchase of puts
and calls, and certain rules which prohibit individuals or
groups acting in concert from buying more than a certain
number of options, limit the individual's ability to leverage
and pyramid an investment. Thus, while the option buyer
cannot imitate the great speculators of the 1920s, the leverage
obtainable through options is still substantial.

Many of the same investors who emphasize the importance
of leverage on the upside in the case of calls, or on the downside in the case of puts, also focus on the importance of an
option's ability to limit the investor's risk. Any buyer of a put
or call knows the maximum loss possible at the time the purchase is made. This limited-risk feature of options has apparently begun to appeal to a few institutional investors. In-
trigued by the potential of a speculative stock, yet concerned
for their fiduciary and quasi-fiduciary responsibilities, a very
few institutional investors have begun to take advantage of
the limited-loss feature of options. Rather than invest $100,000
in the securities of a particular corporation, the institution will
invest $10,000 in call options and put the remaining $90,000
in short-term debt instruments. Interest on the short-term
debt will typically cover about one-third of any possible loss
on the calls. If the stock price advances sharply over the life of
the options, the portfolio participates in this advance. On the
other hand, downside risk is strictly limited to the amount of
the option premium. This use of options will probably expand
as the number of issues with listed options expands and as
institutional investors become more comfortable with options.

The purchase of options to construct a kind of synthetic
convertible bond actually fits the risk-reward requirements of
an institution far better than the more typical institutional
strategy of covered writing. To the extent that an investor's
goal is to limit portfolio risk exposure, the combination of
short-term debt and a long option position has a maximum
risk equal to the amount paid for the options. The covered
writer's risk is reduced by the amount of the option premium

received, but the markets of the early seventies suggest that this is not always enough protection. A quick review of the graphs in Section A should convince the reader that it is the option buyer whose risk is always known and limited to the premium he pays. The option writer, whether or not he also has a position in the stock, can incur almost unlimited losses. The popular view of the option buyer as a risk-taker will change slowly as a new type of buyer appears.

A relatively small number of options are purchased to hedge short or long positions in the underlying common stock. Perhaps the major reason hedging with options has not enjoyed more popularity is that, as we saw in the previous section, buying a call to hedge a short position is functionally equivalent to buying a put. Likewise, buying a put to hedge a long position is functionally equivalent to buying a call. Most investors find it less costly, if not less complicated, to purchase the put or the call outright, rather than construct the hedge.

Over the years option writers have developed a number of explanations and rationalizations for the basic strategies of writing calls, puts, and straddles against positions in the underlying common stock. A very common justification for option writing is that it permits writers to generate additional "income" on their investment portfolio. While it is true that most expired option premiums are taxed as ordinary income to option writers, it is important that writers not lose sight of the fact that they are giving up certain rights in return for this additional income. For example, the writer of a covered call is giving up the right to participate in any appreciation in the underlying stock beyond a price equal to the striking price of the option plus the amount of the call premium. The writer of a straddle gives up similar privileges on the call side of the straddle. The writer of a put, whether written alone or as part of a straddle, incurs an obligation to purchase the stock at a particular price even if the stock is selling at a far lower level at the time the put is exercised.

Given the limited resources and relative lack of sophistication of some option buyers, many observers would expect their analysis of an option position to be superficial. Option writers, however, have long been considered among the most sophisticated participants in the securities markets. To the extent that these investors *really* view their option premiums as additional "income" that accrues to them without significant obligation, their reputation as sophisticates is in danger. Rational analysis, at a minimum, consists of careful examination and weighing of what the investor is giving up in return for what he is receiving. This minimum standard is sometimes more easily satisfied by the option buyer than by the writer, who frequently must evaluate a position in the stock as well as any option he may write. The fact that rational analysis is complicated is no excuse not to undertake it.

If an option premium is too low, the writer who consistently writes such options will find that, despite all his additional "income," his net worth is declining or, at best, growing very slowly. The option premiums he receives during periods when the stock rises will be inadequate to make up for his losses when the price declines. Because the covered call writer agrees to limit his return on the upside, he must earn enough from the option premium to protect his capital during periods when the stock drops.

A classic explanation for writing options is that the investor writes calls in an attempt to hedge his long position in the stock. Frequently, this investor is concerned about the safety of his long position because he expects the stock to decline, yet he does not want to incur a capital gain tax liability by liquidating the position. He may anticipate a modest, temporary decline which would permit him to obtain an option premium with minimal risk of having the stock called away.

Occasionally, an option writer will argue that he is writing calls in the hope of selling his securities at a higher effective price than is presently available. This can be a sound strategy if the investor is happy holding the securities at current or lower price levels, yet would be willing to liquidate the position at slightly higher prices. The chance to sell stock at a higher effective price through receipt of a call premium is appealing. The writer must be certain, however, that the superficial appeal of this argument is not a substitute for careful analysis of both the stock and the option-writing opportunity. If the premium is inadequate to cover the risk of a decline in the stock price, this rationale for option writing becomes questionable and the stock should probably be sold outright.

An argument similar to the "sell the stock at a higher price" thesis motivates certain writers of puts who argue that they write puts in an attempt to lower their effective purchase price. If this writer of puts is correct in thinking that the stock is attractive for purchase, he may be ahead to buy it outright. The put premium would be inadequate compensation for missing the chance to purchase a stock that doubles. Only a careful evaluation of the put premium and the investor's expectations for the stock permit an appropriate decision.

By far the most important rationale for the purchase and sale of option contracts is that, unlike other securities, they provide the investment manager with virtually unlimited flexibility in the risk management of a diversified portfolio. This argument was rarely heard prior to the creation of the listed option, but it has attracted many adherents and should eventually dominate discussions of diversification and portfolio theory as well as option discussions. Using options, a portfolio manager can accept or lay off risk as he sees fit. Neutralization of market risk alone would be considered a worthwhile objective by many investors. Options provide the opportunity not only to neutralize risk but to obtain a superior return as well.

Contrary to an increasingly popular belief, every option writer is *not* guaranteed a 15 percent annual return on his money, nor is every option buyer a lamb being led to the slaughter. Listed options are traded in a reasonably efficient market. If option premiums are higher than fair value, enough writers will be attracted to push premiums down. If premiums are too low, buyers will be attracted. In spite of this mechanism, there is a fairly wide range of prices within which a particular option contract might sell. If he buys options that are underpriced, and writes options that are overpriced, the investor can probably achieve a superior return and simultaneously reduce his market risk exposure.

Because the investor using options can adjust his risk parameters in virtually any way he chooses, the individual option contract should be purchased or sold only if it offers the prospect of superior reward. In this context, the dominant factors in determining a strategy should be the investor's thoughts on the investment merits of the underlying stock and an estimate of the fair value of specific option contracts. While rational evaluation of option contracts is not a simple task, as we shall see in our discussion of option evaluation, the investor who ignores the importance of option value in structuring whatever option-related strategy he may undertake is virtually assuring himself of mediocre long-term results.

Although option evaluation is stressed here, the value of any other analytical process an investor may rely on is not disputed. Whether he feels a stock will go up because it broke out on a chart or because he has done exhaustive fundamental research, the investor should still not ignore option evaluation. Recognizing that his analysis could be wrong and assuming that the investment in question will be only part of his total portfolio, the investor might be ahead if he buys the stock and writes overpriced, out-of-the-money call options instead of buying the same options outright. The covered writing strategy expresses the investor's bullishness on the company's prospects, and the overpriced option works for the investor rather than against him. If he buys the overpriced call option, the investor can control more shares with the same investment, but if his judgment on the stock is only average, the risk-adjusted expected value of the call would be less than the purchase price. In the covered writer's position, an overpriced option will give the investor a superior return with average stock judgment. Similar arguments apply in reverse if the investor expects a stock to decline. Buying an underpriced put reversed from an underpriced listed call is better than writing the underpriced call. Option evaluation can stack the odds in an investor's favor, even if his stock judgment is only average.

None of the arguments examined in this section as reasons for buying or writing an option is adequate without an appraisal of the fair value of the option contract. The option buyer who pays too much and the writer who accepts too little are fighting the investment battle with one hand tied behind their respective backs.

A persistent focus on option evaluation is not an argument

that the investor should scan the exchange closing prices each day in search of temporarily overpriced or underpriced options; the investor should instead seek those options which are consistently overpriced for writing strategies or those which are underpriced for strategies requiring option purchases. Not every investor can be an arbitrageur and profit from small discrepancies in the pricing of options. Every investor can, however, avoid making transactions at prices that give the arbitrageur his opportunities.

Option evaluation is a complex process. We will examine it in detail after we look at some other uses of options, the tax treatment of option transactions, and option participation by various investors.

C. SHORT-TERM TRADING OF LISTED OPTIONS

There are two principal groups of participants in the active short-term trading that has developed in listed call contracts. The first group consists of professional arbitrageurs who attempt to take advantage of temporary disparities between and among the prices of these options, related convertible securities, and the underlying common shares. Arbitrage activity can be based on elaborate calculations or on an intuitive feel developed over years of experience. Through their efforts, arbitrageurs make the market fairer and more efficient for the second large group of active traders, the general public.

In contrast to the arbitrageurs, the nonprofessional trader is more likely to have an opinion on the probable direction of the market or the stock underlying an option than on the suitability of a particular option price–stock price relationship. These individual investors are usually attracted to option trading by the leverage inherent in an option contract. If an individual anticipates a near-term move in a particular stock or in the general market, he can control more shares by buying or writing options than in any other way.

Although the purpose of this section is to provide a few suggestions to the active option trader, a few disclaimers are in order first. The author has never claimed an ability to predict short-term swings in the overall market or the short-term price behavior of an individual stock. Many people do claim such an ability; a few even appear to have it. The author makes no judgment on anyone's claim to trading ability, nor can he advise anyone without this ability how one can acquire it. The author's intent is just to point out a few ways in which the active short-term option trader can improve the odds.

Other things being equal, the short-term trader with access to a rational option evaluation model should try to write options that are overpriced and buy options that are underpriced. Unless his conviction is unusually strong, he should try to find another way to participate in any expected move before taking a position that is at variance with the relationship between the fair value of an option and its market price. Though option valuation can highlight opportunities, most traders will use it only to help them select a particular option contract to trade once they have decided the direction they expect a particular stock or the overall market to move.

It is possible to go one step further and suggest the type of option contract the active trader should consider. The trader who is writing uncovered calls in anticipation of a decline should usually try to write calls that are in the money. This strategy generally maximizes downside leverage per dollar of margin required and may slightly reduce transaction costs. The short-term trader who is a buyer should generally select calls that are slightly out of the money and that have a short remaining life. The premiums on these calls will be small, and the potential is excellent for a large percentage gain *if* the trader's expectations for the underlying stock are correct.

Unfortunately, these leverage-maximizing trading rules (which will be obvious to most active option traders) will frequently result in the purchase of the most overpriced and the sale of the most underpriced options available on a particular underlying stock. Perhaps because of the greater leverage they give to the strongly opinionated buyer and writer respectively, short-term and out-of-the-money options tend to be *relatively* overpriced and in-the-money options tend to be *relatively* underpriced. This is by no means an invariable price pattern, but it does occur quite frequently. There is some evidence that the standardized margin rules for listed option spreads adopted late in 1974 may have modified previously typical price relationships between different options on the same underlying stock. If this apparent change in relative pricing persists, the short-term trader may no longer incur a penalty when he tries to maximize his leverage.

If option evaluation indicates that a particular sector of the option market is temporarily overpriced or underpriced, the trader might find it possible to concentrate activity in that sector. Relevant sectors might include long-term options versus short-term options, options deep in the money versus options out of the money, or options on volatile stocks versus options on conservative stocks. The trader using option evaluation to concentrate activity in particular sectors of the market will usually find that most disparities have a tendency to disappear over time. If they disappear while he has a position, he will obtain an arbitrage profit in addition to any other profit he achieves.

With the possible exception of a particularly attractive listed option spread, the short-term trader should avoid complex hedging strategies because they increase costs. The favorable margin treatment accorded a spread can increase downside leverage if the trader expects a substantial and rapid decline in the stock price. However, the cost of an unsuccessful spread should be weighed against the strength of the trader's conviction. To put the cost in perspective, round-trip commissions on an unsuccessful spread can *easily* exceed the initial margin posted.

These suggestions may or may not appeal to the short-term trader who has a strong conviction. However, if one's conviction is less than overwhelming, these suggestions should be of help.

D. LISTED OPTION SPREADS

1. Short-Term Spreads and Option Arbitrage

Prior to the commencement of trading on the Chicago Board Options Exchange in April 1973, a spread in the option world was a special type of straddle with the put and call exercisable at different striking prices. Though this kind of spread never enjoyed much popularity, the newer listed option spread already accounts for an important share of option trading activity.

A listed option spread consists of a long position in one option, offset by a short or writer's position in another option on the same underlying stock. Numerous combinations of long and short option positions are possible. For example, if an investor feels that premiums on short-term options are high relative to premiums on longer-term options or that the market will be steady or decline for a while before it advances sharply, he can write a short-term option contract against a long position in an option maturing further in the future. Alternatively, an investor who feels that options selling out of the money are attractive relative to options selling in the money, or one who feels that the market is due for a significant decline, could write an option which is trading in the money and buy an out-of-the-money option on the same stock. There is no point in trying to list *all* spread combinations; it is clear that there is a wide variety of possibilities.

For simplicity and to avoid misunderstandings, a *spread* is defined as a partial hedge consisting of a long position in one option contract and a short position in another contract of the same type (put or call) on the same underlying stock. A *call spread* would consist of long and short positions in calls. A *put spread* would consist of long and short positions in puts. This discussion will deal only with call spreads, but many points apply equally to put spreads.

One categorization of spread types that is frequently useful is based on the margin treatment accorded a particular position:

Front spread: The striking price of the long call option is *lower than or equal to* the striking price of the short call option, and the remaining life of the long option is *greater than or equal to* the life of the short option. Both options are listed. Also known as a *bullish* spread.

Back spread: The striking price of the long call option is *greater than* the striking price of the short call option, and the remaining life of the long option is *greater than or equal to* the life of the short option. Both options are listed. Also known as a *bearish* spread.

Unmargined spread: For one of several reasons the short option is margined as a "naked" option rather than as part of a spread: (a) The long option may expire before the short option. (b) The difference between the striking prices of the two options in a back spread may be so great that the margin rules for a "naked" option are more favorable than those for a back spread. (c) One or both of the options may be unlisted.

Many listed spread transactions involve two options with a common expiration date and different striking prices. For simplicity, only this kind of spread will be depicted graphically. Extension of the principles developed here to spreads involving options with different expiration dates is relatively easy. The investor need only estimate the price of the longer-term option at selected stock prices on the date the shorter option expires. To draw a graph, the investor assumes that he closes out his position in the longer option at the estimated price and reflects any gain or loss on that option in his profit-loss line.

Many investors set up unbalanced spreads in which the number of options purchased is different from the number of options sold. The analysis which follows can be adapted to such strategies if care is taken to modify margin requirements when the spread is unbalanced.

The reader may recognize in Figure 4-21 a repeat of Figure 4-20. In this example we assume that the market price of the common stock is $95 on the day the spread is set up and that one of the exchanges lists two options with the same expiration date, one having a striking price of $90 and selling at $16 and the other a striking price of $100, selling for $10. The investor sets up a back spread by purchasing the option with the $100 striking price at $10 and writing the option with the $90 striking price at $16.

As the graph indicates, this spread is profitable before taxes and commissions if the price of the stock declines before the expiration date. In the case illustrated, the maximum possible loss is four points if the stock sells above $100 on the day the option expires and the maximum possible gain is six points if the stock drops below $90 on the expiration date. Calculating the pretax profit or loss on a spread at any stock price is simply

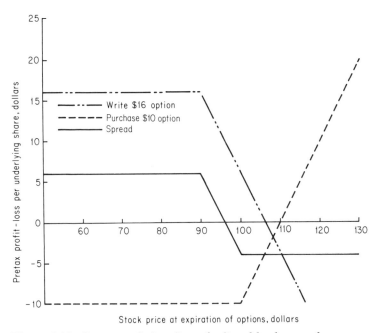

Figure 4-21. Pretax profit-loss line of a listed back spread.

a matter of computing (1) the net premium earned on the option written minus (2) the net loss on the option purchased. If the net premium earned is negative or the option purchased is profitable, the calculation is identical but the algebraic signs change.

The potential pretax profit or loss from a bearish spread is usually quite significant relative to the initial margin requirement. When both options are in the money at the time the spread is set up, the profit from a very-short-term bearish spread, like that illustrated in Figure 4-22, can be enormous if the stock drops dramatically. With the stock price still at $95, as in the previous example, Figure 4-22 assumes an investor pays $6 for a very-short-term option, exercisable at $90. To offset this long position the investor writes an option for a premium of $15.50 with the same expiration date, exercisable at $80. Apart from commissions, the maximum possible loss is $.50 per share. The profitability (again, excluding commis-

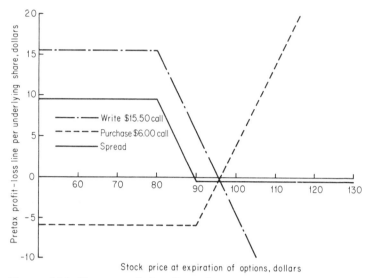

Figure 4-22. Pretax profit-loss line of a short-term bearish spread.

sions) can be as much as $9.50 per optioned share if the stock drops to $80 or lower. On an initial required net margin of $50 per spread or $.50 per optioned share plus commissions, this is an outstanding return on investment over a short period.

Unfortunately, there are two obstacles to realizing the large profit which this kind of spread can provide. First, making any profit at all requires a sharp, immediate drop in the stock price. While such drops have been distressingly frequent over the past several years, they have not been so common that a $15 drop in a $95 stock within a few weeks could be considered common.

A second problem with this kind of short-term spread is the enormous commission cost. In the example cited, if the investor did a spread involving 10 contracts on each side and had to undo the spread near the expiration date with the options at parity and the stock still at $95, the round-trip commission cost would be $701.50, the equivalent of $.70 per optioned share or more than the precommission margin the investor would have to post. The commission cost would be even higher if an exercise notice was delivered for the option written. (Exercise is a distinct possibility on short-term options that are deep in the money and selling at negligible premiums over intrinsic value.) A commission handicap of this magnitude is usually too much for any investment to overcome.

If the options in this example are fairly priced, the expected profit, excluding commissions, should be about as high if the investor buys the deep-in-the-money option and writes the moderately in-the-money option. The indicated potential profit from such a strategy of $.50 per optioned share before commissions suggests that most investors do not think a $5 to $15 drop in the stock price is probable over the remaining life of the options. Short-term spreads of this type should be undertaken only when the investor has an unusual conviction that a stock will drop, *and* when a rational option valuation method shows an unusual relationship between the two options which would permit an arbitrage profit.

Short-term arbitrage spreading based on option valuation is an attempt to profit from temporary price disparities among the various options available on one underlying stock. The arbitrageur need not have an opinion on the probable direction the stock price will take. Theoretically, he can adjust his long and short positions to approximately neutralize the effect of stock price fluctuations. In practice, most arbitrageurs do not set up neutral mixes, preferring to let their positions reflect an opinion on the stock.

Any spread setup using short-term options should have enough of an arbitrage profit built in to cover *at least* two-thirds of the expected in-and-out commission cost. The commission cost of setting up and closing out these spreads is great enough that only with some arbitrage profit offset does the investor stand a good chance of making money even if his opinion on the stock is accurate. In this sense, a sound determination of the relative values of the options involved is a key component of any short-term spreading or hedging strategy. The investor who sets up spreads without being alert to the relative values of the options involved will eventually dissipate his capital in commission charges, no matter how accurate his stock judgments prove to be.

2. Long-Term Spreads

The principal attractiveness of spreading lies not in short-term spreads, unless they are set up with a sizable arbitrage component, but in spreads involving options with more than 6 months of life remaining. Figure 4-21 illustrated the dollar profitability of such a long-term spread unadjusted for commissions and taxes. The pretax profitability of this spread is excellent when the stock price falls, but the investor loses money before taxes when the stock price rises. Unless an investor is confident that the stock will decline over the life of the options, the attractiveness of this long-term spread is not readily apparent.

The tax characteristics of options change the picture completely when the profit-loss line is adjusted for all taxes and commissions. The solid line in Figure 4-23 illustrates the dollar profit-loss line of the same long-term back spread after adjustment for taxes and commissions, under the assumption that the investor is careful not to let losses go long-term. The dashed line illustrates the aftertax and aftercommission effects of reversing the spread to set up a front spread (buying the

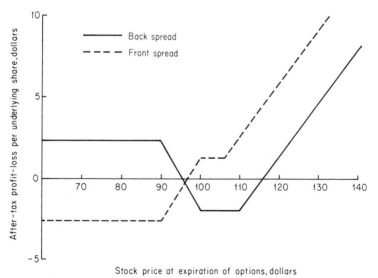

Figure 4-23. Aftertax profit-loss lines of listed option spreads.

option with the $90 striking price and writing the option with the $100 striking price). The calculations assume the investor pays taxes at a 25 percent rate on long-term capital gains and at a 60 percent rate on ordinary income and short-term capital gains. The reason the long-term spread is attractive after tax adjustments is that the investor can obtain long-term capital gains treatment for any profit and short-term capital loss treatment for any loss on the option purchased if the option has a remaining life of more than 6 months when the spread is set up. If the spread is set up in June or July and the purchased option expires in January of the following year, losses can be realized in the current year and profits deferred. The investor achieves this result simply by closing out the unprofitable part of the spread this year and closing out the profitable part next year. If the stock price is in a range where there is some possibility of slippage on the profitable option after the unprofitable side is closed out, the profitable side can be protected by reestablishing a spread using a third option on the same stock. Respreading is usually necessary only when the buy side of the spread is profitable. The profit on the option owned is preserved by writing another option, usually one that is short term and modestly in the money.

Figure 4-24 demonstrates that the high aftertax profitability generated by the long-term gain on the purchased option provides an excellent rate of return on the margin employed. While all previous graphs have shown the dollar profit from a transaction at various stock prices, Figure 4-24 depicts the rate of return on required margin. Rate-of-return calculations are tricky when option writing is involved. For clarity, the rate of return is calculated in terms of aftertax profitability as a percent of the margin required. This calculation tends to understate slightly the actual return on the assets employed in a back spread or uncovered writing. A fuller discussion of this calculation will be found in Appendix C.

More detail on the assumptions underlying Figures 4-23 and 4-24 is provided in the notes to Tables 4-1 and 4-2 which display the calculations used to determine profitability and rate of return on required margin at certain key prices. As the reader can see from Figure 4-24, the aftertax return from the

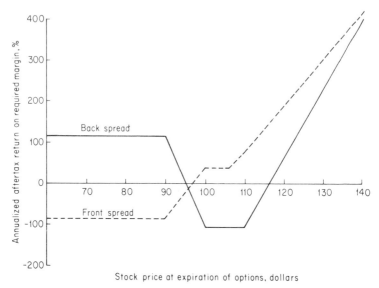

Figure 4-24. Annualized aftertax return on average margin of listed spreads.

back spread can be quite high if the stock moves significantly *either* up or down over the life of the spread. The return on the complementary front spread is positive only if the stock advances, and the pretax loss can equal the entire investment if the stock declines. Obviously, the investment is quite modest relative to the potential profit.

The attractiveness of these long-term spread positions would appear so compelling from Figure 4-24 that the reader may well ask, "Are they legal?" The answer is that they are, indeed, legal and proper if the following simple conditions hold:

1. There are no pertinent changes in the tax treatment of options.
2. The investor has short-term capital gains against which to offset any short-term capital losses which the long side of the spread might generate. Most option traders can meet this requirement if they buy short-term options successfully or if they write straddles.

In addition to these requirements, an IRS agent *may* question the transaction if there does not appear to be any nontax

Table 4-1. Net Profit and Rate of Return Calculation: Long-term Spread (Back Spread) (All figures in dollars unless otherwise labeled and pertain to a spread involving 10 contracts on each side)*

Stock Price at Expiration of Option	$80	$90	$100	$110	$120	$130	$140
Expiration profit (loss) per share:							
Option purchased ($10, $100 strike price)	($10)	($10)	($10)	$0	$10	$20	$30
Option written ($16, $90 strike price)	16	16	6	(4)	(14)	(24)	(34)
Commission:							
Set up position $10 option	172	172	172	172	172	172	172
$16 option	226	226	226	226	226	226	226
Closeout position $10 option			172	172	262	322	332
$16 option				262	322	332	332
Rehedge commission (if necessary to protect capital gain)	300	300	300	300	300	300	300
Long-term capital gain					9,566	19,506	29,496
After tax					7,175	14,630	22,122
Short-term capital loss	10,172	10,172	10,472	344			
After tax	4,069	4,069	4,189	138			
Ordinary income/(loss)	15,774	15,774	5,302	(4,788)	(14,848)	(24,858)	(34,858)
After tax	6,310	6,310	2,121	(1,915)	(5,939)	(9,943)	(13,943)
Net aftertax gain/(loss)	$2,241	$2,241	($2,068)	($2,053)	$1,236	$4,687	$8,179
Required margin (net) (10 contracts)	4,000	4,000	4,000	4,000	4,000	4,000	4,000
Aftertax return on required margin	56.0%	56.0%	51.7%	51.3%	30.9%	117.2%	204.5%
Annualized	112.1%	112.1%	103.4%	102.1%	61.8%	234.4%	409.0%
Commissions as % of required margin	10.0%	10.0%	21.8%	28.3%	32.1%	33.8%	34.1%
Annualized	20.0%	20.0%	43.5%	56.6%	64.1%	67.6%	68.1%

* Notes on page 89 should be studied carefully in connection with Tables 4-1 and 4-2.

Table 4-2. **Net Profit and Rate of Return Calculation: Long-term Spread (Front Spread)** (All figures in dollars unless otherwise labeled and pertain to a spread involving 10 contracts on each side)

Stock Price at Expiration of Option	$80	$90	$100	$110	$120	$130	$140
Expiration profit/(loss) per share:							
Option purchased ($16, $90 strike price)	(16)	(16)	(6)	4	14	24	34
Option written ($10, $100 strike price)	10	10	10	0	(10)	(20)	(30)
Commission:							
Setup position $10 option	172	172	172	172	172	172	172
$16 option	226	226	226	226	226	226	226
Closeout position $10 option			172	172	262	322	332
$16 option				262	322	332	332
Rehedge commission (if necessary to protect capital gain)			300	300	300	300	300
Long-term capital gain				3,512	13,452	23,442	33,442
After tax				2,634	10,089	17,582	25,082
Short-term capital loss	(16,226)	(16,226)	(6,398)				
After tax	(6,490)	(6,490)	(2,559)				
Ordinary income/(loss)	9,828	9,828	9,528	(644)	(10,734)	(20,794)	(30,804)
After tax	3,931	3,931	3,711	(258)	(4,294)	(8,318)	(12,320)
Net aftertax gain/(loss)	($2,559)	($2,559)	$1,252	$2,376	$5,795	$9,264	$12,760
Required margin (net) (10 contracts)	6,000	6,000	6,000	6,000	6,000	6,000	6,000
Aftertax return on required margin	(42.7%)	42.7%	20.9%	39.6%	96.6%	154.4%	212.7%
Annualized	(85.3%)	85.3%	41.7%	79.2%	193.2%	308.8%	425.3%
Commissions as % of required margin	6.6%	6.6%	14.5%	18.9%	21.4%	22.5%	22.7%
Annualized	13.3%	13.3%	29.0%	37.7%	42.7%	45.1%	45.4%

Key assumptions underlying these calculations:

1. Stock price when spread is set up: $95.

2. Option terms

	Striking Price	Option Price	Remaining Life
Higher-priced option	$ 90	$16	More than 6 mos.
Lower-priced option	$100	$10	More than 6 mos.

3. Commissions based on former CBOE minimum commission schedule for 10 contracts on each side of spread.

4. The net cost of respreading to protect any gain on the long side of the spread after the short side is closed out is $300 or about the equivalent of round-trip commissions on a $7 option.

5. Aside from the commission cost, the respreading transaction has no net effect on profit or loss *on average.*

6. No loss is permitted to go long-term and the investor generates sufficient short-term gains to effectively cancel any effect of short-term losses on long-term gains.

7. Any profitable long position in an option is held for long-term capital gains treatment.

8. Rate of return on required margin is calculated by dividing aftertax profit at an expiration price by the margin requirement. For a detailed explanation of this method of calculating a rate of return see Appendix C.

9. The annualized return is derived by doubling the return on what is essentially a 6-month-and-1-day investment.

10. Commission cost as a percent of the required margin employed is listed at the bottom of the tables.

reason for setting up the spread. Though the precise requirements which a long-term spread must meet in order to stand up to review by the tax authorities have not been spelled out, some rough guidelines based on rulings applied to other arbitrage and quasi-arbitrage transactions can be provided. First, the tax advantage of the long-term spread would probably stand up best if, apart from the tax feature, the transaction has a meaningful investment rationale. If an investor sets up spreads in which his expected return would be negative without the tax feature, an alert IRS agent might call the whole structure a sham. Alternatively, the use of long-term spreads as part of a diversified stock and option portfolio should create no tax problems if the tax effect of the spread is supplementary to other investment goals such as portfolio diversification and risk adjustment or where the spread has at least a modest arbitrage advantage.

An excellent investment criterion for a long-term spread would be that the option purchased be undervalued relative to the option written. However, if both options were undervalued, the investor might have reason to expect a large enough price change to permit a profit, apart from any tax advantages.

If the investor has accumulated capital losses, he can still derive tax benefits from spreads, although at a markedly higher commission cost. Specifically, the investor with capital losses will force exercise of options he has written that are about to expire slightly in the money. If the writing side of the spread is profitable, this will convert the profit from ordinary income to a short-term capital gain. A specific example of this type of transaction is provided in Chapter 5, Section C, 2.

If the stock price rises and the option purchased is profitable, the investor using spreads can, in effect, convert ordinary income from option writing or other sources into capital gains. Commodity tax spreads, in other respects the most comparable technique, can only convert short-term capital gains into long-term gains.

Apart from the difference between short-term gain or loss and ordinary income or loss on the short side of the transaction, the listed option spread differs significantly from the commodity tax spread. The side of the option spread the investor takes is extremely important. It is usually irrelevant which side of a commodity spread the investor is long and which side he is short. The investor is largely indifferent between buying February pork bellies and selling May pork bellies. He is not indifferent to the choice between buying a January XYZ $100 call and writing a January XYZ $90 call or taking the other side of the transaction. Clearly, a long position in the option with the lowest striking price gives superior results if the stock advances, while the back spread is superior if the stock declines. This relationship has several implications if long-term spreads become popular. The investor setting up long-term spreads on several stocks should probably do some of each type of spread. Other things being equal, however, the investor should write the relatively overpriced option and buy the relatively underpriced one, unless his conviction on the likely direction of the stock is extraordinarily strong.

If investors concentrate on one type of spread to the exclusion of the other side, they could create an unusual opportunity for short-term trading. When long-term spreading activity is taking place and either the front or the back spread is being emphasized, the astute investor might wish to act as an arbitrageur and temporarily take the unfavored side of the spread for a possible short-term gain when the spreading pressure eases. Spreading pressure might disappear when the spread can no longer provide long-term gains, i.e., when the option purchased has less than 6 months before expiration.

5 TAX TREATMENT OF OPTION TRANSACTIONS

A. TAX TREATMENT OF OPTIONS FROM THE VIEWPOINT OF THE OPTION BUYER

The tables in this section permit the option buyer to evaluate the tax impact of the purchase of an option under virtually any circumstances. To use the tables, the investor need only examine the column labeled *Description of Transaction* and choose the caption which describes the particular case. More complicated transactions than those described in the tables occur frequently in option trading. These complex transactions can usually be broken down into simple segments and the tax treatment of each segment may be determined from the tables.

An investor who uses the tables carefully and follows the procedures described below to avoid "wash sales" will have few tax problems with options. However, the tables are not meant to serve as a substitute for a qualified tax adviser or an annotated copy of the Internal Revenue Code. Any investor who engages in more than an occasional option transaction should consult a professional tax adviser and be familiar with Sections 1091, 1233, and 1234 of the IRS Code and related regulations and rulings. A tax adviser should also be consulted to be certain that the treatment suggested here is applicable to a particular taxpaying entity and that more recent legislation, regulations, and rulings are not pertinent.

Several features of these tax tables require more detailed explanation than that provided on the tables themselves:

1. The designations *short-term* and *long-term* used extensively in the tables refer to periods of less than 6 months and 1 day, and 6 months and 1 day or longer, respectively. A distressing number of taxpayers neglect to wait the extra day necessary to secure long-term capital gains treatment for their profits.

2. The tables were constructed from the point of view of an individual taxpayer who is not a dealer in securities. Under some circumstances a corporation, a member of a partnership, or some other entity will receive different tax treatment.Tax-exempt institutions should exercise particular caution in the writing of options because income from unexercised (or repurchased) option contracts may be unrelated business income and as such is probably taxable.

3. A relatively minor caveat is that any sale of an option contract to register a loss must be made to an unrelated person. The sale of a worthless option to an unrelated buyer for a nominal amount is a perfectly acceptable way to keep a short-term loss from going long-term. If the buyer of an option happens to be the investor's mother, however, the IRS will not allow recognition of the loss.

4. To the extent that an option transaction changes the tax basis or holding period of the underlying stock owned by an investor, the change applies only to the number of shares represented by the option. For example, if the investor buys 1,000 shares of a stock and, within 6 months, buys five puts, the holding period is interrupted on only 500 shares of stock.

5. The most frustrating feature of the tax code for many investors is Section 1091, which sets down the wash sale rule. This rule provides that if an investor acquires (a) substantially identical securities or (b) an option permitting the acquisition of substantially identical securities within a 61-day period beginning 30 days before the sale of securities and ending 30 days after the sale, no deduction for any loss realized on that sale is permitted.

In simpler language, the purpose of the wash sale rule is to prevent the investor from selling a security and repurchasing

Table 5-1. Tax Treatment from Option-Buyer's Viewpoint

		Tax Treatment of Option Premium			
Description of Transaction	Holding Period of Option	Nature of Gain or Loss	Timing of Recognition of Gain or Loss	Effect on Common Stock Holding If Any	Comments (Also See Text)
I. BUY PUT					
A. Having owned related stock less than 6 months and 1 day					
1. Sell put to broker or dealer	Short term	Short-term capital gain or loss	Date of sale of option		Holding period of stock starts when put is sold. Stock position is long-term 6 months and 1 day after stock was purchased
	Long term	Long-term capital gain or loss			
2. Exercise put	Immaterial	Cost of put is deducted from proceeds of sale of stock	Date of exercise	Gain or loss on common stock is short-term depending on the holding period of the stock. The cost of the put is deducted from proceeds of sale	
3. Let put expire	Short term	Short-term capital loss	Date of expiration	Holding period stops on day option is purchased	Holding period of stock starts when put expires. Stock position is long-term 6 months and 1 day after put expires
	Long term	Long-term capital loss			
B. Then buy related stock one or more days later					
1. Sell put to broker or dealer	Short term	Short-term capital gain or loss	Date of sale of option	Holding period starts on day option is sold	
	Long term	Long-term capital gain or loss			
2. Exercise put	Immaterial	Cost of put is deducted from proceeds of sale of stock	Date of exercise	Gain or Loss on common stock is short-term after deducting cost of put from proceeds of sale	
3. Let put expire	Short term	Short-term capital loss	Date of expiration	Holding period of stock starts on day put expires	
	Long term	Long-term capital loss			

Transaction	Term	Tax treatment	Date	Effect	Notes
C. Buy related stock on same day and identify put as intended to be used with this stock position					
1. Sell put to broker or dealer	Short term Long term	Short-term capital gain or loss Long-term capital gain or loss	Date of sale of option	Holding period deferred while put is owned	Stock position is long-term 6 months and 1 day after stock was purchased
2. Exercise put	Same as stock	Cost of put is deducted from proceeds of sale of stock	Date of exercise	Loss is short- or long-term depending on holding period from date of purchase	
3. Let put expire	Same as stock	Add cost of put to basis of stock	Date of sale of stock	Gain or loss on sale of stock is short- or long-term depending on holding period	Holding period of stock starts on day stock and put are purchased
D. Do not own related stock during life of put					
1. Sell put to broker or dealer	Short term Long term	Short-term capital gain or loss Long-term capital gain or loss	Date of sale of option	No holding	
2. Let put expire	Short term Long term	Short-term capital loss Long-term capital loss	Date of expiration	No holding	
II. BUY CALL					
A. Sell call to broker or dealer	Short term Long term	Short-term capital gain or loss Long-term capital gain or loss	Date of sale of option	Can cause wash sale	Short sale of stock does not affect holding period of call. Long-term loss on call can be avoided by exercising call and selling stock even if call has been owned more than 6 months and 1 day
B. Exercise call	Immaterial	Cost of call added to purchase cost to determine basis	Date of sale of stock	Can cause wash sale	Holding period of stock begins on day call is exercised
C. Let call expire	Short term Long term	Short-term capital loss Long-term capital loss	Date of expiration	Can cause wash sale	

95

Table 5-1. Tax Treatment from Option-Buyer's Viewpoint—*Continued*

Description of Transaction	Tax Treatment of Option Premium				Comments (Also See Text)
	Holding Period of Option	Nature of Gain or Loss	Timing of Recognition of Gain or Loss	Effect on Common Stock Holding If Any	
III. BUY STRADDLE		Same as separate put and call		Same as separate put and call	Allocate cost 55% to call and 45% to put unless there is a substantial reason to allocate in another way
IV. ADJUSTMENT OF STRIKING OR EXERCISE PRICE OF OPTION FOR DIVIDENDS, SPLITS OR OTHER CAPITAL CHANGES					No effect on income, gain or loss, or tax basis
V. BUY A PUT OR A CALL FROM A CONVERTER AS PART OF A TRANSACTION IN WHICH THE BUYER HAS SIMULTANEOUSLY SOLD THE CONVERTER ANOTHER OPTION	Same as any option purchased elsewhere			Same as any other option	Holding period begins on date of purchase of any new option. Basis is zero or amount of commission if converter paid cash to holder of option in the conversion. Basis is amount paid to converter if buyer paid cash as part of the exchange.

it almost simultaneously, realizing a short-term loss and reducing the tax basis for possible long-term capital gain treatment of any future profit. The investor does not lose the
deductibility of the wash sale loss forever. The loss is added to
the investor's basis for the substantially identical assets or
options acquired during the 61-day period. The holding period of the original assets is added to the holding period of
the assets acquired during the wash sale period, making fast
action imperative to avoid letting any short-term loss go long-
term.

The investor will avoid trouble with the wash sale rule by
following several rather straightforward rules.

1. Never purchase a common stock, convertible bond, convertible preferred stock, warrant, or option on the securities of any company if
   one has realized a loss on the sale of equity securities of that company within the past 31 days.

2. Never purchase the stock, an option on the stock, or convertible
   securities of a company within about 35 days of the time a position
   one already holds in the securities of that company will go long-term
   for capital gains tax purposes. This policy will permit the investor to
   realize a short-term loss on the position about to go long-term, if that
   becomes necessary, without closing out the newly purchased position.

These simple rules are slightly more restrictive than the tax
code requires with respect to losses realized on the sale of
some convertible securities, but it is probably best to err on
the side of caution. Since it is impossible to reflect all the
nuances of the rule in this brief chapter, the reader is referred
to the IRS Code and Regulations. As the reader will note from
Table 5-2, on the wash sale rule, *any loss realized from the sale
or repurchase of an option is never a wash sale loss under current
law.* This is a distinct advantage in complex option transactions, but the investor should be alert to possible changes in
this situation.

There are several unusual tax characteristics of options from
the buyer's point of view that make them attractive investment vehicles for a large number of investors.

1. Buying a put with a life of more than 6 months and 1 day is the only way to realize a long-term capital gain from a decline in the price of a common stock. The buyer of a put with a life longer than 6 months and 1 day can keep any *loss* on that put from going long-term by selling the put back to the option dealer or to an unrelated third party before 6 months and 1 day have elapsed.

2. The principal reason for the attractiveness of 6-month-and-1-day calls is that they offer an opportunity for the investor to obtain a long-

Table 5-2. Wash Sale Reference Table

Possible Contaminating Transaction within 61-Day Wash Sale Period	Buy Option (Opening or Closing Purchase Transaction)	Write Option (Opening or Closing Sale Transaction)	Buy Common Stock or Convertible Security	Sell Common Stock or Convertible Security
Way in which loss is realized:				
Sell stock	WS	OK	WS	OK
Sell convertible bond	U	OK	U	OK
Sell convertible preferred stock	U	OK	U	OK
Sell warrant	U	OK	U	OK
Cover short sale of stock	OK	OK	OK	OK
Cover short sale of convertible bond	OK	OK	OK	OK
Cover short sale of convertible preferred stock	OK	OK	OK	OK
Cover short sale of warrant	OK	OK	OK	OK
Closing purchase transaction on option	OK	OK	OK	OK
Closing sale transaction on option	OK	OK	OK	OK

NOTE: A husband and wife or a taxpayer and his closely held corporation are ordinarily considered single tax units in determining the applicability of the wash sale rule.

KEY: WS   Wash sale, loss not deductible
U   Uncertain, study regulations carefully or play it safe and avoid the transaction
OK   No risk of wash sale under present law

term capital gain. A particular attraction of options with a life of just slightly more than 6 months is that the option buyer can readily avoid generating any long-term losses by the simple procedure of closing out his option position just before it goes long-term. Theoretically, nearly all gains can be long-term and all losses short-term. The limited life of options can serve as a useful discipline, encouraging the investor to avoid long-term losses by selling the option when it has only a short life remaining, and forcing him to reexamine his thoughts on the outlook for the underlying stock.

B. TAX TREATMENT OF OPTIONS FROM THE VIEWPOINT OF THE OPTION WRITER

Table 5-3, which outlines the tax treatment of options from the viewpoint of the option writer, is similar in format to Table 5-1 which showed tax treatment of option purchases. The warnings, explanations, and definitions which are offered in connection with the option buyer's tax table also apply to the writer's table. In addition to the material in the table, there are several tax consequences of option writing which deserve special attention.

A potentially important but frequently overlooked tax feature of option writing is the favorable tax treatment granted the writer of a straddle. Any side of a straddle which expires worthless is taxable to the writer as a short-term capital gain. While writing straddles may not be an investor's ideal strategy, this tax treatment can be of considerable help to the high-bracket taxpayer who might otherwise be offsetting short-term capital losses with long-term capital gains. To this taxpayer, the short-term gain from the expiration of the worthless side of a straddle is almost the equivalent of a long-term capital gain. The short-term losses can be offset with the short-term gain from the straddle premium, thus preserving the favorable tax treatment of the true long-term gains. This phenomenon is best illustrated with a numerical example.

In Column I, *A* and *B,* of Table 5-4, one assumes the straddle writer has $20,000 *apiece* in short-term losses and long-term gains in one year. Column I, *A* shows that these capital gains and losses cancel out if expired straddle premiums of $15,000 are treated as ordinary income. Short-term capital gain treat-

Table 5-3. Tax Treatment from Options-Writer's Viewpoint

Description of Transaction	Tax Treatment of Option Premium				Comments (Also See Text)
	Holding Period of Option	Nature of Gain or Loss	Timing of Recognition of Gain or Loss	Effect on Common Stock Holding If Any	
I. WRITE PUT					
A. Put expires	Immaterial	Ordinary income	Date of expiration	No effect	
B. Put exercised	Immaterial	Proceeds from sale of put reduce basis of stock purchased	Date stock is sold	No effect	Holding period of stock starts on day put is exercised
C. Put repurchased	Immaterial	Ordinary income	Date of repurchase	No effect	Based on IRS ruling so holding
II. WRITE CALL					
A. Call expires	Immaterial	Ordinary income	Date of expiration	No effect	
B. Call exercised	Immaterial	Call premium added to proceeds of sale to determine gain or loss on stock	Date of exercise	No effect except on lot of stock delivered to buyer	Holding period of stock extends from purchase date to exercise date. If stock is substantially above exercise price writer should try to arrange repurchase of call rather than exercise to get ordinary loss than sell original stock position for long-term gain.
C. Call repurchased	Immaterial	Ordinary income	Date of repurchase	No effect	Based on recent IRS ruling

III. WRITE STRADDLE

A. Side exercised	Immaterial	Basis of stock increased by amount of option premium	Date stock is sold	No effect except on lot of stock delivered to buyer of call or received from buyer of put	Allocate premium 55% to call, 45% to put unless there is a substantial reason to allocate another way.
B. Side expires	Immaterial	Short-term capital gain regardless of holding period	Date of expiration	No effect	See Sec. C, 2 for a detailed discussion of straddle taxation.
C. Side repurchased	Immaterial	May be ordinary income or loss (See Sec. C, 2, p. 119.)	Date of repurchase	No effect	See repurchase of put and call (I, C and II,C)
IV. ADJUSTMENT OF STRIKING OR EXERCISE PRICE OF OPTION FOR DIVIDENDS, SPLITS, OR OTHER CAPITAL CHANGES					No effect on income, gain or loss, or tax basis

Table 5-4. Effect of Short-Term Capital Gain Treatment on Expired Straddle Premium

Assumed tax rates:	Long-term capital gain		25%	
	Short-term capital gain		60%	
	Ordinary income		60%	

	I		II	
	Investor has both short-term losses and long-term gains		Investor has capital-loss carry-forward of $50,000	
	Treat gain on expired straddle as:		Treat gain on expired straddle as:	
	A Ordinary income	B Short-term gain	A Ordinary income	B Short-term gain
Long-term capital gain	$20,000	$20,000		
Short-term capital loss (ex straddle premiums)	20,000	20,000		
Expired straddle premiums	15,000	15,000	15,000	15,000
Tax treatment				
Net long-term Capital gain	0	15,000	0	0
Net short-term Gain or loss	0	0	0	15,000
Net ordinary Income	15,000	0	15,000	0
Aftertax gain from these transactions	$ 6,000	$11,250	$ 6,000	$15,000
Difference	$5,250		$9,000	
Size of capital-loss carry-forward at end of period			$50,000	$35,000

ment of the straddle premiums in Column I, B permits the writer to offset $15,000 of short-term losses with short-term gains from expired straddle premiums. Although $5,000 of the long-term gain is still offset by remaining short-term losses, the bulk of the long-term gain is then taxed at the investor's long-term capital gain tax rate. At the tax rates used in the table, treating the expired straddle premiums as short-term gains improves the aftertax profit by $5,250.

Short-term capital gains treatment of premiums on expired straddles also permits the straddle writer to use any accumulated capital-loss carry-forward more rapidly than might otherwise be possible. This feature of the tax treatment of straddles, illustrated in Column II, *A* and *B*, of Table 5-4, can be important to investors who have built up sizable capital-loss carry-forwards in the difficult markets of the past several years. The investor who occasionally offsets long-term gains and short-term losses or who has a sizable capital-loss carry-forward should study Table 5-4 carefully.

The IRS has ruled that if a writer repurchases a CBOE put or call (and presumably any other listed put or call), closing out his writer's obligation, the difference between the premium received in the original writing transaction and the amount paid in the closing purchase transaction will be ordinary income or loss. Just as short-term capital gains treatment of expired straddle premiums is favorable because a short-term capital gain is always at least as desirable for tax purposes as "unearned" ordinary income, most taxpayers would prefer an ordinary loss to a short-term capital loss. Unless a taxpayer has short-term capital gains that can be offset with a short-term loss, an ordinary loss is preferable to the short-term capital loss because it can be deducted from any other income the investor may have.

The significance of ordinary income and loss treatment for profits and losses generated by writing and repurchasing listed options is enormous. A complete listing of the possibilities this tax treatment opens up is not yet possible, but the following list is suggestive:

1. A high-bracket taxpayer who owns common stock and writes options against his stock positions can cushion any loss on the stock with ordinary income from writing the option. If the stock rises, he has an ordinary loss on the option (after a closing transaction) to deduct from his other income. The profit on his long position in the stock can be a long-term capital gain, depending on his holding period, and he can defer the tax on the appreciation of the stock until he liquidates the stock position.

2. Although the ruling on ordinary income treatment of repurchased options applies explicitly only to listed calls and puts, the principles behind the ruling seem applicable to most conventional options as well. If this assessment is correct, the conventional option writer who can arrange to repurchase an option that is expiring in the

money, rather than let it be exercised, would realize an ordinary loss on the option transaction. If he has written a call on a stock that has appreciated sharply over the option period, he can get *both* an ordinary loss on the option and a long-term gain on the stock by repurchasing the option and selling the stock when it goes long-term. Changing the present option industry practice from exercise of conventional options to repurchase of the option by the writer would enhance the attractiveness of option writing for most taxpaying investors because of the difference between ordinary income and long-term capital gains tax rates.

Table 5-5 illustrates the tax advantages of repurchase versus exercise when the stock advances sharply over the life of the option. Prior to the existence of the CBOE and the receipt of this ruling, the wash sale rule made it necessary for the covered writer to double his stock position at least 31 days before the call was exercised to get the full long-term gain on the original stock position *and* a short-term loss

Table 5-5. Tax Treatment of the Writer of a Covered Option on a Runaway Stock (All figures are per share and ignore commissions)

	A Conventional Call Option Exercised (Current practice)	B Listed Call Option Repurchased (Based on IRS ruling)
Value of stock at time option is written	$ 95.00	$ 95.00
Option premium	$ 10.00	$ 10.00
Value of stock at time option repurchased or exercised	$130.00	$130.00
Calculation of long-term capital gain:		
Proceeds	$105.00	$130.00
Cost basis	($ 95.00)	($ 95.00)
Long-term gain	$ 10.00	$ 35.00
Calculation of ordinary loss:		
Proceeds from writing call		$ 10.00
Cost of repurchasing call		($ 35.00)
Ordinary loss		($ 25.00)
Aftertax gain:		
Long-term capital gain		
@ 25% rate	$ 7.50	$ 26.25
Ordinary loss		
@ 60% rate		($ 10.00)
Net aftertax profit per share	$ 7.50	$ 16.25

on the stock delivered to the buyer of the option. The long-term gain/ordinary loss treatment possible with listed options is preferable and much easier to attain.

One caveat is in order. A 1970 IRS ruling held that a repurchased call option would be treated for tax purposes *as if it had been exercised* if the underlying stock was purchased simultaneously with the granting of the option and sold simultaneously with the repurchase of the option. While the ruling on listed options makes this earlier ruling obsolete, anyone attempting to repurchase a conventional call should consider possible implications of this ruling. Section C of this chapter will deal more extensively with the problems and opportunities of the writer who sells options on a runaway stock.

3. Because short-term gains will be less common than they would have been if writing and repurchasing options had been ruled a short-term capital transaction, greater care must now be taken that short-term losses on stock and option positions do not exceed short-term gains. If they do, long-term gains will be treated as the equivalent of short-term gains. Investment positions that can result in either short-term gains or short-term losses should be monitored carefully. Writing straddles or setting up option or commodity spreads are two of the most reliable ways to generate enough short-term gains to obtain maximum mileage from short-term losses.

4. Investors who write straddles are in a unique position. They can obtain short-term gain treatment of the side of the straddle that expires worthless. The side that has value at expiration may give them ordinary income or loss if they can arrange to repurchase it. Using the conversion process described in Appendix B, it is now possible to write straddles based on listed calls. The tax treatment of such straddles is controversial and will be discussed in Section C, 2 of this chapter.

5. We have already seen (in Chapter 4, Section D) the significance of the ordinary income ruling for the aftertax profitability of listed option spreads. Using spreads or writing calls against long stock positions permits the investor to convert ordinary income from other income-producing activities into long-term capital gains, assuming one is blessed with a rising stock market.

6. This ruling may have the effect of artificially depressing option premiums from time to time. Option writers are *potentially* more numerous than option buyers even without the effect this ruling may have on efforts to turn ordinary income into capital gains. Many writers

may now be less concerned with the risk reduction provided by covered option writing than with the ordinary-income–long-term capital gains conversion possibilities.

7. The tax effects of the interaction of long and short positions in stocks, other convertible securities, and options are so complex it would require another book at least the length of this one to exhaust the possibilities. Section C begins to scratch the surface.

C. USING THE TAX FEATURES OF OPTIONS TO IMPROVE THE INVESTOR'S AFTERTAX RETURN

This section is a supplement to the tax tables and other material in the two preceding sections. The purpose here is to illustrate the usefulness of options in simple and complex investment strategies where their tax features can improve the investor's aftertax return, sometimes quite remarkably. Most of the examples use listed call options, but modified versions of some of these strategies are feasible with conventional options.

1. Some Basic Tax-oriented Uses of Options

The six tables accompanying this section illustrate six specific uses of options, each motivated partly by the promise of a better aftertax return to the investor. In each of the six cases discussed in detail, one assumes that the investor-taxpayer bought 200 shares of a stock selling at $95 a share on January 4, 1974. Subsequent action depends upon (1) the behavior of the stock following the purchase and (2) the investor's changing opinion of the investment merits of the stock. The tables show ways an investor can use options to make the portfolio structure consistent with personal risk preferences and to maximize aftertax profit. If the strategy chosen in any one of these cases is an alternative to another possible course of action, the rate of return is calculated versus the alternative. The aftertax rate of return from a particular strategy is calculated as a percentage of any incremental margin or equity which the investor must deposit with the broker. This aftertax rate of return on incremental margin is annualized where appropriate. The rationale behind this rate-of-return calculation is discussed in detail in Appendix C.

A calculation on the tables for each of the six examples, which both the investor and the registered representative may find of interest, is an attempt to estimate the incremental commission cost associated with each strategy under discussion. The incremental commission cost is also expressed as a percentage of the average incremental margin.

Because all of these strategies involve options, one assumes the investor has determined that an option appropriate to the strategy is available at a satisfactory price. Satisfactory price means that an investment position calling for the purchase of an option should be set up by purchasing a fairly valued or undervalued contract. If writing an option is called for, the position should be set up by writing an option which is fairly valued or, if possible, overvalued. If the investor already owns the underlying stock, the tax effect of the strategy may be so great that the investor must disregard the implications of option valuation. To the extent that the value of the option is inappropriate, the investor should keep in mind that the expected rate of return will be less than the strategy would otherwise provide.

Any investor adopting a strategy illustrated here may not enjoy the returns indicated because the profits in the examples result from a specific sequence of price movements of the underlying stock. The aftertax return will usually be higher if the stock appreciates after a hedged or a "risk-neutralizing" position is established, and lower if the stock declines.

Case 1: Stock Appreciates Sharply after Purchase: How to Protect and Defer Gain

In this case one assumes that the stock, purchased at $95 per share on January 4, 1974, appreciates sharply within a matter of a few months to $130 per share. The owner of the stock finds that his ebbing enthusiasm for the prospects of the company does not justify owning the stock at this price. He is even reluctant to maintain his position until early July to obtain long-term capital gains tax treatment for the $35 per share profit he has achieved.

Given the basic decision that the investor is no longer willing to risk exposure to fluctuations in the price of the stock, he has at least three choices. The simplest solution would be to sell the stock, realize a sizable short-term capital gain, and pay taxes at a 60 percent rate. The investor could then reinvest the tax-diminished proceeds in another situation.

An only slightly less conventional course of action would be

Table 5-6. Case 1. Stock Appreciates Sharply After Purchase: How to Protect and Defer Gain

Date	Description of Transaction	Assumed Price of Stock	Net Margin Required After Credit for Option Premium Received*	Profit/(Loss) Realized	
				Ordinary or Short-Term	Long-Term
1/4/74	Buy 200 shares of stock	$ 95	$ 9,500		
5/20/74	Write 4 Jan. $130 calls @ $17	$130	$14,000		
1/4/75	Sell 200 shares of stock —Repurchase 4 Jan. $130 calls@ $2.50	$130	$ 0	$5,800.00	$ 7,000.00
	Net profit before tax and commission			$5,800.00	$ 7,000.00
	Adjustment for commissions			$ 156.20	$ 299.00
	Pretax profit			$5,643.80	$ 6,701.00
	Long-term gain after tax at 25% rate				$5,025.75
	Ordinary income after tax at 60% rate				$2,257.52
	Net aftertax profit				$7,283.27
	Increased aftertax profit vs. realizing short-term gain				$ 4,602.87
	Average incremental margin required vs. immediate sale				$14,000.00
	Aftertax return (vs. realizing short-term gain) on average margin				52%
	Annualized aftertax return				83%
	Total option commission cost				$ 156.20
	Incremental commission cost as % of average margin				1.1%
	Annualized incremental commission cost				1.8%

* All margin figures based on 50% initial and maintenance margin for stocks and 30% for options.

to sell the stock short against the box. While the short sale would interrupt the holding period and eliminate any possibility of obtaining a long-term capital gain, it could defer the short-term gain to the following tax year. Unfortunately, this example deals with a sale to be made in the spring. Maintaining a short position against the box until the following January will be costly unless the investor expects to experience a materially lower tax rate on short-term gains in the following year.

A third possibility, which is illustrated in Tables 5-6 and 5-7, is based on the investor's ability to neutralize future stock

Table 5-7. Case 2. Stock Appreciates Sharply After Purchase: How to Protect Gain Until It Goes Long Term

Date	Description of Transaction	Assumed Price of Stock	Net Margin Required After Credit for Option Premium Received*	Profit / (Loss) Realized	
				Ordinary or Short-Term	Long-Term
1/4/74	Buy 200 shares of stock	$ 95	$ 9,500		
5/20/74	Write 4 Jan. $130 calls @ $17	$130	$19,200		
7/6/75	Sell 200 shares of stock —Repurchase 4 Jan. $130 calls at $16	$130	$ 0	$400.00	$ 7,000.00
	Net profit before tax and commission			$400.00	$ 7,000.00
	Adjustment for commission			$210.80	$ 299.00
	Pretax profit			$189.20	$ 6,701.00
	Long-term gain after tax at 25% rate				$5,025.75
	Ordinary income after tax at 60% rate			$ 75.68	
	Net aftertax profit			$5,101.43	
	Increased aftertax profit vs. realizing short-term gain				$ 2,421.03
	Average incremental margin required vs. realizing short-term gain				$14,000.00
	Aftertax return (vs. realizing short-term gain) on average margin				17.0%
	Annualized aftertax return				138%
	Total option commission cost				$ 210.80
	Incremental commission costs as % of average margin				1.5%
	Annualized incremental commission cost				12.0%

* All margin figures based on 50% initial and maintenance margin for stocks and 30% for options.

price changes by constructing a neutral option hedge. To be specific, on May 20, 1974, the investor writes 4 January (1975) $130 calls at $17. In Case 1 he maintains this hedged position until January 1975, when he sells the stock position and repurchases the calls. Both the long-term gain on the stock position and the ordinary income from writing the calls are deferred to 1975. If the sole purpose were to protect the gain on the stock until it went long-term in July, the investor could close out the hedge at that time. Case 2 (Table 5-7) illustrates the latter possibility.

If the stock price remains at $130 for the balance of the year, as was assumed in Case 1, the investor would probably write additional calls over the period between May 1974 and January 1975 to maintain the neutrality and the protection of his hedge. As a result of the artificial assumption that the investor makes no further option transactions, the estimates of the total option commission cost and of the total aftertax return are probably low.

Attempting to neutralize the effect of future stock price changes through construction of a neutral option hedge is usually very attractive relative to realizing a short-term gain immediately or maintaining a short-against-the-box position for a long period. The strategy is particularly attractive when an investor has a large short-term gain early in a tax year.

Case 2: Stock Appreciates Sharply After Purchase: How to Protect Gain Until It Goes Long-Term

If the investor's only interest is to protect the gain in the stock until it goes long-term, he can close out the hedge set up in Case 1 as soon as the gain is long-term. Any gain or loss on the option contracts is ordinary income or loss no matter how long the option position is outstanding. Case 2 in Table 5-7 illustrates the result of closing out the hedge as soon as the stock goes long-term. As the reader will note, the return on average margin from converting the short-term profit into a long-term capital gain is lower than in Case 1 (17 percent versus 52 percent), but the annualized return on the incremental margin is much higher (138 percent versus 83 percent) because the margin is tied up for a relatively short period of time. The commission charges are higher, both unadjusted and annualized. Case 2 will probably appeal to more investors than Case 1, although either approach can serve as a useful introduction to the option hedge. Careful comparison of Tables 5-6 and 5-7 should help the reader appreciate both the versatility of option hedges and the overwhelming desirability of long-term capital gains tax treatment.

If a careful evaluation of option contracts available on the stock reveals that these contracts are generally underpriced (i.e., that setting up an option hedge is not attractive from an investment viewpoint as opposed to a tax viewpoint), the investor can achieve approximately the same tax effect as in Case 2 by writing in-the-money calls priced near their intrinsic value. If he adopts this strategy, the stockholder might write one call option with a striking price of, say, $110 for each 100 shares of stock he is long. With the stock at $130, he will receive a premium of over $20 per optioned share. Before any tax effect and disregarding transaction costs, his position is neutralized unless the stock drops precipitately. He has frozen his pretax profit at $35 per share if the stock stays above $110 per share. By maintaining this stock/option position until the stock goes long-term, the portion of the profit represented by the gain in the price of the stock from the $95 purchase price is a long-term capital gain. Any gain or loss on the option transaction is an ordinary gain or loss.

Case 3: Stock Which Investor Owns Drops Sharply: How to Realize a Short-Term Loss While Maintaining the Investment Position

Cases 3 and 4 illustrate two of many ways for using options to deal with "wash sale" problems. As indicated in the discussion of the wash sale rule (Section A, page 92), if a stock declines sharply soon after purchase, the investor may want to realize a short-term loss while maintaining his position. In Cases 3 and 4, one assumes the stock price drops from the $95 purchase price to $60. The principal differences between these examples are the different attitudes they reflect toward the near-term appreciation potential of the underlying stock and the amount of equity or margin the investor is willing or able to commit. Case 3 suggests a continuing positive attitude toward the underlying stock combined with a willingness to allocate additional capital to the situation as long as the effective risk to total capital is no greater than the risk associated with the initial purchase of 200 shares of stock. In Case 3 (Table 5-8) the investor sets up an option hedge on May 20, 1974, consisting of a long position in 200 shares of newly purchased stock plus a writer's position of 5 October $70 call

Table 5-8. Case 3. Stock Which Investor Owns Drops Sharply: How to Realize a Short-Term Loss While Maintaining the Investment Position

Date	Description of Transaction	Assumed Price of Stock	Net Margin Required After Credit for Option Premium Received*	Profit / (Loss) Realized Ordinary or Short-Term	Long-Term
1/4/74	Buy 200 shares of stock	$95	$ 9,500		
5/20/74	Buy 200 shares of stock. Write 5 Oct. $70 calls @ $5	$60	$10,300		
6/24/74	Sell 200 shares of stock vs. purchase Jan. 4, 1974	$60	$ 5,900	($7,000.00)	
7/27/74	Repurchase 5 Oct. $70 calls @ $4	$60	$ 6,000	$ 500.00	
	Net profit/(loss)			($6,500.00)	
	Adjustment for commissions			($ 441.50)	
	Net			($6,941.50)	
	Aftertax loss based on 60% short-term rate			($2,776.60)	
	Average incremental margin required (approx.)				$2,000.00
	Total commission cost (ex initial purchase commission)				$ 441.50
	Commission cost as % of average incremental margin				22%
	Annualized incremental commission cost				132%
	Aftertax saving over letting loss go long-term				$2,473.40
	As % of average incremental margin				124%
	Annualized return on incremental margin				742%

* All margin figures based on 50% initial and maintenance margin for stocks and 30% for options. No additions to margin requirements are made for losses.

options sold at a price of $5. If one considers the risk characteristics of the original stock investment separately, this new position is an approximately risk-neutral option hedge as long as the stock price does not change dramatically. The margin requirement is $800 more than the margin requirement on the original stock purchase or, perhaps more relevantly, $4,300 more than the margin that would be required if the initial 200-share position were just being established at the lower price of $60 per share. On June 24, after more than 31 days have passed, the investor sells the 200 shares of stock originally purchased at $95. He carefully designates the sale order "versus purchase January 4, 1974." For the next month the investment position is neutral. Although the investor still owns 200 shares of stock, his writer's position in 5 October $70 call options neutralizes this investment. On July 27, 1974, after more than 30 additional days have elapsed, the investor repurchases the 5 October $70 calls at a price of $4. As a result of timing transactions to avoid a wash sale, the investor has realized a short-term loss of $7,000. Under the tax-rate and stock and option price assumptions used here, the investor has achieved an aftertax saving of $2,473.40, instead of the alternative of letting the loss go long-term. As a return on the average incremental margin of about $2,000 over two months, this works out to 124 percent or, when annualized, some 742 percent after all costs. The registered representative has not done badly, either, obtaining total commissions of $441.50 in addition to the initial purchase commission. The additional commission cost works out to 22 percent of the average incremental margin for an annualized commission rate of some 132 percent of the incremental margin commitment. There are very few occasions in the securities business when both the investor and the broker benefit so handsomely.

Case 4: Stock Which Investor Owns Drops Sharply: Alternative to Case 3

Case 4 (Table 5-9) carries the assumption that, in the same circumstances as Case 3, the investor is unable or unwilling to provide the margin required to construct the option hedge

Table 5-9. Case 4. Stock Which Investor Owns Drops Sharply: Alternative to Case 3

Date	Description of Transaction	Assumed Price of Stock	Net Margin Required After Credit for any Option Premium Received*	Profit/(Loss) Realized	
				Ordinary or Short-Term	Long-Term
1/4/74	Buy 200 shares of stock	$95	$9,500		
5/20/74	Buy 2 July 60 calls @ $5	$60	$7,000		
6/24/74	Sell 200 shares of stock	$60	$1,000	($7,000.00)	
7/27/74	Buy 200 shares of stock. Let 2 July 60 calls expire	$60	$6,000	($1,000.00)	
	Net profit/(loss)			($8,000.00)	
	Adjustment for commission			($ 336.00)	
	Net			($8,336.00)	
	Aftertax loss based on 60% short-term rate			($3,334.00)	
	Average incremental margin required (approx.)				($2,000.00)
	Total commission cost (ex initial purchase commission)				$ 336.00
	Commission cost as % of average incremental margin				Not meaningful
	Annualized incremental margin				Not meaningful
	Aftertax saving over letting loss go long-term				$1,691.35

* All margin figures based on 50% initial and maintenance margin for stocks and 30% for options. The required margin for a *long* option position is 100% of the cost of the option. No additions to margin requirements are made for losses.

for slightly longer than the 61-day period necessary to avoid a wash sale. Furthermore, in spite of the decline of the stock, the stockholder is more optimistic about near-term stock price behavior than he is in Case 3. Instead of setting up an option hedge on May 20, the investor buys 2 July $60 call options at a price of $5 for an investment of $1,000. In addition to requiring a smaller capital commitment than the option hedge, this strategy increases the investor's participation in any upward move the stock might make while he is maneuvering to realize the short-term loss.

More than 30 days later, on June 24, the investor sells the original 200 shares of stock, realizing a $7,000 short-term loss and reducing his investment. Through ownership of the 2 July $60 call options, the investor still has exposure to any upward move the stock might make. After slightly more than an additional 30 days have passed, on July 27, he purchases 200 new shares of stock at $60. Shortly thereafter, he permits his 2 July $60 options to expire (or, if possible, sells them) realizing an additional $1,000 short-term loss.

The investor could exercise the options to reestablish his stock position, but, if he did, the cost of the options would be added to the cost basis of the stock purchased and he would not be able to realize the $1,000 short-term loss. If the stock is selling above $60 as the options are about to expire, he should sell the options at approximately their parity value, realizing any short-term loss. Only if the stock is selling very close to $65 should the investor exercise the calls instead of buying stock on the market to reestablish his stock position.

In a return-on-investment sense, the results of Case 4 are too good to be meaningful because the net incremental margin requirement is negative. The aftertax saving versus the alternative of letting the loss go long term is only $1,691.35, about $800 lower than the saving in Case 3, and is largely due to the fact that the investor lost money on the options purchased in Case 4, and made money on the options written in Case 3. The intriguing features of Case 4 are that the average incremental margin or investment required is lower than the case of simply holding the stock and that over a period of slightly more than 30 days, from May 20 to June 24, the investor has upside exposure to more than his original 200 shares of stock. At no time is the investor a nonparticipant if the price of the stock moves upward. As in Case 3, the commission generated is substantial, particularly relative to the size of the investment involved. Here again, both the investor and the broker benefit from imaginative use of options to realize a short-term loss while maintaining the investment position.

Another technique used by some investors to keep a loss from going long-term while, in effect, maintaining their position in the stock is to sell the stock to realize the loss and simultaneously to write a short-term, deep-in-the-money put. The put is nearly certain to be exercised, and the premium received for the put reduces the tax basis of the stock acquired. This is simply one more way to avoid the frustrations of the wash sale rule at a somewhat higher total commission cost.

Case 5: Stock Advances Sharply, Making Option Hedge Unprofitable

Cases 5 and 6 (Tables 5-10 and 5-11) illustrate some of the tax features of option hedges and the corrective measures that can be taken when an option hedge does not work out as anticipated in spite of the careful calculations that went into setting it up. The investor who monitored this hedge position with any care would undoubtedly have taken corrective action more quickly than one assumes in these examples, but to

Table 5-10. Case 5. Stock Advances Sharply Making Option Hedge Unprofitable

Date	Description of Transaction	Assumed Price of Stock	Net Margin Required after Credit for Option Premium Received*	Profit/(Loss) Received	
				Ordinary or Short Term	Long Term
1/4/74	Buy 200 shares of stock. Write 5 July $100 calls @ $10	$ 95	$11,550		
6/25/74	Repurchase 5 July $100 calls @ $33. Write 5 Jan. $130 calls @ $16	$130	$16,700	($11,500.00)	
1/14/75	Sell 200 shares of stock. Repurchase 5 Jan. $130 calls @ $2.50	$130	0	$ 6,750.00	$7,000.00
	Net profit/(loss) Adjustment for commissions			($4,750.00) ($ 479.75)	$7,000.00 ($ 299.00)
	Net Aftertax return based on 60% short-term rate Aftertax return based on 25% long-term rate			($5,229.75) ($2,091.90) $5,025.75	$6,701.00
	Net			$2,933.85	
	Total commission cost				$ 778.75
	Average margin required				$15,000.00
	Aftertax return on average margin				19.6%
	Commission cost as % of average margin				5.2%

* All margin figures based on 50% initial and maintenance margin for stocks and 30% for options.

Table 5-11. Case 6. Stock Declines Sharply Making Option Hedge Unprofitable

Date	Description of Transaction	Assumed Price of Stock	Net Margin Required after Credit for Option Premium Received*	Profit / (Loss) Realized	
				Ordinary or Short-Term	Long-Term
1/4/74	Buy 200 shares of stock. Write 5 July $100 calls @ $10	$95	$11,550		
6/24/74	Sell 200 shares of stock	$60	$ 3,750	($7,000.00)	
7/27/74	5 July calls expire (or repurchased @ 1/16)	$60	0	$5,000.00	
	Net profit/(loss) Adjustment for commissions			($2,000.00) ($ 396.00)	
	Net Aftertax return based on 60% rate			($1,604.00) ($ 641.60)	
	Total commission cost				$ 396.00
	Average margin required (approx.)				$18,000.00
	Aftertax return on average margin				(6.84%)
	Commission cost as % of average margin Annualized commission cost				5.0% 8.5%

* All margin figures based on 50% initial and maintenance margin for stocks and 30% for options. No additions to margin requirements are made for losses.

illustrate the effect of frequently readjusting the risk characteristics of the hedge as the price of the underlying stock changes would make the examples unnecessarily complicated.

In Cases 5 and 6, the investor begins by buying 200 shares of stock at a price of $95 and simultaneously writing 5 July $100 calls at a price of $10. The initial margin required for this option hedge is $11,550. In Case 5, by late June the stock price has appreciated to $130. While the investor has a profit on his long position in the stock, he has suffered a substantial loss on the calls he wrote. Furthermore, the calls are so deeply in the money and have so little time left to expiration that the position is no longer a hedge; it is almost equivalent to being long 200 shares and short 500 shares of the same stock.

The imbalance should have been corrected earlier—but better late than never. On June 25th, the investor repurchases 5 July $100 calls at a price of $33 and writes 5 January $130 calls at a price of $16. He realizes an $11,500 ordinary loss on the July calls. One now assumes that the stock trades in the $130 range until January 14, 1975, when the investor sells the original 200 shares of stock for a $7,000 long-term capital gain, and repurchases the 5 January $130 calls at $2.50, realizing ordinary income of $6,750.

After adjustment for commissions and taxes, the investor realizes a creditable net aftertax return of some $2,933.85 or 19.6 percent of the approximate average margin he had to post over the course of the year. If he had corrected the imbalanced hedge sooner or written more options as the January $130 calls neared expiration, the return would have been better. For his part in the transactions the registered representative has obtained gross commissions equal to 5.2 percent of the average margin posted. This is a highly satisfactory outcome for an option hedge that did not work on the first attempt.

If an evaluation of the January $130 calls indicates that they are underpriced, the investor can still accomplish his tax objectives by repurchasing only three of the July $100 calls. The two remaining July $100 calls will hedge his stock position until it goes long-term if they retain enough premium over intrinsic value to discourage premature exercise.

Case 6: Stock Declines Sharply, Making
Option Hedge Unprofitable

Just as the option hedge in Case 5 did not work because the stock advanced too sharply, in this case the hedge does not work because the stock declines too sharply. While Case 6 does not give the investor a profit, writing the options sharply reduces his loss from what it might have been. As in Case 5, the investor sets up his option hedge on January 4, 1974. On June 24 he sells the 200 shares of stock at a price of $60, realizing a short-term loss of some $7,000. As the chance that the stock will appreciate some $40 per share in 1 month is a bit remote, there is no purpose to be served in hedging his profitable option-writing position. The investor lets the options run until the end of July when they expire and he realizes ordinary income of about $5,000. After adjustments for commissions and taxes, the investor realizes a $641.60

aftertax loss. Given that the option hedge was an investment disaster, this result is not bad. If the hedge had been initiated in June rather than January, the investor might have been able to realize his loss in the first year, deferring the gain into the next. The broker enjoys better luck than the investor, receiving commissions equal to 5 percent of the average margin or about 8 percent on an annualized basis.

Implications The reader is urged to examine the tables that display the results of each of these six cases for implications that can be of use in his or her own activities. Care should be taken to avoid too casual extrapolation of these cases. In adapting Cases 3 and 4 to a real investment situation, the investor should be certain that the magnitude of a stock's decline is sufficient to make it worthwhile to take the steps necessary to realize a short-term loss and reduce the tax basis of his stock position. It should be obvious that a decline of a few points is inadequate to justify what can become a fairly complex and costly series of transactions.

One further note of caution: If the possible tax benefits of a particular option strategy seem too good to be true, there may be an error in the calculations. Before committing large sums to a seemingly foolproof scheme, consult a tax adviser, re-evaluate the alternatives, and recheck the numbers at various possible stock prices.

2. Generating Short-Term Capital Gains

Even a casual examination of the first part of this section suggests that writing options usually permits the investor to generate ordinary income or losses and to protect capital gains with hedges until they go long-term. We also see that the investor can use options to maintain a stake in a particular company while realizing a short-term loss. These six typical examples indicate that many option-oriented investments lead to one of four tax consequences: ordinary income, ordinary loss, short-term capital loss, and long-term capital gain. Short-term capital losses are offset dollar-for-dollar against long-term capital gains if the investor does not have enough short-term gains to offset short-term losses. It does not help to keep all losses short-term unless a taxpayer has enough short-term gains to fully absorb them.

Fortunately, there are several steps one can take to generate short-term gains when they are needed. To the extent that they can be undertaken on attractive terms, short-term reverse option hedges and purchases of short-term straddles can generate net short-term gains. If the investor engages in short-term trading and is correct in judging the direction of the market, he *can* realize substantial net short-term gains; but, unless the investor is either extremely astute or unusually careless, he will probably find himself generating the same combination of net long-term gains and net short-term losses from reverse hedging and the purchase of straddles that he should generate from other kinds of option trading.

One reliable, though temporary, source of short-term gains is a commodity spread. Commodity tax spreads are usually designed to defer short-term gains from one year to the next and, it is hoped, to convert them into long-term gains. A commodity spread can also be used to defer excess short-term losses until the following year, if the taxpayer is confident of his ability to generate offsetting short-term gains the next year and does not object to increasing his current tax bill. Because it generates no net profit and increases the investor's current tax bill, the commodity spread is a desperation method of generating short-term gains.

Another way to generate short-term capital gains is to write in-the-money calls against a position in the underlying stock or against another option in a back spread. If the stock rises, it or the long option position can be sold for a capital gain and any loss on the short option position is deductible from ordinary income. Unless the stock drops below the striking price of the call written, the writer can force exercise. When the call is exercised, the call premium is added to the cost basis of the stock and any profit becomes a capital gain. One disadvantage of this technique is that the size of any capital gain it might generate is unpredictable. Also, the required investment and the commission costs relative to the size of the probable net capital gain can be large.

One of the most reliable ways to obtain short-term gains is

to write straddles. As noted in Section B of this chapter, there is a special tax rule for writers of straddles which makes the profit on any expired option written as part of a straddle a short-term gain. Unlike the commodity or stock trader, a straddle writer can predict his short-term gains with a fair degree of precision. He knows that exercise of both sides of a straddle is rare. Therefore, his short-term gain will equal the premium from the least valuable side of his straddle at a minimum, and may be as much as the premium from the most valuable side (or even more under some circumstances). The principal drawback to a conventional straddle has always been that the writer cannot close out the unfavorable side of the straddle to minimize his loss on that side of the combination option. Furthermore, the side of the straddle that is ultimately exercised could give him a capital loss that is as large as or larger than the capital gain on the side that expires unexercised.

Though the exchanges do not yet trade puts or straddles as such, an investor can write a hybrid straddle by simultaneously selling a call on one of the exchanges and a comparable conventional put to a converter. The converter concurrently buys the stock and sells a second call on the exchange. Either side of this hybrid straddle, unlike the conventional straddle, can be repurchased whenever the writer so desires. If the reasoning behind the tax ruling on ordinary gain or loss from the repurchase of an option can be extended to the repurchase of either or both sides of this hybrid straddle, it would be possible to obtain short-term capital gains treatment of any profit and ordinary loss treatment of any loss.

The tax treatment of this hybrid straddle is probably the most controversial feature of the taxation of options. Any investor who considers undertaking such a transaction should first explore all the implications with a qualified adviser.

It is not certain that an investor can combine short-term gain and ordinary loss treatment with this hybrid straddle. Even if this interpretation is correct, this is a quirk in the tax law, and the IRS will surely act to prevent its use for very long. The real question is how the IRS will move to settle the issue. If the apparent anomaly can be resolved by the issuance of a ruling, setting up hybrid straddles makes no sense from a tax viewpoint, though they might still be attractive investment positions. On the other hand, there is a substantial body of opinion which holds that a change in the Internal Revenue Code may be necessary to eliminate this unusual situation. If the Code must be changed, investors can probably count on using this device for a year or two before Congress acts.

In the author's view, the IRS could attempt to upset this tax treatment of straddles with a ruling based on one or more of three contentions:

1. Writing a listed call and a conventional put or (when trading begins) a listed put cannot qualify as a straddle.

2. The intent of Congress when it enacted Section 1234(c) was to provide equitable treatment to writers of straddles who otherwise might have a combination of ordinary income and capital losses. Congress did not visualize the effect of the listed option.

3. The reasoning behind the ordinary income or loss treatment granted in the option repurchase ruling does not apply to options granted as part of a straddle.

The author leaves to professional tax advisers the task of evaluating the strength or weakness of each of these possible grounds for an adverse ruling. The author does believe it is easily possible to satisfy every *statutory* requirement necessary to have the transactions qualify as straddles.

If the IRS concludes that a change in the statute is necessary, it might, nonetheless, issue an adverse ruling and take a few cases to tax court to discourage use of hybrid straddles while the legislative process is under way. The fact that amending legislation was under consideration by Congress would seem to strengthen the position of any taxpayer whose use of a straddle was questioned.

While an attempt has been made to sketch the possible tax risks, investors and their tax advisers must determine for themselves whether or not to use the strategy. The only further help which can be provided here is a numerical example to illustrate how straddles might be used to generate a combination of short-term capital gains and ordinary losses. In the remainder of this section, it is assumed that this tax treatment is possible. The example should also help clarify the investment risks and opportunities inherent in the technique.

On August 28, 1974, Eastman Kodak common stock closed at $75\frac{1}{2}$. The Kodak October $80 CBOE call option, which represented the right to buy 100 shares of Eastman Kodak common stock until 10:30 A.M. on October 28, 1974, closed on the CBOE at $3\frac{7}{8}$ or $387.50 per contract. From these stock and option prices, it is possible to calculate the net proceeds to the writer of a straddle with a striking price of $80 and the same expiration date as the CBOE October $80 call. The actual calculations have been omitted to keep the example simple:

Stock price on NYSE	75\frac{1}{2}$
Striking price	$80
Call price on CBOE	3\frac{7}{8}$
Size of transaction	5 straddles
Net premium received by straddle writer after costs	$5,147.77 or $10.29 per share
Allocated to call side after costs	$1,870.27 or $3.74 per share
Allocated to put side after costs	$3,277.50 or $6.55 per share

There are other possible methods for premium allocation between the two sides of a straddle; but allocation based on the respective market values of the two options is preferable when these values can be determined.

Now we are ready to examine what happens if the stock price changes during the life of the straddle. If the stock price drops to $70 per share during the next month, we estimate that the price of the October $80 call will drop to about $1 on the CBOE. To protect himself from a further decline in the stock, the investor may repurchase the puts from the option converter at a total cost of $5,687.50 or $11.38 per share. His loss on the put side of the straddle will be $2,410.00 ($5,687.50 minus $3,277.50). This loss will be an ordinary loss, fully deductible from other income. If the call position is then permitted to expire unexercised, the call premium of $1,870.27 is a short-term capital gain. If the investor has excess capital losses, this gain is untaxed. Assuming a 50 percent tax rate on ordinary income, the net aftertax profit on the *overall* transaction is as shown in the following table.

	Before Tax	After Tax
Loss on put	($2,410.00)	($1,205.00)
Gain on call	$1,870.27	$1,870.27
AFTERTAX PROFIT		$ 665.27

If the market price of Eastman Kodak is close to the striking price of the straddle at the end of the option period, the profitability can increase markedly because *both* sides of the straddle can generate short-term capital gains. When the market price and the striking price are very close as the options near expiration, the writer does not repurchase the side of the straddle that is in the money. Instead, he forces the holder of the option to exercise it. When the option is exercised, the writer immediately closes out the resulting stock position. Under the tax rules for gains and losses on exercised options, he has a short-term capital gain on this side of the straddle *as well as on the side that expires unexercised.* If the put side of the straddle discussed earlier was exercised when Eastman Kodak sold at $79 per share, the position of a straddle writer with excess capital losses would look like the following table after allowing for all costs.

		Before Tax	After Tax
Cost of 500 shares purchased on exercise of put	$40,403.65		
Less proceeds from sale of put	3,277.50		
Net cost basis of stock purchased	$37,126.15		
Received on sale of stock	39,070.56		
Short-term gain on put		$1,944.41	$1,944.41
Gain on call		1,870.27	1,870.27
NET PROFIT		$3,814.68	$3,814.68

To simplify these examples, all profits and losses after costs have been calculated without listing each expense item separately. The total transaction costs paid by all parties in the two cases cited are approximately as shown in the following table.

	Put Repurchased w/Stock at $70	Put Exercised w/Stock at $79
Floor brokerage charged by converter	$ 22.50	$ 22.50
Converter's breakout charge	125.00	
Transfer tax	25.00	50.00
Option commission to:		
Sell call	67.19	67.19
Sell put	62.50	62.50
Repurchase put	62.50	
Commission on exercise of put		403.65
Commission on stock sold		403.65
SEC fees	.04	.83
TOTAL TRANSACTION COST	$364.73	$1,010.32

The investor should note the significantly higher costs incurred when an option is exercised. In this case these costs are easily justified by the resultant tax savings. If the put had been repurchased, the gain would have been ordinary income. In addition to the transaction costs listed above, there is an imputed interest carrying charge of about $800 for the put conversion. This charge will be largely offset by interest earned on the straddle premium the writer receives and by any earnings from the collateral he deposits as margin. All expenses considered, this is a relatively low-cost method of converting capital losses to ordinary losses and, perhaps, generating net capital gains.

These two cases highlight the major investment risks and opportunities inherent in straddle writing. The investor should look at least as hard at the risks as at the opportunities before deciding to proceed.

Risks

1. If the investor is unable or unwilling to close out the unprofitable side of the transaction before the stock moves dramatically away from the striking price, he could lose money, even after the tax saving.

2. If the stock moves sharply in one direction and then in the other, the investor could lose money on both sides of the straddle.

3. One side of the straddle might be exercised before the investor can repurchase it. Any time an option is exercised, transaction costs increase and pretax profits decline. Any short-term listed option that has substantial intrinsic value should probably be repurchased at least a week before expiration or an ex-dividend date (if the dividend is large) to prevent exercise.

Opportunities

1. If the stock does not move dramatically in either direction, the investor could have ordinary income rather than a loss on the side of the straddle that is repurchased or an additional capital gain on the side that is exercised. Rarely, both sides might expire unexercised.

2. While the magnitude of any short-term gain and ordinary income or loss is not perfectly predictable in advance, writing straddles is a relatively low-cost way to utilize capital losses to reduce an investor's current tax bill.

3. Unlike many tax-oriented investments, writing straddles can and *should* always be attractive from an investment as well as from a tax viewpoint. Ideally, straddles should be written only when the options involved are overpriced. If this rule is followed, an investor will find that in the long run short-term gains will *exceed* ordinary losses. No other method of changing capital losses to ordinary losses offers this potential.

The author is occasionally asked, "Why should I write straddles on common stocks when I can adjust my capital gain or loss position with commodity tax spreads?" Before answering this question, he always takes care to point out that the kind of straddles discussed in this section are not like commodity spreads. A commodity spread is a long position in one commodity contract offset by a short position in another. In this respect, a commodity spread is more like a listed option spread than an option straddle, though the tax characteristics of an option spread are slightly different, as noted earlier. Occasionally, commodity positions can be used to generate a combination of ordinary losses and capital gains; but usually they simply defer short-term gains until the following tax year and, perhaps, convert them into long-term gains. With rare exceptions, the pretax impact of a commodity straddle is that the investor loses an amount approximately equal to commission costs. Investment risks and possible pretax returns are practically nil.

As we saw in Figure 4-12 and in the example above, a straddle on a common stock is an investment position. It exposes the investor to investment risk and, if one's judgment is sound, can provide an excellent economic profit even before any tax effect. While a commodity tax spread might be ruled a sham transaction and many tax advisers urge their clients to avoid commodity maneuvers on that basis, writing a straddle on a common stock exposes the investor to real economic risk and could never be attacked on the grounds that the position has no investment justification apart from its tax effect.

In the context of the emphasis in this book on option evaluation, the investor who writes straddles when the component options are overpriced should *on average and in the long run* earn a pretax profit. This opportunity for profit before any tax effect should make up for the higher margin requirements and the investment risk inherent in the stock option straddle.

3. Converting Ordinary Income into a Long-Term Capital Gain

The single tax feature of option writing that deserves the most attention is the ability of the option writer to convert ordinary income into a long-term capital gain with some help from a rising stock market. Option writing is not unique in its ability to generate ordinary losses and long-term gains. Cattle breeding and petroleum exploration can accomplish approximately the same results. Listed options have the advantage over most cattle and oil programs of a public auction market which determines the price an investor will pay or receive for an option and known commission rates. In short, option writing has a lower "hanky-panky" coefficient.

The keys to the simplest method of converting ordinary income into long-term gains with options are (1) the IRS ruling that the gain or loss on a call option written and then repurchased on the CBOE is ordinary income or loss, and (2) a rising price on the underlying stock. If the stock declines or rises by no more than the option premium, the premium will provide the writer with additional ordinary income rather than generate an ordinary loss. Table 5-12 illustrates how the process works, using the standard stock and option characteristics adopted in Chapter 3, Section A.

In the example in Table 5-12, the investor obtains a long-term gain of $3,500 and an ordinary loss of $2,100 before taxes and commissions. The tax rate on the long-term gain will be no more than one-half of a taxpayer's marginal tax rate, while the ordinary loss is fully deductible from adjusted gross income and reduces tax payments at the full marginal tax rate.

Trying to convert ordinary income into long-term capital gains through one-for-one option writing as shown in Table 5-12 has two weaknesses. First, it requires the investor to

Table 5-12. Conversion of Ordinary Income into Long-Term Capital Gains

Purchase shares of stock at $95 per share	$ 9,500
Write 1 call with 6 mos. remaining to expiration. Option price is $10; striking price is $100	$ 1,000
Net investment	$ 8,500

Assume stock price rises to $130 shortly before the option is due to expire; if the stock has been owned for more than 6 months and 1 day, the tax treatment is as follows:

Sell 100 shares of stock at $130 per share	$13,000
Deduct cost basis	($ 9,500)
Long-term capital gain*	$ 3,500
Repurchase 1 call with striking price of $100 at $1 over parity	($ 3,100)
Deduct premium received	$ 1,000
Ordinary loss*	($ 2,100)

* The ordinary loss is deductible from any other income the taxpayer has received, and the long-term gain is taxed at a reduced long-term capital gain tax rate.

make a substantial investment and involves the risk of a price decline in the stock. While the risk of decline is mitigated by the option premium received, the premium offers little protection if the *decline* is as large as the *gain* hypothesized in this example. The second weakness of the example in Table 5-12 is that it only works if the stock price rises. Both these weaknesses can be overcome with option spreads.

The front spreads and back spreads discussed in Chapter 4, Section D, can generate long-term gains and ordinary losses if the stock price rises. In a declining market, the same effect can be achieved by constructing a put spread. The investor could buy one long-term call and convert it into a put. He could then write a put analogous to a different long-term call and sell it to a converter who would convert it to a call and sell the call. The investor is now long one put and short another with a different striking price. His position is very much like a call spread except that he will not enjoy favorable margin treatment, and the put spread will generate long-term gains and ordinary losses only if the price of the underlying stock declines.

The put spread probably has limited current applicability because of its high margin requirement and high transaction costs, but it does extend the flexibility of options by converting ordinary income to long-term capital gains if the stock declines. When puts are traded on the exchanges and appropriate margin rules apply, the put spread may be widely used to supplement the call spread as a mechanism to convert ordinary income into long-term capital gains.

4. Tax Features of a Neutral Hedge

Throughout this chapter and elsewhere in the book, the author has adopted the nearly universally accepted convention that a neutral option hedge is a long position in the underlying stock offset by short positions in enough options that any small increase or decrease in the value of the long position is approximately offset by an equal decrease or increase, respectively, in the value of the option position. To illustrate, assume an investor is long 100 shares of a $95 stock and short two options with striking prices of $100, selling at $10. If this is a neutral hedge and the stock rises or declines by, say, $5, the investor's position should look like the following table.

Stock Price	Value of Stock Position	Option Price	Value of Option Position	Net Value of Total Position
$ 90	$ 9,000	$ 7.50	($1,500)	$7,500
95	9,500	10.00	(2,000)	7,500
100	10,000	12.50	(2,500)	7,500

The hedge would be exactly neutral only for a limited time period and only for a limited range of stock prices. Obviously, if the stock rose or fell quickly by $30 or if a significant amount of time passed and the value of the options declined, the hedge would no longer be neutral and the stock-option ratio would have to be adjusted.

This definition of a neutral hedge ignores the fact that any long-term gain on the stock will be taxed at a much lower rate than the ordinary income or loss from the option premium. The neutral hedge is defined in terms of *pretax* profit and loss. Because the investor is interested in his aftertax profit, he may want to adjust the hedge ratio to reflect taxes. The appropriate adjustment will depend on the investor's ordinary income and capital gains tax rates and the holding period of the stock. Assuming that any gain or loss on the stock is already long-term or that a large gain is very close to going long-term, the investor should multiply the pretax neutral hedge ratio by the fraction

$$\frac{1 - \text{long-term capital gains tax rate}}{1 - \text{ordinary income tax rate}}$$

If the individual's tax rates are 25 percent on long-term gains and 60 percent on ordinary income, the value of the fraction is

$$\frac{1 - .25}{1 - .60} \quad \text{or} \quad \frac{.75}{.40} = 1.875$$

The pretax neutral hedge ratio, 2 in our example, is multiplied by 1.875 to give an aftertax neutral hedge ratio of 3.75. If the stock position in the hedge is not yet long-term, the appropriate neutral hedge ratio will lie between the pretax and aftertax ratios.

Because most investors prefer to structure even a hedged portfolio so that it performs better in a bull market than in a bear market, it is doubtful that many readers will want to adjust the pretax neutral hedge ratio. The reason for discussing the point at all is that most users of option hedges assume their downside risk and upside reward are roughly symmetrical when they use the pretax neutral hedge ratio. When the tax features of the investment are considered, complete symmetry requires a larger short position in the options.

D. CALCULATING THE EFFECT OF TAXES ON A COMPLEX OPTION TRANSACTION

The six cases in the previous section illustrated the effect of tax features of options under carefully controlled assumptions about stock price fluctuations. The time has come to present a comprehensive example in both tabular and graph form to illustrate the adjustments which must be made when tax factors and changing stock prices affect an option investment strategy. Theoretically, tax adjustments are necessary whenever the investor has an opportunity to achieve a long-term capital gain on an option or its underlying stock. In practice, it is only necessary that the investor understand the nature of the changes in profitability caused by taxes.

To permit readers to test their understanding of the graphic technique developed in Chapter 4, Section A, and the mechanism of tax adjustment, the example chosen (Figure 5-1) uses stock and option prices consistent with the model used to explain the graphic approach. The investment position itself is similar to Case 1, outlined in Section C.

An investor buys 1,000 shares of a stock at $75 per share. In a very short time the stock runs to $95. If there were no tax considerations, the investor would sell the stock without hesitation. Unfortunately, as noted in the discussion which accompanied Case 1, if he sells the stock immediately, he will realize a short-term capital gain which will be taxed at his full

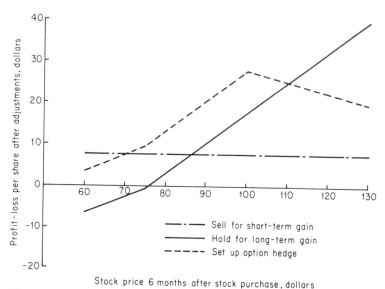

Figure 5-1. Tax and commission adjustment to a complex option strategy.

marginal tax rate. If he sells the stock short-against-the-box, he simply defers realization of the short-term gain into the following year. If the investor holds the position in the hope that the price will be maintained or that further appreciation will occur, he runs the risk of a price decline. Since one of the reasons for his dilemma is that he feels the stock is now fully priced, this choice is not attractive.

Assuming the stock has listed options, the investor can write one or more options against the stock position. If he had no opinion on the underlying stock, he might construct a neutral hedge. If, as was indicated, the investor feels the stock is overpriced, he may wish to write enough options to create a bearish hedge. The example which will be discussed at length here is a moderately bearish hedge when pretax results are considered. (A high-bracket taxpayer has to write a large number of call options to create a hedge that is bearish after taxes unless he elects to write a smaller number of in-the-money calls.)

With the stock at $95, the investor writes 2.5 options for

each 100 shares of stock he is long or 25 options in total against his 1,000-share position. The option premium is $10, the striking price of the options is $100, and the options have about 6 months of life remaining. The calculations in Table 5-13 depend on the investor's maintaining the hedge until the options expire, which may be slightly longer than necessary to let the stock position go long-term. In Table 5-13 and Figure 5-1, this strategy (the dashed line on the graph) is evaluated and the profit from it is compared to the investor's other choices: selling the stock immediately for a short-term gain (the dot-dash line on the graph) and holding the stock until the gain goes long-term (the solid line). Unless the investor's marginal tax rate will drop in the next fiscal year, selling the stock short-against-the-box will look very much like the dot-dash line, i.e., selling the stock for a short-term gain. The profits depicted by each line are adjusted for commissions and taxes (marginal short-term and ordinary income tax rate, 60 percent; long-term capital gains tax rate, 25 percent). The profit figure is expressed in dollars and is not annualized. On the graph, no attempt is made to convert the profit or loss figure from dollars into a rate of return on investment.

These calculations are based on several simplifying assumptions that do not detract materially from the usefulness of the illustration. For example, the investor refuses to let a loss go long-term under any circumstances. Also, the hedge is set up and not modified unless a loss is in danger of going long-term. This assumption forces the investor to pass up opportunities to improve the protection and the profitability of the hedge by writing additional options as the 25 original options approach expiration. This assumption also prevents repurchase of some options if the stock continues to move up.

To determine the shape of the graph, the net profit (after taxes and commissions at key prices) is calculated as indicated in Table 5-13. The exact profit at a particular stock price between those selected might vary slightly from the figure shown on the graph, but the deviation will be minor. Because the lines on the graph change slope a number of times when tax adjustments are made, the easiest way to plot the graph is to calculate the profit or loss at key prices and connect the

Table 5-13. Tax and Commission Adjustments to a Complex Option Strategy (See text and footnotes for assumptions)

Price of Stock at Expiration of Options:	$65	$75	$95	$100	$110	$120
Base Case: Sell stock @ $95 per share for short-term gain						
Sale price	$95.00	$95.00	$95.00	$ 95.00	$ 95.00	$ 95.00
Less: Cost of stock	75.00	75.00	75.00	75.00	75.00	75.00
Commissions	1.25	1.25	1.25	1.25	1.25	1.25
Taxes	11.25	11.25	11.25	11.25	11.25	11.25
Profit after tax	$ 7.50	$ 7.50	$ 7.50	$ 7.50	$ 7.50	$ 7.50
Alternate Case A: Hold stock in attempt to get long-term gain, sell stock to keep loss short-term if stock drops						
Sale price	$65.00	$75.00	$95.00	$100.00	$110.00	$120.00
Less: Cost of stock	75.00	75.00	75.00	75.00	75.00	75.00
Commissions	1.11	1.15	1.25	1.27	1.32	1.36
Taxes	6.67 cr	.69 cr	4.69	5.93	8.42	10.91
Profit after tax	$ 4.44 loss	$ .46 loss	$14.06	$ 17.80	$ 25.26	$ 32.73

Alternate Case B: Set up option hedge until gain on stock goes long-term, sell stock to keep loss on stock short-term if stock drops

Option premium received	$25.00	$25.00	$25.00	$ 25.00	$ 25.00	$ 25.00
Less: Repurchase of option					25.00	50.00
Option commissions	.35	.35	.35	.35	.70	.75
Taxes on option profit	14.79	14.79	14.79	14.79	.42 cr	15.45 cr
Profit/(loss) after tax	9.86	9.86	9.86	9.86	(.28)	(10.30)
Plus profit from stock Case A	(4.44)	(.46)	14.06	17.80	25.26	32.73
Total profit Case B	$ 5.42	$ 9.40	$23.92	$ 27.66	$ 24.98	$ 22.43

NOTES:
1. All figures per share
2. Commissions calculated on a 1,000-share stock position and 25 option contracts
3. Stock purchased @ $75. At decision point, stock price is $95
4. Option premium $10, striking price $100
5. Investor's marginal tax rates: 60% on short-term gains and ordinary income, 25% on long-term capital gains
6. No capital loss is permitted to go long-term

135

points with straight lines. Straight lines connecting the profit points calculated at the following stock prices will give a good picture of the aftertax profit-loss line of any strategy:

1. The striking prices and break-even prices of any options used

2. The purchase price of any stock position

3. Prices five or ten points above the highest and below the lowest of other prices used

To maximize the usefulness of this example, the reader should study it with care to understand why the option hedge is an attractive alternative to realizing a sizable short-term capital gain. Careful examination of the tax and commission adjustments is particularly important. Even though he will probably not make such meticulous adjustments in evaluating each investment considered, the investor should understand the qualitative and approximate quantitative effect they have on his results.

This example illustrates the importance of examining both an investment position for possible uses of options and any option strategy for tax implications.

It is worth observing that if a stock is purchased in June or July and the hedge is set up using January options, the investor might not only protect short-term gains until they go long-term, but can defer the gain until the following tax year as well. Furthermore, the investor can probably arrange to deduct any losses in the current year.

A number of the strategies discussed in this chapter use long-term options. The reader who has traded actively in listed options might point out that a strategy using long-term options is conceptually interesting but not necessarily practical. The option price summaries in *The Wall Street Journal* suggest that there is very little trading activity in options with a life longer than 6 months. While this inactivity can be a problem at times, there should not be any real difficulty in establishing a modest position in long-term options, for reasons which will be outlined in the next section.

E. TAX CONSIDERATIONS AFFECTING THE LIQUIDITY OF LISTED OPTION MARKETS

An interesting subject for a short article in one of the academic journals or for a student of finance in need of a topic for a paper would be the effect of taxation on trading activity in listed call options. A glance at option trading summaries in *The Wall Street Journal* indicates that activity is concentrated in short-term options with relatively little interest apparent in options with more than 6 months remaining before expiration. This phenomenon seems peculiar in view of the advantageous tax treatment accorded buyers of long-term options. Ironically, this characteristic of option trading activity is probably due to the interaction of the tax laws and the weak, erratic stock markets of the past 5 years.

The fact that trading activity is low in long-term options does not mean that these contracts have been totally neglected. The ratio of trading volume to open interest (number of contracts outstanding) is generally lower for the longer contracts, reflecting a tendency for at least some holders of longer options to concentrate on the possibility of obtaining a long-term capital gain. Short-term arbitrage activity accounts for much of the high trading volume relative to the open interest for the shorter option maturities. Nonetheless, the conclusion is inescapable that long-term capital gains are somehow less important than they used to be.

Probably the best explanation for this trading pattern is that the markets of the past several years have gratuitously provided many investors with sizable capital-loss carry-forwards. Some of these stock market victims will be very fortunate if they have to pay taxes on any capital gain, short-term or long-term, for the next several years. This very sizable group of market participants is indifferent to a choice between short-term and long-term capital gains. In time, long-term capital gains will recover their importance for most investors and the interest in longer options will expand.

Another important reason for the present neglect of longer option contracts is that many of the techniques and tactics discussed in this book are not widely appreciated or understood. Many option strategies were either not feasible prior to the start of listed option trading or locked an option writer into a position until the buyer elected to exercise. As familiarity with options increases, there will be more interest in what are now strange and exotic uses of options.

A frequently voiced doubt about the viability of large-scale option trading is concern over a potential shortage of option buyers. The implied premise behind this argument is that all rational, risk-averse investors will write options, but only the unsophisticated public will be gullible buyers. At first glance, this appears to be a cause for real concern. Many individual and institutional investors are willing to write options, but historically the "small" investor has been the primary buyer of options. The weak markets of the early 1970s have dampened the enthusiasm and decimated the portfolios of many traditional call option buyers. As more institutions, now foreclosed from any activity in options, obtain the necessary regulatory and legislative approvals to enter the option market as writers, there is reason to suspect that option premiums which were too high in the early months of the CBOE may be chronically too low.

Fortunately, as one of the leading figures in the option business once said to the author, "Markets work." Premiums on individual contracts or on all options may be temporarily too high or too low, but arbitrageurs will detect and correct these inappropriate valuations. The correction will not be instantaneous, however, and overvaluations and undervaluations may persist for some time as writers adjust slowly to the mercurial moods of buyers. The greatest opportunities will be available to the flexible investor who can *either* write *or* buy to take advantage of a supply-demand imbalance.

One of Wall Street's most widely held beliefs is that option buyers consistently lose money and option writers consistently make money. Like most bits of conventional wisdom, this statement has a kernel of truth. The covered option writer will make money with reasonable consistency but will typically make money because the stock he owns appreciates, not because the options he writes expire worthless. By writing options he levels out his return. He will never see his assets appreciate by 50 percent in 1 year. Likewise, he will rarely experience a devastating loss because option premiums protect him on the downside. In contrast, the option buyer typically experiences either feast or famine.

During the first year and one-half of CBOE trading, uncovered call writers fared relatively well and call buyers, as a group, lost badly. Studies made during strong bull markets have shown call buyers to be winners while covered writers underperform the market averages. The behavior of the market over the life of any such study is the primary determinant of which side of the option contract looks most desirable.

Putting the conflicting historical evidence aside for a moment, it is important to understand that the option buyer enjoys many of the same inducements that attract the option writer. For example, if the writer wants to set up an option hedge to protect a recent sharp gain in the stock until it goes long-term, anyone who buys the option must feel that the purchase is worthwhile. The buyer is presumably aware of the recent price history of the stock. He knows that it has advanced sharply in the past few months. Stocks that exhibit this kind of volatility appeal to option buyers if the premiums are reasonable. Even if a potential buyer agrees with the writer that a stock is vulnerable, he might still find the call option attractive. The buyer can set up a reverse option hedge, use the call to hedge a short sale, or convert the call into a put. These possibilities can provide the option buyer with some of the same tax and risk management benefits the writer enjoys.

Just as the option writer may be anxious to write long-term options against a stock position in June or July to permit him to realize short-term or ordinary losses in the current year and long-term or ordinary gains in the following year, the call buyer can also influence the timing of his realization of gains and losses by buying options at midyear. There is a strong tax incentive to the potential option buyer to buy precisely the option which the writer wishes to write. Both parties will want to set up transactions in January options at approximately midyear so that any losses can be kept short-term and deducted in the current year, and any gains allowed to go long-term, if possible, and deferred to the following year. This commonality of interest helps assure each party of an efficient market.

There is an even more important reason why there will rarely be a persistent shortage of option buyers at fair premiums. Figure 5-2 is a graph of the option writer's and option buyer's profit-loss lines for the $10 option premium, $100 striking price call option used throughout the book. The unique feature of Figure 5-2 is that it shows an investor's profit or loss on the option *after taxes.* The aftertax value of the $10 option premium is $4 if the applicable tax rate of both buyer and writer is 60 percent on short-term capital gains and ordinary income, respectively. If the option is purchased with more than 6 months of life remaining, the buyer's and writer's positions are different if the stock sells for more than the striking price plus the option premium. If the buyer makes a profit, it is a long-term capital gain, taxable, in the graph, at a 25 percent rate. Under this set of tax assumptions, *the call is worth more to the buyer than to the writer even if they have identical tax positions and identical expectations for the underlying stock.*

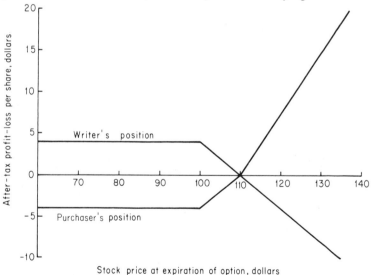

Figure 5-2. Aftertax profit-loss lines of long-term call buyer and writer.

The fact that the tax laws make calls attractive to buyers at a *higher* price than would be necessary to induce a rational writer to sell them indicates that option volume should expand steadily as more investors become aware of the advantages of options.

Figure 5-2 also suggests a subtle but potentially important effect of taxation on option valuation and liquidity. Fischer Black has pointed out in an article in the *Financial Analyst's Journal* (see Bibliography) that the value of an option will always be greater from the viewpoint of a high-tax-bracket investor than from the viewpoint of a low-tax-bracket investor. While the difference in valuation due to taxes is usually quite small, this feature of options does suggest that tax-exempt institutional investors should be buyers rather than writers of options, other things being equal. Because the tax-related value differential is small and because other things are rarely equal, it is doubtful that pension funds will soon replace individuals as the principal buyers of options.

6 REGULATION AND THE ROLES PLAYED BY VARIOUS MARKET PARTICIPANTS

A. THE ECONOMIC FUNCTION OF OPTIONS AND PROBLEMS IN REGULATING THEIR USE

Critics of option trading occasionally argue that the securities options market serves no economically useful purpose. In earlier chapters we saw evidence that options permit investors to modify the risk-reward posture of their portfolios in practically any way they choose. In our view, risk modification is ample justification for option trading. Unfortunately, this rationale for options does not satisfy critics who argue that option buyers are either innocent victims being fleeced of their hard-earned savings or gamblers who see calls as an alternative to the numbers or the ponies. This argument imposes a moral tone on the discussion that defies rational response. In spite of the hazards of trying to answer such an argument, it is at least possible to provide an alternate interpretation of the option buyer's motives.

Apart from moral issues, some observers argue that option trading disrupts the market in the underlying stock and that options somehow increase the volatility of the stock. Another potentially damaging criticism is that speculation in options reduces investors' interest in American Stock Exchange and over-the-counter stocks, making capital more costly and more difficult for smaller companies to raise. Excellent answers to each of these criticisms emerge as soon as the critic understands the role of options in the investment universe.

Understanding the motivations of option buyers is central to dealing with most of the emotional criticism of options. Granted, there are undoubtedly a few option buyers who consider buying a Xerox January $80 as an alternative to a $100 win ticket on Secretariat. If the option buyer *is* a gambler, he is a smart one. Option commissions consume a smaller fraction of his "bet" than the track or an underworld syndicate takes out. In most cases, however, the option trader does not see himself as a gambler.

Options are nothing more than investment tools for the acceptance or elimination of risk. Most buyers have considered the risk-reward features of call options and have concluded that calls are appropriate to their risk preferences. Consider for a moment the young executive or doctor who has very little capital but is reasonably certain to earn a substantial and rising income. Calls offer him the opportunity to amass enough wealth to start his own business or build his own clinic without giving up his chance for a more modest, yet still satisfactory, future. He knows he can never lose more than the call premium and the possible profit is theoretically unlimited.

The high interest rates and erratic securities markets of the past several years have increased the population of another type of option buyer. This buyer has invested most of his assets in high-yielding debt instruments because the risk of equity investment appears too great in an uncertain environment. To provide some exposure to equities if the outlook improves, the buyer invests a small portion of his assets in calls.

While there are always some speculators who go overboard for any investment medium that becomes popular, most of the current crop of call buyers appear to have a fair grasp of the risks as well as the rewards associated with options. The exchanges and their member firms have done an outstanding job of increasing public awareness and understanding of call options. Broader knowledge of options should attract more sophisticated participants to both sides of the option contract, making the "horse players" a small factor in the total market.

It is widely believed that option buyers are suckers and that only writers make money on options. Actually, as noted in the previous chapter, the empirical studies that have been made are inconclusive. Some studies made during bull markets show the buyer with a clear advantage. Regardless of past experience, the existence of an active secondary market for options should cause most listed options to sell close to their fair value, giving buyers and writers approximately equal expected profits after adjustment for risk. In fact, as more institutional investors begin to write options, it would not be surprising if options became consistently underpriced.

There is nothing inherent in option trading that harms either buyer or writer. Existing rules for option trading suitability do an adequate job of protecting most investors. A broker who encourages inappropriate trading can be disciplined. On the other hand, an investor who is determined to find a way to increase leverage can easily find a more dangerous technique than buying call options or writing "naked" options.

Turning to the effect of options on the market in the underlying common stock, an important benefit of listed option trading can be an improvement in the liquidity of the stock market. Liquidity is defined as a measure of the average amount by which a buy or sell order pushes the price of a stock up or down. To the extent that increased option volume leads to arbitrage activity between the option and the stock, an efficient option market should have the effect of moderating stock price fluctuations. Definitive evidence of the impact of option trading and option-stock arbitrage on stock price action is not yet available. As trading procedures and business relationships become more firmly established, the option market should improve the liquidity of the market in the underlying stock.

One mechanism by which the option market improves the liquidity of the stock market merits at least a brief discussion. Assume for a moment that a block positioning house or an institution permitted to write options is asked to bid on a block of stock. To the extent that the buyer can write call options on part or all of the block, his risk is reduced and the price he can offer the seller may increase. Regardless of the size of the trade or the direction of the buying or selling pressure, the ability to lay off some of the risk is important. Any financial instrument that permits investors to reallocate risk among themselves to suit their diverse risk preferences should have the effect of improving overall market liquidity and efficiency.

One of the major criticisms that has been leveled at secondary trading of options is that this activity tends to reduce the level of stock trading activity on the Amex and in the over-the-counter market. The concern behind this argument is that option trading may restrict the ability of smaller companies to obtain financing through public offerings of equity securities. This criticism is based on the hypothesis that many buyers of options would alternatively buy $2 stocks on the American Stock Exchange or be prime candidates for an offering of a speculative new issue.

Evidence on either side of this argument against option trading has not been assembled. Without any hard evidence, one would argue that most option buyers are not candidates for Amex or OTC issues in the recent market environment, and many will never be prospective buyers of such securities. Conservative option buyers have most of their assets in saving accounts or fixed-income securities. With some care, they are investing small amounts in conservative stocks or options to provide what they feel is an appropriate degree of exposure to the equity markets. The fact that the companies with listed options are among the major names in American industry is important to these investors. They have no interest now and may never have any interest in the secondary and tertiary companies whose ability to obtain financing concerns the critics.

More aggressive option buyers are interested in maximizing the leverage their small capital base can give them. They might be candidates for Amex and OTC issues in a different market environment. Today, their alternative to options would probably be commodities. The uncertain business environment is probably the most important reason for the aggressive option buyer's present lack of interest in smaller companies. If the environment improves, this investor can be attracted to equity issues from smaller companies.

In measuring the impact of option trading on the market for securities of smaller companies, it is important to keep in mind that none of the money spent on options leaves the market. For every option buyer there is a writer, and every dollar the buyer spends on options goes to a writer after a minor deduction for commission charges. The writer who receives the premium is free to invest it in securities of smaller companies *if they promise attractive returns.*

The commission revenues which are the only drain on the transfer of funds between buyer and writer are a major source of profit for many brokerage firms. If small and medium-sized companies are to obtain financing when market conditions improve, options may turn out to have played a role in the survival of the firms that will be called upon to underwrite these offerings. In short, the argument that the option market may detract from the ability of smaller companies to obtain financing simply does not hold up. The fact of the matter is that the prices of shares in these companies would be no higher if options did not exist.

There is one real regulatory problem created by trading in listed option contracts. Some of the people who are buying and writing these contracts do not thoroughly understand the risks they are taking. Time and experience with options will help resolve this problem. In the extreme, option investors might be required to pass a simple written examination based, perhaps, on the Options Clearing Corporation prospectus. If an investor demonstrates that he knows what he is doing, he should be permitted to accept whatever risks he deems appropriate. To the extent that participation by investors mentally incapable of understanding or financially incapable of accepting the risks of option trading is the result of a zealous securities salesman overselling a product, the traditional regulatory mechanisms can deal with the problem. If the SEC and NASD can police the scattered over-the-counter market, they can easily regulate the relatively centralized option market.

B. OPTION TRADING BY INSTITUTIONAL INVESTORS

Before turning to a discussion of the potential role of options in the management of institutional portfolios, a brief review of some of the obstacles to institutional participation in option trading seems in order. Legal and tax counsel should be consulted by any institutional-type investor who is considering buying or writing options. This summary is intended to provide general information, not to serve as a definitive guide to institutions interested in options.

One of the principal deterrents to institutional participation in the option market is the speculative taint associated with options. Thanks to such diverse undercurrents as the Dutch tulip bulb mania and the focus of most written material on the investment leverage options can provide, option trading of any sort is frequently viewed as a highly speculative pursuit. Even institutions which are not bound by strict fiduciary restrictions such as legal lists or the prudent-man rule must consider the lawsuits option trading might encourage before they decide to participate. To the extent that the prudent-man rule in a modified form applies to every fiduciary, nuisance lawsuits are a universal possibility.

Another serious deterrent to many large institutions is a rule adopted at the suggestion of the SEC which limits the number of listed options on a single underlying stock that one investor or a group of investors acting in concert can write or buy. With minor qualifications, the present limits on each underlying stock are 500–1,000 contracts for each expiration date and 1,000 contracts in toto. While the precise meaning of acting in concert has not been spelled out, it is relatively clear that options will never have much of an impact on the total portfolios managed by Morgan Guaranty or Manufacturers Hanover if this rule remains in effect.

When institutions do move into options, they are far more likely to come as writers than as buyers. There are many reasons for this bias toward writing, including these:

1. It is the popular view that option writing is conservative and option buying is speculative.

2. Fiduciary guidelines can be more readily extended to covered option writing than to option buying.

3. Covered writing typically reduces exposure to market fluctuations; buying options typically increases it. Most institutions want to reduce their market risk exposure.

4. An option buyer pays for a privilege that may expire totally worthless. Its value declines inexorably over time unless the stock moves up.

Initially the only significant purchases of options by institutions are likely to be made by aggressive corporations, investment partnerships, and mutual funds and by a few conservative institutions which will buy in-the-money options selling at very modest premiums over intrinsic value. Buying these in-the-money options can limit downside risk if the stock drops sharply before the option expires. The net acquisition cost of stock acquired by exercising an in-the-money option might be about the same as an outright purchase.

In addition to general obstacles affecting the option trading policies of all institutional investors, there are a number of specific barriers peculiar to certain institutions. This listing is by no means all-inclusive.

Nonfinancial Corporations. The only possible obstacles to option trading by a nonfinancial corporation would be an obscure statute in its state of incorporation or a restrictive clause in the corporate bylaws. Ordinarily these restrictions can be removed by the directors or the stockholders of the corporation.

Mutual Funds. The principal obstacles to mutual fund participation in the option market are restrictive provisions in most fund prospectuses and certain limitations on a fund's sources of income that must be observed if the fund is to be treated as a regulated investment company for tax purposes. With the exception of a few extremely aggressive funds, most investment companies are prohibited by a statement in the prospectus from buying or writing puts and calls. In most cases, these provisions could be changed at the next annual meeting or at a special shareholders' meeting called for that purpose and an amended prospectus could be published. The prohibition against any trading in puts and calls has historically been inserted in mutual fund prospectuses to give them a solid, conservative sound and to avoid a registration delay while the SEC looks more closely than usual at the fund and its management.

A more serious barrier than the fund prospectus is a provision of the Internal Revenue Code which permits an investment company meeting certain requirements to collect interest and dividends and realize profits from the sale of stocks and bonds without paying taxes on this income. Provided that the fund's income comes from appropriate sources and the fund is adequately diversified, the fund acts as an untaxed conduit for any income it generates. The shareholder pays taxes on income distributed by the fund as if he were the owner of a pro rata share of the fund portfolio.

Two of the criteria that a fund must meet to qualify for this pass-through of earnings are called the 10 percent rule and the 30 percent rule. The 10 percent rule requires an investment company to obtain no more than 10 percent of its income from sources other than dividends, interest, and gains on the sale of securities. The 30 percent rule states that to avoid double taxation of the income of an investment company, at least 70 percent of the gross income before deduction of losses must come from dividends, interest, and capital gains on securities held more than 90 days. Other sources of income, including realized capital gains on securities held less than 90 days and profits from put and call transactions, cannot account for more than 30 percent of gross income before deduction of losses. While a fund that actively purchased call options could avoid a conflict with these rules by exercising profitable options and holding the stock for more than 90 days, such a procedure is cumbersome and forces the fund to accept exactly the investment risk that buying the call option is designed to avoid. Not only does the option premium received by a writer count as part of both the 10 percent and the 30 percent limitations, option premiums earned will usually be highest when the overall market is weakest and long-term capital gains are scarce. If the fund should fail to meet the investment company requirements and incur a tax liability, the fund's management company could expect a shareholder suit to recover the taxes paid.

Several prospectuses have been filed for funds which would specialize in trading options and related underlying stocks. The regulatory and tax problems which must be ironed out before these funds are offered to the public are enormous. At this time several small mutual funds with sizable loss carry-forwards have received the necessary approvals to write options. Though additional small funds with accumulated losses will probably begin writing options soon, existing or newly offered mutual funds are not likely to account for a significant share of option activity for at least a year or two.

Tax-Exempt Organizations. Pension funds, charitable organizations, and other tax-exempt institutions are effectively excluded from writing options by a provision of the Internal Revenue Code which implicitly defines unexercised option premiums as unrelated business income subject to tax. Legislation has been proposed to exempt option premium income from taxation as unrelated business income, but it is impossible to predict when or if this legislation will pass.

Bank Trust Departments.   Unless forbidden to do so by state law or a clause in the trust agreement, individual trust accounts managed by banks may write covered options. A preliminary ruling by the Comptroller of the Currency prohibited national banks from any option activity for a number of months before the ruling was reversed to permit covered writing.

Insurance Companies. Some insurance companies were active option writers for years before listed option trading began. The only obstacles to option writing by most insurance companies are inertia and a few insurance commissioners who consider options speculative. Active participation by insurance companies will probably expand slowly until these commissioners are converted.

Most of the restrictions which prevent institutional investors from participating in the options market will be lifted in time. As these restrictions disappear, there will probably be a gradual increase in institutional participation in option writing. Options provide something which the institutional investor has consistently sought but rarely found: A method of structuring the risks and rewards of an equity portfolio to give it a measure of independence from market fluctuations.

One of the most frequent criticisms that institutional portfolio managers hear is that they have shown no ability to provide the ultimate owners of the portfolio with either consistent or superior returns on equity investments. As was seen in the diagrams of possible option strategies, writing options permits the institutional investor to be free from lockstep dependence on the vagaries of market trends. While writing options does not guarantee that a portfolio will never have a down year, it can smooth out the fluctuations. Furthermore, if only overvalued options are written, the portfolio should enjoy a superior as well as more consistent performance.

Writing options can also enable an institution to modify its risk exposure without making massive changes in the portfolio. If an institutional portfolio manager feels that the stock market will be flat or that it may decline, he usually sells the more volatile stocks in his portfolio and invests a modest fraction of the equity portfolio in short-term debt securities until he is more sanguine about the outlook for the market. If he writes options, he can reduce the volatility of the portfolio without selling his volatile stock positions or shifting the portfolio into short-term debt.

If options are actively traded by institutions, not only will their clients enjoy more consistent investment results, the destabilizing effect of some institutional trading decisions on stock prices might be reduced. A portfolio manager who was uncertain about the outlook for a company but not strongly negative on the stock could temper his risk by writing options. He would not have to disrupt the market in the stock.

The goal of many institutional portfolios can be roughly defined as protection of portfolio capital against erosion by inflation while the portfolio assets are earning a sufficient current return to meet certain fixed obligations such as pension payments or insurance claims. If this statement of purpose is even approximately correct for a large number of institutions, unhedged exposure to volatile stock prices is not an appropriate investment strategy. One could even go so far as to state that rational management of most institutional equity portfolios practically requires the extensive use of options.

As the first legal barriers to institutional participation in the option market begin to crumble, the pressure on all regulatory agencies to relax the remaining barriers will increase. Whether institutional portfolio managers like it or not, the existence and use by their competitors of an efficient option market will force them to include options in their investment thinking. There will be growing competition to attain a consistency of equity performance that can only be achieved with options.

The beneficiaries of greater use of options will be the ultimate owners of institutional portfolios. Their pensions and the payments from their trust accounts will be more stable and more certain as a result of the institutional portfolio manager's ability to restructure risks and rewards in a manner appropriate to the needs of his ultimate clients. If the portfolio manager uses option evaluation carefully, his clients should also enjoy higher average returns.

At the end of 1974, the market value of the stock necessary to cover every open CBOE option contract was less than $2 billion. If institutions with their multibillion-dollar portfolios become active option writers, premiums are likely to be minimal and option buyers will be assured of favorable terms. In this context it is appropriate to examine the role of the individual investor who is, and will probably remain, the primary option buyer.

C. THE ROLE OF THE INDIVIDUAL INVESTOR

Historically, individual investors have accounted for most of the option contracts written and nearly all of the contracts purchased. Typically, writers have been wealthy individuals who see option writing as a way to stabilize and perhaps improve the rate of return from their equity portfolios. Option buyers have been small investors or executives with high incomes and little capital. The buyer typically sees options as a way to increase investment leverage and to limit possible loss when the risk-reward characteristics of an option contract fit his expectations for the price action of a particular stock better than owning the stock outright. There are obviously exceptions to these generalizations but they are approximately correct descriptions of the majority of conventional option market participants.

The success of the Chicago Board Options Exchange promises to increase institutional participation and profoundly change many historic relationships between option market participants. Institutional investors will soon participate actively on the writing side of the option market, but less frequently, if at all, on the buying side. Their presence as writers may tend, over the long run, to depress option premiums. In the past a burst of speculative option purchases has generally caused option premiums to rise sharply because buyers have tried to expand their participation more rapidly than new writers could be found. With wider institutional participation, option premiums will probably fluctuate less dramatically. In fact, option buyers may ultimately have a consistent advantage over option writers unless institutional investors are more flexible in their use of options than it now appears they are likely to be.

If premiums do become chronically low, there is a very conservative option-buying strategy designed to take advantage of low option premiums. This strategy is suitable for investors who ordinarily would not consider purchasing an option.

When option premiums are too low, it means that the premium the buyer is called upon to pay is lower than the premium justified by the risk-adjusted expected value of the reward that might be gained from appreciation in the price of the stock. If premiums are low, conservative investors can enjoy most of the protection of a debt portfolio combined with some of the reward potential of equities. The investor simply puts most of his assets in fixed-income securities and purchases underpriced call options with a small portion of his capital or with part of his interest income. This investor is protecting himself from the risk of losing his capital. Should the stock on which he has bought options go up, he will participate in the rise.

This strategy could also be adopted by the trustees of a pension fund which has a modest required rate of return that can be locked in with fixed-income securities. Rather than accept the downside risk associated with outright stock ownership, the trustees could obtain equity participation by purchasing options with any interest income that exceeds the actuarially required return. Though the risk-reward characteristics of this strategy are very similar to those of a high-quality convertible bond, it is doubtful that many pension funds will adopt this strategy until they have had a few years' experience writing options.

Though institutional purchases of options will develop slowly, investing most assets in short-term debt and buying a few options to give equity market exposure will become increasingly common among conservative individual investors over the next several years. Because of the magnitude of the individual and institutional money involved, conservative option purchases of this type will ultimately be larger than the strictly speculative purchase of options by the small investor. These uses of options are part of a longer-term trend, however, not an overnight development.

7 EVALUATION OF AN OPTION CONTRACT

A. THE SIGNIFICANCE OF OPTION EVALUATION

Throughout this book, the importance of careful evaluation of the specific option contract has been stressed. Rational evaluation of an option relative to the risk-reward characteristics of the underlying stock is the single most important step an investor must take to achieve superior investment performance using options.

Many option services and option users stress calculations based on (1) the leverage inherent in a particular option contract, (2) the option premium as a percent of the stock price or the striking price, or (3) the stock price parameters within which an option writing strategy is profitable. While it can occasionally be helpful to know the leverage potential of an option relative to a possible price change in the underlying stock, the option premium as a percent of the stock price, or the range of prices over which a given strategy will be profitable, a far more useful approach is to try to arrive at a single figure for the *fair value of an option*. Not only will that figure tell the investor whether, other things being equal, he should buy or write that option, but, based on that single figure, he can easily make any other appropriate calculations.

Whether the fair value of an option is expressed in dollars and cents or the desirability of the option to a buyer or writer is appraised by calculating the ratio of the market price of the option to the fair value of the contract, the important thing is to arrive at a single figure which provides meaningful guidance to the use of that option in a possible investment strategy. The purpose of this and subsequent evaluation sections is to describe and analyze the various methods of option evaluation in widespread use by arbitrageurs and advisory services. While many option and warrant advisory letters base their recommendations exclusively on an opinion on the underlying stock, the better services attempt to evaluate the option contract or warrant in its own right. Although it is not possible to determine the accuracy of a stock recommendation in advance of the period for which the recommendation is made, it *is* possible to determine the *relative* attractiveness of the stock and an option on that stock. Any advisory service which does not attempt to *evaluate* the option relative to an investment in the stock should be viewed with suspicion.

An appropriate standard against which to judge the usefulness of the assorted option valuation techniques, which will be examined in subsequent sections, is a simplified version of what most academic economists agree is the theoretical value of an option. Although this theoretical formulation was outlined briefly in the Introduction, it is now appropriate to expand upon those abbreviated remarks.

In Figure 7-1 and in the discussion to follow, an attempt is made to avoid visual clutter and confusion by dealing with the value of an option from the viewpoint of the buyer. Evaluation of the writer's position is essentially similar. This discussion deliberately omits several points which bear importantly on any practical application of this approach or on any advanced discussion of the theoretical value of an option. The sole purpose of these omissions is to improve the clarity of the explanation.

The buyer's profit-loss line begins in the lower left-hand corner of Figure 7-1, runs parallel to the horizontal axis until

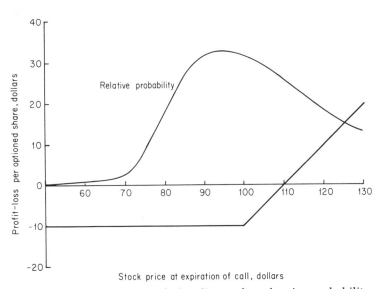

Figure 7-1. Call buyer's profit-loss line and stock price probability distribution.

it reaches the striking price (in this case $100 per share), then rises toward the upper right-hand corner of the page. The approximately bell-shaped curve superimposed on the graph is a hypothetical probability distribution of the stock price on the day the option expires. The shape and location of the stock price distribution curve are a function of the price of the stock at the time the option is purchased, interest rates, the volatility of stock price changes, and the time remaining before the option expires. In the present instance, the price of the stock is assumed to be $95 on the day the buyer purchases the 6-month call at an option price of $10. The interest rate is the intermediate-term, low-risk interest rate. For simplicity, the volatility of the stock is assumed to be the average volatility over some past period.

While it is not possible to determine the exact price of the stock on the date 6 months in the future when the option will expire, it is possible to estimate the *probability* that it will sell at any particular price. This probability estimate is based largely on the way common stock prices have behaved in the past. The probability estimate should not be confused with technical analysis of stock price behavior. Derivation of the probability curve neither requires nor provides a forecast of the *direction* of any change in the stock price. It is concerned only with the likely *magnitude* of stock price changes.

Certain characteristics of this probability distribution are intuitively obvious if given even a little thought. For example, most observers, whether they are avid chart readers or exponents of the random walk hypothesis, would agree that the price of a typical stock is more likely to be close to the present price 6 months from today than it is to be selling for either twice or half the present price. As the time period is extended from 6 months to, say, 2 years, the probability distribution will tend to spread out. Over the longer period, doubling or halving the stock price will become more likely events.

Some stocks are more likely to double or collapse than others. Both McDonald's Corporation and American Telephone and Telegraph were selling near $50 per share in early 1975. Regardless of their opinions on the merits of the two issues, most market participants would expect McDonald's stock to trade over a broader price range than AT&T over the next several years. Beyond these areas of agreement, there is considerable controversy over the exact shape of the probability distribution of future stock prices. The curve shown here is for illustrative purposes only, though it does approximate the shape of observed probability distributions.

Once the difficult task of estimating the characteristics of the probability distribution has been completed and the shape and location of the probability curve is determined, it is a relatively simple matter to calculate the expected profitability of a call option. Using the example in Figure 7-1, we divide the probability curve into small segments. The area under the curve in each segment, say in the stock price range between $70 and $71 per share, is divided by the total area under the curve. The resulting fraction is multiplied by the profit or loss to the buyer ($10 loss) if the stock sells in the range of $70 to $71 per share on the day the option expires. When the results of these calculations over the range of all possible stock prices are added up, the total is the profit or loss the buyer of that call can expect.

This explanation of the calculation of the expected profit or loss from buying a call will seem quite straightforward once the reader understands the basic principle of multiplying the fraction of the total area under the probability curve times the profit or loss associated with the price range under that part of the curve. In practice, the calculation is very time-consuming unless the probability distribution curve is similar to one of a family of curves which can be defined by a simple equation. Readers will appreciate the complexities of option evaluation when they consider that calculation of the expected profit or loss occurs only after an analyst has carefully esti-mated the shape and location of the probability distribution and has made a myriad of adjustments to the probability dis-tribution and/or the profit-loss line for the effect of commis-sions, dividends, interest rates, and risk.

Before we can compare an option valuation method with this theoretical model, we must convert the expected profit or loss figure into an estimate of the value of the call. This is simply a matter of adding the buyer's expected profit *to* or sub-tracting his expected loss *from* the market price of the call to determine the call price at which he could expect to break even.

The fair value or expected break-even price of the call is the single figure most rational option evaluation techniques attempt to derive. Our appraisal of these techniques will be largely an assessment of how closely they approximate the value that the theoretical model would generate. Most of the option evaluation techniques in widespread use are the result of attempts to short-cut the process by simplifying the calcula-tions or, more commonly, by finding the value of the option indirectly through a formula that does not explicitly incor-porate the probability distribution of stock prices.

The importance of the fair value or break-even value of an option contract is hard to overestimate. Once this value has been determined, it can serve as the foundation for any fur-ther work the investor might wish to do. It can also serve as part of a simple decision rule such as:

A call option is never written unless the premium received by the writer exceeds the fair value of the call, and a call option is never purchased unless the premium falls below the fair value of the option.

The fair value of a call or the ratio of the call price to fair value can serve as the basis of a whole series of calculations which permit the investor to structure the risk and return parameters of his investment position in virtually any desired way. Some of these calculations will be illustrated in Section F of this chapter.

If we use an expected value calculation, such as the fair value of a call, as the sole criterion for a decision, we implicitly assume that the investor is neutral toward risk. Stated another way, relying solely on the expected value of an option implies that an individual is indifferent to the choice between, say, a 100 percent chance of gaining $1 and a 10 percent chance of gaining $10 combined with a 90 percent chance of no gain. While there is considerable evidence that this assumption is not valid when the amounts of money involved are quite large, the calculation of expected value provides a useful starting point. An individual's risk preferences can be reflected in the development of an investment strategy once the "risk neutral" expected value has been calculated. Information about the fair value of a call option, combined with the graphic representations developed in Chapter 4, Section A, should help the investor select a strategy with a high expected return that is also appropriate to his risk preferences.

From the explanation in Chapter 4, Section A, of the graphic representation technique, it should be clear that it is possible to calculate the profit or loss from any investment if we know the stock price at the end of the period. A profit-loss calculation at a particular stock price can be made in a few seconds. If the investor is willing to spend a bit more time, he can construct one of the simple graphs that was used to illustrate profit or loss at various stock price levels. When the data on the graph are processed to reflect the probability distribution of future stock prices, the investor can rationally evaluate the investment from the viewpoint of expected rate of return in addition to building a portfolio that reflects risk preferences and subjective stock price expectations.

Few investors will rely strictly on an expected value calculation in devising a portfolio strategy. It is important, however, that the rational investor understand the nature of the probability distribution of stock price changes and the possible cost of each deviation from a strategy based on expected value. Graphic representation of risks and rewards combined with an expected rate-of-return calculation permits the most intelligent evaluation of the possible results. The graphs need not be fancy to help the investor judge the appropriateness of a strategy to his expectations and risk preferences.

Before turning our attention to the variety of evaluation techniques that have been devised to deal with the problem of determining the appropriate price to pay or receive for a call option, we will examine some other approaches to option selection which are in widespread use but which do not attempt to compute or estimate the fair value of the option contract as a prelude to an investment decision. These approaches are espoused by a number of advisory services and are used by some experienced investors. While each of these approaches provides some useful information, none of them is adequate when used without an appraisal of the fair value of an option contract.

Leverage calculations generally attempt to estimate the effect of a given change in the stock price on the option price. For example, a 20 percent rise in the price of a stock by the time an option expires may lead to a 100 percent profit on the option; or a 10 percent rise in the stock price may be necessary to give the call buyer a 10 percent return on investment. Such calculations are prepared by a variety of option services and are frequently used to justify the speculative purchase of options by investors with limited resources.

The problem with leverage calculations is that they tend to be misleading. In any given 6-month period the probability of a 20 percent advance in AT&T is far lower than the probability of a 20 percent advance in the price of Brunswick. As obvious as this statement may be and as unlikely as it may seem that any reasonably intelligent investor would be misled, the fact that leverage calculations ordinarily fail to discriminate among stocks with different degrees of volatility is, at best, confusing. At worst, the naive investor could be led to make an erroneous decision. Unless the investor is deliberately seeking risk, the fact that a given option provides unusually high leverage will not be useful information. The rational investor is much more likely to be interested in expected profit or rate of return. To get these numbers the investor must try to put a value on the option itself, not on its leverage.

A large number of covered option writers base their writing decisions on a calculation of the option premium as a percent of the stock price or, alternatively, on the rate of return if the stock they own is called away from them. Using our standard example of a $95 stock and its related option, the $10 option premium for a 6-month option at $100 is 10.5 percent of the $95 stock price. If the stock is called away, the writer gets a return of

$$\frac{\$100 - \$95 + \$10}{\$95}$$

or 15.8 percent over 6 months. The annualized return would be about 31.6 percent *if the call is exercised.*

In spite of its *apparent* attractiveness, writing this option may not be a sound strategy. This call writer is giving up any incremental profit he might earn if the stock rises above $110 per share by the end of the option period. The call writer can *never* earn more than an annualized return of 31.6 percent. If the stock is extremely volatile, there is a high probability that the stock will sell for more than $110 and, *conversely, a high probability that it will sell below $85 per share, giving him a loss even after he receives the option premium.* The option premium is the covered writer's compensation for giving up the chance to participate in any appreciation of the stock beyond $110 per share on the upside, and his insurance protection if the stock declines. If he sells the option too cheaply, he may be giving up too much potential appreciation relative to the risk he is accepting in the event the stock declines. The tricky feature of the single-point rate-of-return approach to option writing is that the writer *always* gets a good return if the stock rises and is *always* better off having written the call if the stock declines. If the stock is sufficiently volatile, however, the overall return will be inadequate in the long run because the writer will not make enough when the stock advances to recover losses from periods when the stock declines.

Many arbitrageurs and option writers use another "non-evaluation" approach to options that has a little more to recommend it than the simple leverage calculation, or dividing the option premium by the stock price. This is the so-called "parameter" approach; it involves calculation of the range of prices over which a strategy is profitable. For example, if an investor buys 100 shares of stock at $95 and writes two options with a striking price of $100 and an option premium of $10, this strategy will be profitable if the stock sells between $75 and $125 per share on the day the options expire. The range—$75 to $125—defines the profitability parameters of this strategy.

To the extent that the investor tries to evaluate the risk that the stock price will rise above or fall below this range, the parameter approach can be sensible. Unfortunately, we are all familiar with remarks such as: "The absolute maximum downside risk on this stock is 10 points." As most investors who have made such statements are painfully aware, stocks do drop or rise further than one might think possible. Unless the assessment of the risk that the stock will violate the profit parameters is done conscientiously and quantitatively, it is useless.

The principal danger of the parameter approach is that option writers who are addicted to it have a tendency to try to write their way out of any problem. Suppose that the stock in our example dropped to $65 per share, putting it outside the profit parameters the investor originally set up. The devotee of parametric analysis will often yield to the irresistible temptation to write additional options, frequently with only minimal consideration for the adequacy of the premium, to extend the lower parameter below the $65 price level. This reduction of the lower parameter can be accomplished *only by reducing the upper parameter as well*. If the stock price recovers after the upper parameter is lowered the investor can easily be whipsawed. Furthermore, as the investor writes more options on this stock, he ties up more of his capital in a situation which his machinations prove he does not understand. Unless the underlying stock goes to zero, fluctuates violently, or moves up rapidly and steadily for a long enough period of time to bankrupt him, this investor should *eventually* earn at least a small profit. He could have a substantial fraction of his assets committed to a low-return investment by the time that happens, however.

Another problem with the use of parameters is that two strategies with similar parameters may vary greatly in attractiveness. If, in the example cited earlier, the investor purchased the stock at $120 instead of $95 and wrote two options with striking prices of $100 for premiums of $22.50 per share, the profit parameters would still be $75 to $125. Unless the investor expects the stock price to decline, this strategy is probably less attractive than the earlier example. The point of maximum profitability ($100) is well below the $120 stock price, and even a modest advance in the stock price will make the strategy unprofitable.

A more serious flaw in the parametric approach is that it provides no way except "gut feel" to compare strategies involving options with different striking prices or positions involving different stocks. Only if a fair value is calculated for each option can the investor rationally compare two strategies involving different options on the same stock or strategies involving different stocks.

The sophisticated reader may feel that the author has attacked straw men in criticizing the devotees of leverage calculations, premium percentages, and parametric analysis. Nothing could be further from the truth. There are numerous investors who consider one or another of these techniques to be a sound method of managing an option portfolio. Many option buyers look primarily at leverage calculations to determine where they can get the most return on their dollar. Numerous experienced option writers are convinced that as long as the option premium is a large enough percentage of the stock price, or as long as they readjust their profit-loss line to bracket the current stock price with their profit parameters, they are bound to make money in the long run. The fact that these writers may tie up a disproportionate amount of their equity in a single situation, or that the ultimate return on investment may be very small, does not seem to bother them.

On the assumption that the reader is convinced of the importance of evaluating the option contract itself as a first step in the analysis of any option strategy, we turn to the consideration of the wide variety of techniques various authors have devised to compute the fair value of an option. The reader who is not persuaded of the overwhelming importance of option valuation should reread the Introduction and Chapter 4.

B. GRAPHIC EVALUATION TECHNIQUES

Graphic techniques for the analysis of option investment strategies vary greatly in usefulness and sophistication. Some investors accept the market's appraisal of the value of options and use graphs of the type examined in Chapter 4, Section A, to estimate the profitability of a strategy at specific stock prices. These investors see graphs as tools to restructure the risk characteristics of a portfolio rather than as part of an evaluation technique. If the investor is a disciple of the parameter school, he can use graphs to determine the stock price range over which a strategy will be profitable. Regardless of the approach, drawing a graph can help the investor crystallize his views on the probable course of the stock price and integrate these views with his attitude toward risk.

To take things one step further, an investor might superimpose on a graph (see Chapter 4, Section A) his personal estimate of the probability curve of the distribution of stock prices on the day the option expires. This graph might look very roughly like Figure 7-1. If, based on the investor's visual assessment of such a diagram, there is high probability that the expected return on investment will be satisfactory and the risk characteristics of the investment are acceptable, the investor will take the position. Most graphic analysis techniques used for option evaluation are simpler than the diagrams used in this book and require less input data from the user. These graphic techniques spring from efforts to simplify the decision-making process.

One of the most widely used sets of graphs for the evaluation of conventional options was prepared by Zaven A. Dadekian for his book, *The Strategy of Puts and Calls*. The charts actually published in the book are obsolete because interest rates and commission charges have changed significantly since 1968 and, even with new charts, the results are only approximate. Nonetheless, Dadekian's graphs can be the foundation for one of the few rational option analysis techniques which the average investor can apply to the appraisal of conventional options. There is no intent to suggest that Dadekian's charts are the answer to the public's option evaluation needs. In fact, certain features of Dadekian's technique are misleading. For example, he calculates an annualized return on investment which is really a return on equity *if* the option is exercised. In spite of such weaknesses, the thinking behind Dadekian's charts can be more useful than most of the material available to the small investor.

Dadekian's contribution lies in his analysis of conventional option premiums (bids to writers) for stocks at various price levels. He collected data on a large number of conventional option transactions and divided the data into quartile rankings at ten-point stock price intervals. He found, for example, that about 25 percent of the option premiums paid to writers for a 6-months-and-10-day call on a $40 stock fell below $417 or $4.17 per share, 50 percent fell below $455 or $4.55 per share, and 75 percent fell below $492 or $4.92 per share. Figure 7-2 is Dadekian's graph for premiums on 6-months-and-10-day call options. It is easy to be overly critical of Dadekian's study from a technical viewpoint, but the approach can be helpful. From Dadekian's charts the would-be option writer can conclude that a $450 premium offered him on a $40 stock with average volatility is probably a fair bid, but a $475 bid on an extremely volatile stock is probably too low.

One of the problems with Dadekian's charts is that they must be updated frequently and the user must subjectively evaluate such factors as volatility and dividend payments in his examination of each proposed transaction. Another problem is that the charts are only useful for conventional options for which the market price and striking price are identical. They are almost useless for listed options or "special" options for which the two prices are different.

Because the Dadekian charts assume that, on average, option bids to writers are fair, it is possible for a writer using the charts to accept a bid that was relatively better than most bids

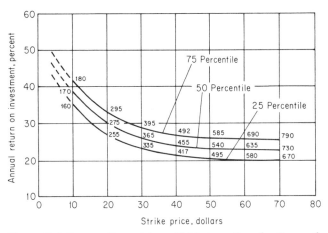

Figure 7-2. Percentile ranking of bids to writers for 6-month-and-10-day call options. Reprinted by permission of Charles Scribner's Sons from *The Strategy of Puts and Calls* by Zaven A. Dadekian. Copyright © 1968 Zaven A. Dadekian.

available, but still too low, or to reject a bid that did not appear attractive on the charts, but was actually higher than the fair value of the call. The charts are most likely to give inappropriate indications when a major change is occurring in the economy or a particular company. The intelligent option writer can probably incorporate such a change into his thinking and compensate accordingly in reaching a decision. If he is writing conventional options on a small scale and does not have access to better information, an investor can do far worse than rely on this kind of chart.

The buyer or writer of listed options, where the market price of the stock and the striking price of the option can be quite different, needs more information than can be obtained from the Dadekian charts. He needs a graph which relates the value of a particular option contract at one stock price to the value of that same contract at any other price on the underlying stock. The rest of the diagrams in this chapter illustrate attempts to construct this type of graph.

To use a graph which relates the value of a listed call to the market price of the underlying stock, the investor must know or estimate the value of the call at one stock price, usually the striking price. Determining this key value requires a non-graphic valuation approach or a Dadekian-type chart. Many investors claim to have a good "feel" for option values, with or without a Dadekian chart, when the stock price and striking price are equal. Investors who are more at home with the identical striking and market prices of the conventional option market than with the divergent market and striking prices of listed options will be comfortable using a graph that permits them to locate a curve based on a single valuation point where the striking and market prices are equal.

Although both models were designed for the analysis of long-term warrants, the Shelton and Kassouf econometric models, which will be examined in detail in Section D of this chapter, have occasionally been adapted to graphic evaluation of warrants and options. Neither author would approve of this adaptation of his work; however, these models were chosen to illustrate some of the problems of evaluating options with graphs, primarily because the popularity of the Shelton and Kassouf models might lead investors to misuse them. While our discussion of the graphic adaptation may point to some weaknesses in the related econometric model, failure of the graphic adaptation does not condemn the econometric model.

The series of graphic models begins with an adaptation of the Shelton model. Figure 7-3 depicts an option value line derived from the Shelton model for warrant evaluation. The reader who wishes to experiment with the Shelton line as a graphic technique for option evaluation should first draw a graph similar to Figure 7-3 for some stock and option of interest. The triangle *OAB* in Figure 7-3 is drawn by connecting the three points in this table:

Point	Stock Price	Option or Warrant Price
O	0	0
A	Exercise price	0
B	4 × exercise price	3 × exercise price

The reasons Shelton chose these particular points will be discussed in the detailed analysis of his model. The focus of in-

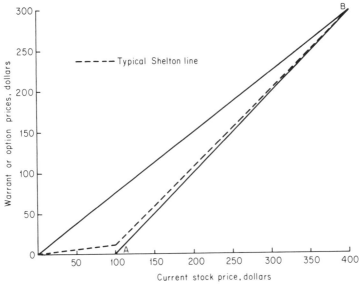

Figure 7-3. An evaluation "curve" derived from the Shelton econometric model.

terest here is strictly on how well the model works as a graphic valuation method for options.

Once the points have been located and the lines drawn, the investor must determine the fair value of any call he wishes to evaluate at one specific stock price. As noted earlier, most active option traders claim they can assign an appropriate value to a call as long as the stock price and the striking price are identical. Evaluation techniques are most useful (and most necessary for the typical investor) when these two prices differ. In the example illustrated, the investor has concluded that a 6-month option with a striking price of $100 is worth $12.50 per share when the stock is selling at $100. Plotting this point on the graph, the investor has one of the points on the Shelton line. All that remains is to calculate the values at several more points and draw in the curve. The known point is $12.50/ $75.00 or 16.7 percent of the distance between what Shelton calls the minimum value of the warrant or option (line *OAB*) and what he calls the maximum value (line *OB*). To estimate the value of the option at any stock price other than $100, the investor merely multiplies this percentage by the distance between the minimum value and the maximum value and adds the result to the minimum value. For example, if the stock is selling at $80, the calculation is as follows:

Value of option = % of range × (value at maximum
$$- \text{value at minimum}) + \text{value at minimum}$$
$$V_c = 16.7\% \times (\$60 - 0) + 0$$
$$= \$10.02$$

This value is clearly too high. If one makes the same calculation for this option at a stock price of $120, one will get an option value of $31.69, which is also far too high. Part of the reason for this sizable discrepancy between the values computed for the Shelton line and the prices at which options actually change hands may be accounted for by the fact that the Shelton line was derived for the evaluation of long-term warrants. For short-lived options, a graph of the Shelton line has little to offer as an evaluation tool.

Just as his entire model is more complex than Shelton's, Kassouf's basic curve is slightly more difficult to derive. For mathematically inclined readers, the formula for the curve is:

$$V_c = S\left[\sqrt[z]{\left(\frac{P_s}{S}\right)^z + 1} - 1 \right]$$

where V_c = value of call or warrant
S = striking price of call or warrant being evaluated
P_s = price of stock at which option is being evaluated
Z = location parameter of curve which reflects all determinants of option or warrant value such as interest rates, dividends, stock price, time remaining to expiration, and stock volatility

The reader who fears we are about to depart on a mathematical tangent at this point can relax. The only purposes in writing out the formula are to provide interested readers with more information and to show that the formula for the curve assumes that the value of a particular call is completely determined by the stock and striking prices of the option once the value of Z, which defines the shape and location of the curve, is known. In other words, Z describes the curve for various values of the ratio P_s/S.

The formula suggests that once the user of the formula or graph knows the value of the stock price and the striking price, he can determine the value of the call. Unfortunately P_s (stock price) is one of the variables determining Z. Thus, a given Z curve might provide a better fit to the observed data over a narrow range of values for the option than any other Z curve, yet still not fit very well if the stock price and option value move out of that range. Figure 7-4, illustrates a typical, though hypothetical, relationship between observed data and Kassouf's Z curve. When we examine Kassouf's econometric model in detail we will see that, unlike the graph, the model can accommodate this drift off the Z curve.

The difficulty with both the Kassouf and the Shelton lines is that they are derived from equations that do not incorporate the probability distribution of stock price changes. These figures represent their respective creators' attempts to fit a curve or a line to observed warrant price/stock price relationships. As part of the Shelton and Kassouf econometric models, these curves can give useful results, particularly in estimating

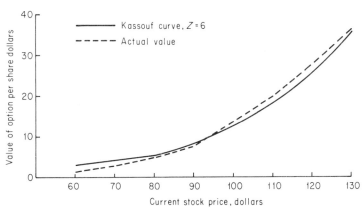

Figure 7-4. Comparison of a Kassouf Z-curve with actual option values.

the expected price of a long-term warrant. The curves themselves are of little use in option evaluation.

Figure 7-5 depicts a set of option curves based on the Gastineau-Madansky option valuation model. Unlike the Shelton and Kassouf models, there is no simple formula for the derivation of this set of curves. The curves in Figure 7-5 have been fitted by hand to selected points calculated by a computerized model. Although the reader will understand the lack of a simple formula better after the Gastineau-Madansky model is discussed at greater length, the principal reason no simple formula is available is that the probability distribution used in the Gastineau-Madansky model is empirically derived. As a consequence, no simple function will describe the curve with appropriate precision.

Figure 7-5 is set up in much the same way as the Shelton and Kassouf curves. The major difference is that the Gastineau-Madansky curve should fit any observed data rather well. Under normal circumstances, the market price of an op-

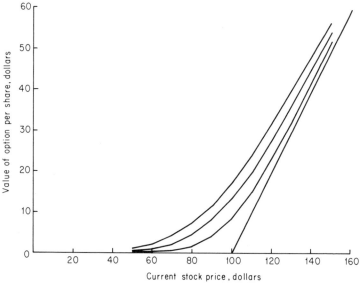

Figure 7-5. Option value curves based on the Gastineau-Madansky model for option valuation; adjusted for expected commissions, assumes no dividend paid.

tion should roughly approximate the value an investor might extract from the curves, provided he has selected the proper curves. Although any departure of the option price from the value indicated by the curve *might* represent an opportunity for arbitrage profit, the user of the graph must exercise care that the option has not "jumped" to another curve.

These curves have only limited practical value to the investor because of the restrictive assumptions on which they are based. Discussion of these assumptions and limitations will aim as much at discouraging indiscriminate use of the graph as at helping the user adjust his thinking to the graph's idiosyncrasies. The most important single assumption underlying any graphic evaluation technique is that, with the exception of the stock price, the basic determinants of option value are unchanged from the moment a specific curve is selected to the moment the curve is used to derive the value of an option. This assumption is frequently invalid. Time usually passes after a particular curve is chosen, and time is one of the most important determinants of option value. If much time passed, the value of the option would lie on a different curve, not at a different location on the same curve.

The graph is most likely to be used when the stock price has changed significantly from an earlier value which was used to select an appropriate curve. Unfortunately, many of the factors that cause stock price changes also cause changes in the relative value of options. For example, gyrations in interest rates cause option values as well as stock prices to fluctuate. Other things being equal, an increase in interest rates increases the relative value of an option, and a decrease in interest rates causes the value of the option to fall. In addition, an outbreak of military activity in the Middle East could cause the price of an international oil stock to fall. Because the outlook for the oil company is now less certain and the stock is likely to be more volatile, the value of an option contract might decline *less* than the graph would predict.

Apart from these problems with the effect of external changes on the choice of an appropriate curve, graphs are difficult to adjust for commissions and dividends. A commission adjustment can be built in, but the investor will still need separate sets of curves for conventional and listed options and for high-yield stocks and low-yield stocks. This litany could continue, but it should be clear by now that a set of sophisticated valuation graphs could do as much to confuse and mislead the average investor as to help him. If Figure 7-5 helps readers appreciate the relationship between stock price and option value over a range of stock prices, it will serve its purpose. To use this graph directly in decision making is inappropriate.

C. EVALUATION RULES AND FORMULAS

To differentiate the numerous rules of thumb and simple formulas that are proposed for option evaluation from the more sophisticated econometric models of Shelton and Kassouf, a rule or formula used in option evaluation is defined as any numeric or analog relationship that does not directly incorporate an adjustment for either dividends or stock price volatility. Formulas may attempt to derive an option value from scratch or they may only describe appropriate adjustments for differences between the market price of the stock and the striking price of the option. They may be expressed as algebraic expressions or they may be reduced either to tables designed for easy reference or to mechanical devices. In the latter category, the author has in his possession two completely different "warrant slide rules" and has seen an "option slide rule" and an option "computer."

At a very slight risk of overgeneralization, one may state that most of these rules and formulas are dangerous. While many of the specific examples criticized come from the extensive literature on warrants, similar techniques have been and will be applied to options now that exchange listing has focused interest on these shorter-term warrantlike instruments. Developments in the option market are proceeding so rapidly that new formulas, rules, tables, and other gimmicks will appear regularly.

To simplify the discussion, the formula approaches are divided into two groups: first, the techniques designed to define the value or price of an option or warrant in relation to the price of the underlying stock; second, attempts to adjust a given warrant or option premium to reflect differences between the stock price and the striking price. This second group of formulas received little critical attention until recently because conventional call options are generally written with the striking price equal to the current market price of the stock and are rarely resold or exercised by the original purchaser until just prior to expiration.

One formula originally developed for the evaluation of long-term warrants was proposed by Guynemer Giguère in *The Analysts Journal* of November 1958. Modifying Giguère's symbols to conform to those used previously, his equation is $V_c = P_s^2/4S$. To state the formula in words, Giguère argues that the value of a warrant (V_c) is equal to the price of the stock (P_s) squared, divided by four times the exercise or striking price (S). The curve which this formula describes is a parabola with a value of zero when the stock price is equal to zero. The shape of the function is illustrated in Figure 7-6. The premium over intrinsic value disappears completely when the price of the stock reaches twice the exercise or striking price. Empirical

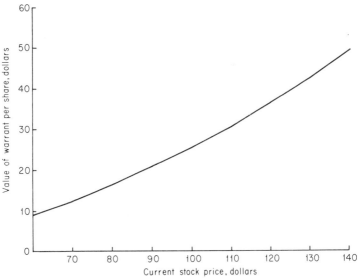

Figure 7-6. Guynemer Giguère's warrant valuation parabola for $S = \$100$.

studies using this formula indicate that, as a general rule, warrants with more than 3 to 5 years of life remaining will usually sell at prices higher than those predicted by the formula. Options with less than 1 year of life will usually sell at lower prices. Giguère suggests modifying the formula for shorter- or longer-term options or warrants by adding to or subtracting from the denominator of the equation. The results this modification gives are not consistently useful, however. Giguère's formula is more an historic curiosity than a practical method of evaluating either warrants or options.

A more recent discussion of warrant valuation using a tabular approach was published in *Value Line Selection and Opinion*, July 1968. Though no equation is given in this article, a table suggesting the degree of positive and negative leverage in warrants at various prices is provided. An implicit fair value line for long-term warrants is obtainable from the table. Although it is not possible to say definitely, the Value Line formula appears to be a modification of either the Shelton or the Kassouf model, probably the former.

Several writers have published tables designed to show the relationship between option premiums and stock prices. Most of these tables of option values give an average or maximum premium for options of various lives. As the composite listing in Table 7-1 indicates, the appropriate premium assigned to a stock is primarily a function of the stock price. Apart from some modest evidence that there is an inverse relationship

Table 7-1. Estimated Maximum Premiums* Paid by Buyers for New Conventional Calls at the Market

Stock Price	3 Months	6 Months	1 Year
10	$137.50–150	$175–237.50	$300–337.50
20	$212.50–225	$312.50–350	$400–450
30	$300–325	$400–450	$500–550
40	$400–425	$525–600	$700–750
50	$475–525	$625–700	$800–875
75	$700–775	$925–1100	$1200–1300
100	$900–1025	$1225–1350	$1450–1700

* These premiums are composites derived from several sources. Any resemblance to actual premiums is coincidental. Most authors of such tables indicate that premiums on American Stock Exchange or over-the-counter stocks will be higher.

between stock price and volatility that makes options on lower-priced stocks more expensive than those on higher-priced stocks, the principal reason for the indicated relationship between stock prices and conventional option premiums is the extraordinarily high transaction cost of a conventional option on a low-priced stock. Readers should regard these tables of option values with suspicion. Even though they may reflect option prices, they will not usually reflect option values. If an investor is careful, these tables can be used much like the Dadekian charts. Table 7-1 is based on the premiums paid by buyers in contrast to the premiums paid to writers as in the Dadekian chart in Figure 7-2. Though the data came from different sources, the principal difference is the put and call broker's spread.

With the present interest in options it was inevitable that a number of advisory services would begin to publish tables showing expected option prices at various combinations of striking price, market price, and time to maturity for listed options. Such tables could be useful to the investor if properly derived and frequently updated. Three sets of such tables with which we are familiar have been prepared by the FRA Warrant Service, by Computerized Investment Services Corporation (OPSYS), and by Fischer Black of the University of Chicago.

The FRA Warrant Service tables are apparently based on a Kassouf-type econometric model. Judging from the author's limited analysis of several of these tables, they offer only a fair indication of actual option price–stock price relationships.

The OPSYS tables also appear to be based on an econometric analysis of price relationships. Like the FRA tables, the OPSYS approach frequently provides misleading predictions of actual relationships. The virtue of the OPSYS tables is that the distortion appears to be consistent: The values assigned to deep out-of-the-money options are far too high. Furthermore, the tables do not adequately adjust for dividends.

The tables published by Fischer Black in an article titled "Fact and Fantasy in the Use of Options" (see Bibliography) are probably the most useful tables readily available to the student of options who is willing to do the necessary work to use tables intelligently. In contrast to the material accompanying the other sets of tables, the assumptions behind each of Black's tables are spelled out in detail. Although he does not simplify the user's task by pointing out which table should be used with which stock, Black does discuss how an appropriate table should be selected and how necessary adjustments for dividends and taxes can be made. Careful study of Black's article will help the reader understand the hazards of blind dependence on a set of option tables.

The option slide rule and the option computer have little to recommend them. The author has yet to see a warrant or option slide rule that can accommodate enough variables to give meaningful results. Most of the money spent on these is wasted. The Option Computer sold by ISEC of Princeton, New Jersey, appears to be a technical market service in an option disguise. Stock price volatility is a component of the model, or, if one prefers, an input to the computer; but the instruction manual clearly states that the focus of the model is technical market analysis. In fact, it appears from the instruction manual that the "computer" does not even consider option price or option value in reaching a buy or sell recommendation.

We turn next to the rules of thumb. It is an article of faith with many long-time traders in conventional options that if the striking price of an option and the market price of the underlying stock are close, the price of the option should change by about one-half as many points as the stock price changes. In other words, if an option with a striking price of $30 is worth $5 when the stock is selling at $30, it will be worth $2.50 with the stock at $25 and $8 with the stock at $36. To the extent that investors use rules of thumb like this one, they may provide the astute investor with trading and arbitrage opportunities.

Not all rules of thumb are simple. In his book, *Stock Options*, James B. Cloonan provides a brief table of adjustment factors for in-the-money options. Briefly, he argues that if the stock is selling above its striking price and if the option has 9 months to go before expiration, the investor should expect the option price to rise by only one-half of the amount by which the option trades in the money. The reader will note that, so far, this is the same as the old rule of thumb mentioned above. Though his statement of the "new" rule is complicated, Cloonan basically argues that the percentage by which the option price will change increases as the option approaches expiration. Cloonan's estimates of the percentage of the stock price move by which the option price will move are given in Table 7-2. Though rules of thumb are frequently misleading,

Table 7-2. Cloonan Factors for Option Price Change of In-the-Money Options

Months remaining to expiration	9	8	7	6	5	4	3	2	1	0
Percentage of any stock price move that will be reflected in an option price move	50	55	60	65	70	75	80	85	90	95

even a cursory examination of actual option price behavior suggests that the old rule is more accurate than Cloonan's table. In general, option prices seem to move between one-half and two-thirds as much as stock prices when the striking price and market price are roughly equal. This rule works fairly well almost regardless of the time remaining in the life of the options.

The relationship between stock price and option price is too complicated to be reduced to a simple formula or rule of thumb. Simplicity is a virtue if a simple model or rule provides good results. Unfortunately, none of the simple option models accurately describes or predicts the relationships found in the real world. Greater complexity in the model and the aid of a computer to handle the calculations are necessities.

D. ECONOMETRIC MODELS

1. The Shelton Model

In a two-part article in the *Financial Analysts Journal* beginning in the issue of May/June 1967, John Shelton reviewed much of the then existing literature on warrant evaluation and presented an econometric model which, in its most general form, permits evaluation of warrants and options with virtually any period of life remaining. Unlike the Giguère formula which is difficult to adjust for variations in remaining life, dividend yield, and other parameters, the Shelton model can be modified to handle virtually any warrant or option contract.

As was noted in the discussion of graphic techniques for option evaluation, Shelton argues that there are minimum and maximum theoretical values for any option or warrant. The minimum value is the intrinsic value. If the striking price of an option or warrant is $100 and the stock is currently selling at $110, then the intrinsic value is $10, or the difference between the current price of the stock and the striking price or exercise price of the option or warrant. If the stock is selling below the striking price, the intrinsic or minimum value of the option or warrant is zero. Largely from examination of warrant and stock price relationships, Shelton and other observers have found that a long-term warrant rarely sells at any significant premium over intrinsic value when the price of the stock is more than four times the exercise price. Furthermore, when the stock price is below this level, the maximum value of the warrant appears to be about 75 percent of the price of the stock.

Within the range determined by the minimum of either zero or the intrinsic value of the warrant and the maximum of 75 percent of the stock price, Shelton finds that a good approximation to prices of long-term warrants is given by the following expression:

$$\sqrt[4]{\frac{M}{72}} \left(.47 - 4.25\, \frac{D}{P_s} + .17\, L\right)$$

where M = number of months remaining to expiration

D = annual dividend payment

P_s = current price of stock

$\frac{D}{P_s}$ = annual dividend yield

L = 1 if warrant is listed, 0 if it is traded over the counter

Once the value of this expression has been calculated, the resulting decimal fraction is multiplied by the difference between the maximum and minimum values of the option as computed above, and the product is added to the minimum value. An example of a warrant value calculation using the Shelton model can be found in Table 7-3.

Unlike Giguère's formula and many of the rule-of-thumb warrant-stock relationships, Shelton's formula has the important advantage that it adjusts explicitly for the effect of the dividend on the common stock. A further advantage of the Shelton formula is that it permits ready calculation of a warrant price by the average investor. All the information needed is in the daily newspaper.

A major drawback of the Shelton formulation, based on our earlier discussion of the theoretical valuation of an option, is that the Shelton formulation makes no adjustment for the volatility of the stock. If the dividend, stock price, and remaining life were identical, the Shelton model would give identical predicted prices for warrants on American Telephone & Telegraph and Gulf & Western. As strange as this result may appear, stock price volatility does seem to have less of an impact on longer-term warrant prices than on option prices. Shelton

Table 7-3. Sample Shelton Warrant Valuation Calculation

Issue: Fibreboard Corporation warrants

Expiration date: December 1, 1978

Exercise price: $22.50

Date of calculation: May 24, 1974

Months to expiration (M): 54

Dividend (D): $.90

Stock price (P_s): $16.50

Dividend yield $\left(\dfrac{D}{P_s} \right)$: 5.5%

Warrant is listed on the American Stock Exchange: (L) = 1

Substitute in Shelton formula:

$$\sqrt[4]{\frac{54}{72}} \ (.47 - 4.25 \times .055 + .17) = 38.1\%$$

Value of warrant (V_c) = 38.1% × ($12.38 + $0) + $0
= $4.72

Actual price of warrant: $5.13

tested the effect of stock price volatility on warrant prices and found it did not materially affect the prices actually paid for long-term warrants. Volatility is absent from Shelton's formulation not because he ignored it, but because he concluded it did not matter very much in the appraisal of long-term warrants.

Besides missing a volatility factor, Shelton's model gives values for options that appear to be too high. Again, part of the problem is that the model was designed for long-term warrants. Casual observation of listed option trading suggests that any premium above intrinsic value disappears long before the stock price reaches 4 times the exercise price. The price at which the premium over intrinsic value disappears varies with the remaining life of the option, but it is probably between 20 and 40 percent over the striking price in most cases.

The reader has probably begun to suspect that he is being led to the conclusion that while the published Shelton model was not designed for use on options and gives absurd results when applied to any short-lived option or warrant, it can be reformulated to give useful results. The parameters of the valuation triangle must be changed, perhaps as implied by the line OC in Figure 7-7, and the multiple regression analysis which was used to devise the expression for calculating the position of the option line within the triangle must be done with option data instead of long-term warrant data. It is likely that the revised expression will contain the level of the stock price and stock volatility as important factors affecting option value in addition to dividend yield and time remaining to expiration which appear in the warrant version of the model. When these modifications are made, it would be interesting to compare the results from Shelton's model with those from the Kassouf model. Kassouf's formulation is more applicable to options than Shelton's approach and has consequently been more widely used. There is little reason to suspect that the Kassouf approach is inherently superior, however.

Someday an ambitious doctoral candidate will undertake a study of the two approaches to determine how results from each deviate from the theoretical fair value of an option or

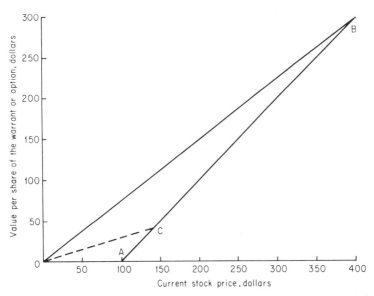

Figure 7-7. A possible modification to Shelton's econometric model to apply it to options.

warrant. Some deviation is inevitable in both cases because these econometric models use historic stock and warrant price relationships as the basis for calculation of *expected* warrant or option *price*, not *fair value*. If premiums were higher than fair value during the period used to construct the model, applying the model at a later date will typically show predicted prices that are higher than fair value. This weakness is inherent in the econometric approach. It has less significance when a model is applied to warrant evaluation because overvaluation or undervaluation in warrant price may correct only very gradually. A prediction of relative warrant price may, in the short run, be as useful as a prediction of fair value. Options have a very limited life, however, and a model that predicts prices rather than values could lead to erroneous decisions. For example, if a model constructed during a period of high premiums is applied to data from a period of lower premiums, it might indicate that a particular option should be bought when in reality the option is still overpriced.

A further weakness of econometric models is that they provide no simple mechanism to adjust a coefficient if a change in the company's position occurs and is not adequately reflected in the input variables. Changing a coefficient arbitrarily could easily do more harm than good. The limitations of econometric models will be clearer after examination of the Kassouf model, which is somewhat more complex than the Shelton model and consequently somewhat more difficult for the average investor to use.

2. The Kassouf Model

The Kassouf econometric model is widely used by professional arbitrageurs and by a few of the more sophisticated advisory services. The basic model was developed by Sheen T. Kassouf in a doctoral dissertation submitted to Columbia University in 1965. Though the model, as originally developed, was used to estimate the value of warrants, Kassouf and others have used it to evaluate virtually every kind of convertible security.

Kassouf's approach has been more widely used by professionals than Shelton's, less because of any inherent superiority in Kassouf's approach than because the rules for a doctoral dissertation require the author to reveal his methods in detail. The work behind Shelton's model may have been as sophisticated as Kassouf's work, but Shelton did not elaborate on his methods in the articles describing his model. In contrast to Kassouf, Shelton wanted a simple approach that anyone with a daily newspaper could use. Some of the material Kassouf has published is also designed for the average investor, but the backup information in his thesis has always been available. Shelton published only one simplified version of his model while Kassouf has emphasized the importance of periodic reexamination of the model to check how well an earlier formulation fits present circumstances. The detailed material he has published facilitates these checks.

For mathematically inclined readers, Table 7-4 presents the basic Kassouf equation and the coefficients Kassouf calculated for warrant evaluation for two separate time periods. Even

Table 7-4. The Kassouf Warrant Evaluation Model

$$V_c = S\left[\sqrt[z]{(P_s/S)^z + 1} - 1\right]$$

$$Z = k_1 + \frac{k_2}{t} + k_3 R + k_4 d + k_5 E_1 + k_6 E_2 + k_7 x + k_8 S + a$$

V_c = expected price of warrant

S = striking or exercise price

P_s = price of underlying stock

$k_1 \ldots k_8$ = coefficients derived by multiple regression analysis

t = number of months before expiration

R = dividend yield on common stock

d = number of outstanding warrants divided by number of outstanding shares (i.e., potential dilution ratio)

E_1 = slope of least squares line fitted to logarithms of monthly mean price of common stock for previous 11 months

E_2 = standard deviation of natural logarithms of monthly mean price of common stock for previous 11 months

$x = \dfrac{P_s}{S}$

a = random variable

Calculated values for Z:

1945–1957

$$Z = -1.061 + 6.922\left(\frac{1}{t}\right) + 8.768R + 1.876x + 0.357d + 0.074S$$

1958–1964

$$Z = 1.526 + 2.717\left(\frac{1}{t}\right) + 13.421R + 0.301x - 1.340E_2$$

those readers without mathematical interest or aptitude should examine the two formulas Kassouf devised to estimate warrant prices for the years 1945–1957 and 1958–1964, respectively. The formulas for the two time periods are quite different. Moreover, the warrant prices they predict are quite different when warrants with similar characteristics are evaluated. Using average values for the explanatory variables, Kassouf finds that a comparable warrant would have sold for $4.87 in the earlier period and $6.50 in the later period.

While there are several possible explanations for this difference, the most plausible is that supply and demand and other factors caused warrant premiums to be higher in the later period. Unfortunately, the Kassouf approach cannot tell us whether the buyers of the warrants or the short sellers had better chances of success *in either period.*

The Kassouf model predicts a normal or average price, not a fair value. The distinction may not be critical for a warrant that has 5 or 10 years of life remaining. An investor has little reason to expect that a long period during which average values have exceeded fair value will come to an abrupt end while he owns the warrants. On the other hand, options have short lives, usually less than a year. Overvaluation or undervaluation of an option cannot last longer than the option. If an investor regularly buys options at normal or average prices that are higher than fair value or writes options at normal or average prices that are below fair value, he will earn an inferior rate of return.

The Kassouf model or any other econometric model generates a figure that is not equivalent to the fair value generated by the theoretical option value model; this fact sharply reduces the usefulness of the econometric valuation methods. If options on a particular stock are overpriced during the period used to calculate the coefficients in the Kassouf equation, the estimated normal value from the model will probably be above the fair value level until the coefficients are recalculated. Only in a very approximate way does the Kassouf model indicate when an option premium is higher or lower than the price one should rationally be willing to pay. The model assumes that past option price–stock price relationships were appropriate.

Although the result it produces is not exactly the number we are looking for, the Kassouf model has at least three important advantages over either the Giguère formula or the Shelton warrant model:

First, it explicitly considers more variables. Any factor from interest rates and stock price volatility to dividends has an opportunity to demonstrate its importance when a multiple regression analysis derives the equation for Z. If a factor drops out of the equation, it drops out because it does not appear to have affected price relationships during the period under study.

Second, the Kassouf model explicitly considers the effect of stock price volatility. Stock price fluctuations are extremely important in option evaluation. None of the other methods examined assign any significant weight to this variable, though Shelton would have used volatility if he had found it meaningful.

Finally, unlike the other two equations, the Kassouf model is not wedded to a particular curve. Although the basic price relationship curve is fixed, as was noted in the discussion of graphic techniques for option analysis, Kassouf introduced stock price as a variable affecting Z, the exponent in the equation, to permit the warrant or option value to drift from one curve to another. This considerably loosens the tie to a particular price relationship equation and improves the predictive value of the model.

The Kassouf model, from the time of its publication until today, has been the only reliable and practical method for estimating the average or normal price of a wide variety of convertible securities. Its principal weakness is that the value it generates is only an approximation, based on past price relationships, of what the price of a convertible security *might* be, not a statement, based on the behavior pattern of the underlying common stock, of what the value *should* be.

We turn next to the probability models, a group of approaches that try to determine what the price of an option or other convertible security should be, based on the probability distribution of the price of the underlying stock.

E. PROBABILITY MODELS

1. Sprenkle, Samuelson, Merton, and Others

A number of leading economists have, at one time or another in their careers, written articles on option or warrant pricing. Most of this work has used options or warrants as a tool to study some other phenomenon which interested the author. To the reader who appreciates the nuances of academic literature, few of the option value models developed by these economists are exactly identical. To the reader less concerned with nuances, the similarities among these models are either comforting or boring, depending on one's mood.

Tables 7-5 and 7-6, below and on the next page, describe two of the more important probability models. The first of these models, outlined in Table 7-5, was derived by Case M. Sprenkle in his doctoral dissertation at Yale University in 1960. Sprenkle's work was published in *Yale Economic Essays*, Vol. 1, No. 2(1961), and reprinted in *The Random Character of Stock Market Prices*, edited by Paul Cootner. The Sprenkle model is similar in most respects to other classical option and warrant models based on the probability approach. Apart from a few practical considerations that limit its usefulness, Sprenkle's model describes fairly well the relationship between the probability distribution of stock price changes and

Table 7-5. Sprenkle Probability Model (as restated by Black and Scholes)

$$V_c = k\, P_s\, N(b_1) - k^*\, SN\, (b_2)$$

$$b_1 = \frac{\ln\left(\dfrac{kP_s}{S}\right) + \frac{1}{2}v^2\,(t^* - t)}{v\sqrt{(t^* - t)}}$$

$$b_2 = \frac{\ln\left(\dfrac{kP_s}{S}\right) - \frac{1}{2}v^2\,(t^* - t)}{v\sqrt{(t^* - t)}}$$

V_c = fair value of option

k = ratio of expected value of stock price at time option or warrant expires to current stock price

P_s = stock price

$N(b)$ = cumulative normal density function

k^* = discount factor that depends on risk characteristics of stock

S = striking or exercise price

$\ln$ = natural logarithm

v^2 = variance rate of return on stock

t^* = maturity date of option or warrant

t = current date

Table 7-6. Samuelson-Merton "Util-Prob" Model

$$V_c = e^{r(t-t*)} \int_{\frac{S}{P_s}}^{\infty} (ZP_s - S) \, dQ \, [Z; \, (t* - t)]$$

V_c = fair value of option

r = interest rate

t = current date

t^* = maturity date of option or warrant

$\int_{\frac{S}{P_s}}^{\infty}$ = integral over interval from $\frac{S}{P_s}$ to ∞

S = striking or exercise price

P_s = stock price

Z = random variable return per dollar invested in common stock

$dQ \, [Z; (t* - t)]$ = risk-adjusted probability density function of Z over a time period of length $t* - t$

e = base of natural logarithms = 2.71828

option or warrant values. The Sprenkle model approximates the description of the probability approach already given and soon to be developed further.

The other model, outlined in Table 7-6, was developed by Paul Samuelson and Robert Merton of M.I.T. and described in an article in the Winter 1969 issue of *Industrial Management Review*. The unique feature of this model is that it is based on what the authors call a "util-prob" or combined utility and probability distribution. Though most observers would argue that some of the complexities of the Samuelson-Merton model are rendered obsolete by the work of Fischer Black and Myron Scholes, which will be discussed in the next section, this model in its most general form is one of the most flexible approaches to warrant and option evaluation.

The purpose here is not to compare and contrast the myriad of theoretical option and warrant pricing models suggested by various economists. The material in Tables 7-5 and 7-6 is provided strictly for the benefit of readers who are mathematically inclined. For the majority of readers, the simplified version of the general probability model for warrant and option evaluation which was used in earlier chapters will be expanded on. This simplified model lacks the refinements and the complexities of the mathematical formulations favored by the authors of the works cited. The intention is not to give the reader an elegant formula, but to help him understand relationships. Consistent with the goal of making option evaluation understandable to the reasonably sophisticated investor who does not necessarily have a strong grounding in mathematics, the continued emphasis will be on graphic, rather than algebraic, explanations. Some of the simplifying assumptions of the basic probability approach are deliberately glossed over to avoid entanglement in some important but nonetheless confusing refinements. The author's goal is to be understood, not to present a comprehensive model of option valuation in exhaustive detail.

Figure 7-8 is a reproduction of Figure 7-1 which shows the profit-loss position of a call buyer with a stock price probability distribution superimposed on the diagram. This diagram will be used to review and expand upon the basic explana-

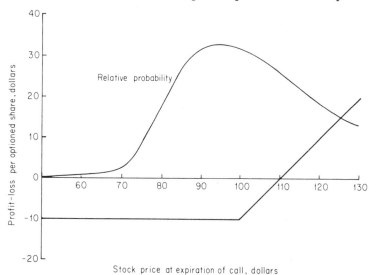

Figure 7-8. Call buyer's profit-loss line and stock price probability distribution.

tion of the probability model outlined in the first chapter of this evaluation section.

The reader will recall that once the characteristics of the profit-loss line and the probability curve are known, calculation of the expected profit or loss and the fair value of the call is straightforward, if perhaps a bit time-consuming. As noted earlier, the expected profit or loss to an option buyer is calculated by adding up the results obtained by multiplying the profit or loss over a particular range of stock prices by the probability that the price will fall in that range when the option expires. To phrase it another way, the expected profit or loss is equal to the sum of all possible outcomes multiplied by their respective likelihoods of occurring. The fair value of the call before adjustments is simply the call price less any profit or plus any loss to the buyer.

The key to superior common stock investment performance is usually superior ability to predict the direction and magnitude of stock price changes. The investor who can accurately estimate the shape and location of the probability curve of the stock price changes should enjoy superior results using options even if he is completely unable to predict a specific stock price move. Buying options that are selling for less than fair value and writing those that are selling for more than fair value is the key to these superior results. With this in mind, it is time to examine some of the basic characteristics of the curve in Figure 7-8.

If we draw a line vertically through an expiration price of $100 per share on the graph, we see that approximately half of the area under the curve falls to the left of this price and approximately half falls to the right. In other words, if we neglect the effect of commissions, there is approximately a 50 percent probability that the option will expire without being exercised and an equal probability that it will be exercised. If the option does expire without being exercised, the buyer will lose the entire premium. The buyer does not begin to recover the premium paid until the stock price at expiration moves into the right half of the probability curve.

When we examine the curve carefully it becomes clear why the size, shape, and location of the probability distribution of future stock prices become so important. It is theoretically possible for the stock price to increase by almost any amount over the 6-month life of this call option. In actual practice, the stock price will rarely even double. As the graph is drawn in this example, even a price of $130 per share on the expiration date of the call option would have to be considered unusual. Yet it is these extreme values that the call buyer must count on to make the investment worthwhile. When large profits are weighted by low probabilities, the resulting impact on the call buyer's profit position can be material.

If there were only a 5 percent chance that the stock price would exceed $130 and the mean of expected prices over $130 was $140, this sector of the curve would add 0.05 × $40 or $2 to the call buyer's expected profit. If this segment of the curve accounted for 6 percent of all possible stock prices, the expected profit contribution would be $2.40. The additional $0.40 is 4 percent of the option price. If the curve in this example moved a single percentage point to the right, the expected profit to the call buyer would increase by about $0.25 or $2\frac{1}{2}$ percent of the option price. Clearly the shape and location of the curve are important.

Since the first paper on the modern theory of options was published by Louis Bachelier in France in 1900, economists have debated the shape and location of the curve representing the probability distribution of future stock prices. A thorough discussion of this controversy would involve mathematical relationships beyond the scope of a book which is designed for practitioners. Nevertheless, any student of options should have a basic understanding of what the argument is about.

Most arguments over the shape of the probability distribution of stock prices have resulted from attempts to simplify calculations by postulating a particular mathematical function as an approximation of the empirical relationship. The purpose here is to help the reader understand certain generalizations about the shape and location of the probability curve. After an intuitive discussion of the stock price distribution, we will examine the mathematical functions that have been suggested as approximations to the actual stock price distribution.

One important characteristic of the probability distribution curve drawn in Figure 7-8 is that its arithmetic mean or average lies at least slightly above the current stock price. This characteristic of the curve reflects the fact that, in spite of the experience of the past several years, there is a definite secular uptrend in stock prices. It also reflects the fact that this stock must compete with other possible investments. No investor would hold the stock if he did not expect it to appreciate. Over the 6-month period depicted in this example, the expected increase is not very great, but the present price of the stock will discount an expected increase related to such factors as the size of the dividend, the level of interest rates, and the likely volatility of the stock price.

A second characteristic of this curve is that it reflects the tendency for a stock price 6 months from today to be close to today's stock price. The tails of the curve suggest that there is a significant probability that the stock price will diverge materially from the current level, but the stock price 6 months from today will more likely be close to today's price than far away from it.

A third characteristic of the curve is that it is slightly skewed in a positive direction. That is, if we pick a price $10 higher and another price $10 lower than today's price, the probability of reaching the higher price is somewhat greater than the probability of reaching the lower price. There is nothing esoteric about this characteristic of the stock price probability distribution. It simply reflects the nature of stock price changes. While it would not be common for the price of a stock selling today at $95 a share to rise by $100 over the next 6 months, a price change of this magnitude is possible. It is not possible for the stock price to decline by $100 because the price cannot drop below zero.

Most techniques that attempt to estimate the fair value (as opposed to the average or normal price) of an option approximate the shape of the stock price probability curve with one of two mathematical functions used as the probability distribution. The simplest of these distributions is the so-called normal distribution which is the basis of most statistical analysis. The other widely used probability distribution is the lognormal distribution. The lognormal distribution is simply the normal distribution applied to the logarithms of the data, in this case, stock prices.

Although the lognormal distribution is slightly more difficult to use than the simple normal curve, most economists have used it in their option models because it more closely approximates the process by which stock prices change. The normal distribution assigns equal probabilities of occurrence to a $100 increase in stock price and a $100 decrease. With the lognormal distribution a 100 percent price rise is as probable as a 50 percent decline. The lognormal distribution appropriately reflects the skewness in the actual distribution of stock prices.

While economists are satisfied that the lognormal distribution provides a better approximation to the actual probability distribution of stock prices than the standard normal distribution, the lognormal distribution does not fit observed data on stock prices well enough to permit its use for all purposes. Empirical studies have shown that the probability distribution of future stock prices differs from the lognormal approximation in several ways. First, there is a slight tendency for future stock prices to cluster more around the current stock price than might be expected on the basis of the lognormal distribution. Second, and even more significant when options are involved, there is a pronounced tendency for stock prices to be more concentrated in the tails of the distribution than predicted by the lognormal curve.

Figure 7-9 illustrates for comparative purposes the difference between the lognormal distribution (dashed line) and the observed distribution with its higher peak and fatter tails (solid line). If the reader will compare these distributions and consider the earlier discussion of the theoretical evaluation of an option, it will be clear that if the striking price of the option and the market price of the stock differ materially, these two distributions will give considerably different values for an option.

Option evaluation techniques based on the lognormal distribution give reasonably satisfactory results as long as the market price and the exercise price are identical. When these

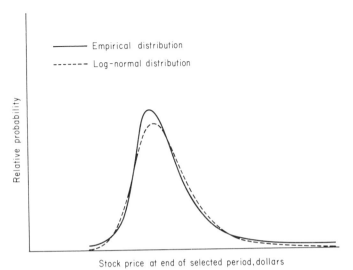

Figure 7-9. Comparison of empirical distribution of stock prices with lognormal distribution.

prices differ materially, however, an option valuation based on a lognormal distribution of expected stock prices is subject to substantial error. For example, an option selling well out of the money might appear, from the lognormal distribution, to have little value. The "skinny" tails of the lognormal distribution suggest a low probability of a large-price advance. Using the empirical distribution with its fatter tails, the value of the out-of-the-money call would be much higher.

Although very little has been said about the problems of estimating the precise characteristics of the probability distribution applicable to a particular stock at a particular time, the reader should appreciate that practical use of a probability model for option evaluation is difficult and time-consuming even with the help of a computer. Adjustments for dividends and commissions present a further complication. It is small wonder that most models designed for practical use in the appraisal of stock options and warrants have bypassed the probability approach for econometric models. Publication of the Black-Scholes model, to be discussed in the next section, has been instrumental in focusing renewed attention on the probability models.

2. The Black-Scholes Model

Almost as if it were timed to coincide with the opening of the CBOE, a theoretical valuation formula for options, derived by Fischer Black and Myron Scholes, was published in the *Journal of Political Economy* for May/June 1973. The principal difference between the Black-Scholes formulation and the techniques proposed by other economists over the years is that Black and Scholes focus on the neutral option hedge as the key to the determination of option value. The Black-Scholes formula and its major assumptions are outlined in Table 7-7. While the mathematical derivation of the formula is an important feature of the Black-Scholes article, the focus here will be on the principle behind the Black-Scholes approach and its usefulness as a practical method of evaluating options.

The Black-Scholes model is based on the fact that it is possible, subject to a number of assumptions, to set up a perfectly hedged position consisting of a long position in an underlying stock and a short position in options on that stock, or a long position in the options and a short position in the stock. By perfectly hedged, they mean that over a stock price interval close to the current price, any profit resulting from an instantaneous increase in the price of the stock would be exactly offset by a loss on the option position or vice versa. The Black-Scholes formula, then, is developed from the principle that *options can completely eliminate market risk from a stock portfolio.* Black and Scholes postulate that the ratio of options to stock in this hedged position is constantly modified at no commission cost to offset gains or losses on the stock by losses or gains on the options. Because the position is theoretically riskless, the option premium at which the hedge yields a pretax return equal to the risk-free short-term interest rate is the fair value of the option. If the price of the option is greater or less than fair value, then the return from a risk-free hedged position could exceed the risk-free interest rate. The reader may detect a subtle but significant difference between this definition of fair value and the simpler definition used elsewhere in this

Table 7-7. Black-Scholes Model

$$V_c = P_s N (d_1) - S e^{r(t-t^*)} N(d_2)$$

$$d_1 = \frac{\ln \left(\dfrac{P_s}{S} \right) + (r + \frac{1}{2}v2) (t^* - t)}{v \sqrt{(t^* - t)}}$$

$$d_2 = \frac{\ln \left(\dfrac{P_s}{S} \right) + (r - \frac{1}{2}r2) (t^* - t)}{v \sqrt{(t^* - t)}}$$

V_c = fair value of option

P_s = stock price

S = striking or exercise price

$N(d)$ = cumulative normal density function

r = "risk-free" interest rate

t = current date

t^* = maturity date of option or warrant

v^2 = variance rate of return on stock

e = base of natural logarithms = 2.71828

ln = natural logarithm

Key Assumptions of the Black-Scholes Model

1. The short-term interest rate is known and is constant through time.
2. The stock price follows a random walk in continuous time with a variance rate proportional to the square of the stock price.
3. The distribution of possible stock prices at the end of any finite interval is lognormal.
4. The variance rate of return on the stock is constant.
5. The stock pays no dividends and makes no other distributions.
6. The option can only be exercised at maturity.
7. There are no commissions or other transaction costs in buying or selling the stock or the option.
8. It is possible to borrow any fraction of the price of a security to buy it or to hold it, at the short-term interest rate.
9. A seller who does not own a security (a short seller) will simply accept the price of the security from the buyer and will agree to settle with the buyer on some future date by paying him an amount equal to the price of the security on that date. While this short sale is outstanding, the short seller will have the use of, or interest on, the proceeds of the sale.
10. The tax rate, if any, is identical for all transactions and all market participants.

SOURCE: From Fischer Black and Myron Scholes, "The Pricing of Options and Corporate Liabilities," *The Journal of Political Economy*, May/June 1973, pp. 637–654. Copyright © 1973 by the University of Chicago. All rights reserved.

book. Though the Black-Scholes definition is more appropriate in several respects, it seems to be harder for most people to grasp. The Black and Scholes articles are an appropriate starting point for anyone wishing to examine the distinctions in greater depth.

This brief chapter is not intended to provide a detailed critique of the Black-Scholes model. Readers can examine the accompanying table and list of assumptions (Table 7-7) and judge the realism of the model for themselves. Some of the Black-Scholes assumptions can easily be relaxed to make the model more realistic. For example, the assumption that the option can only be exercised at maturity is not critical. Likewise, it is not overly difficult to adjust for commissions and other transaction costs or even taxes. Conversely, a number of the Black-Scholes assumptions are both difficult to accept and difficult or impossible to modify within the framework of their model. Unless these assumptions are relaxed, however, the model is likely to encourage misleading option evaluations.

Some of the same features of the Black-Scholes model which contribute to its computational efficiency detract materially from its practical usefulness. While some of the weaknesses of the Black-Scholes formulation are too technical for a clear nonmathematical explanation, most of the problems with the Black-Scholes model are easy enough to understand. First, in its basic form, the model assumes that the stock pays no dividend. On the assumption that we are dealing with listed options, it would appear at first glance to be a simple matter to adjust the formula for dividends by subtracting the dividend yield from the interest rate used in the computation. Unfortunately, while interest usually accrues steadily over time, dividend payments are discrete sums, usually paid once a quarter. Timing of the dividend payment can have an important effect on the value of a short-term option when the market price of the stock is above the striking price of the option. As if the *timing* of dividends were not enough of a problem, many companies pay irregular quarterly dividends. The dividend in the final quarter or two quarters of the year may be materially larger than the dividend paid in the first half. Correctly adjusting the Black-Scholes formula or any probability model for dividends is complicated yet critically important for some of the higher-dividend-paying stocks with listed options.

A second weakness of the Black-Scholes model is its use of a single "risk-free" interest rate as the discount factor in the formula. The risk-free rate causes several problems which are beyond the scope of this book. However, there are a few simple reasons why the strictly risk-free rate is inappropriate.

While it is theoretically possible to iron out all fluctuations in the value of the investor's equity in a hedged position by continuously changing the ratio of options short to shares long, or vice versa, few investors will actually modify their option hedges so frequently. Frequent minor adjustments of the hedge ratio would lead to an intolerable level of commission cost. The fact that the actual rate of return will fluctuate as a result of the fact that frequent adjustments in the hedge ratio are impractical suggests that a rate slightly higher than the risk-free interest rate should be used. Black and Scholes argue that any deviations from the risk-free rate will be unsystematic (unrelated to the market trend), and that they can be eliminated through diversification. Empirical studies suggest that even unsystematic risk requires a higher rate of return than the so-called "risk-free" rate.

Another problem with the Black-Scholes single interest rate is that an investor cannot really borrow and lend at the same rate. If the rate an investor receives on short-term debt instruments is 7 percent, he may find that he is paying 9 percent or more for money borrowed in his margin account. A related problem is that the short-sale assumption adopted by Black and Scholes is unrealistic. The short seller will not usually have access to the proceeds of his sale. Interest on the proceeds of the short sale technically belongs to the owner of the shares the short seller borrowed to deliver to the buyer.

Probably the most important shortcoming of the Black-Scholes model is that it relies heavily on the assumption that the probability distribution of future stock prices is a lognormal distribution. As we saw earlier (p. 194), the lognormal distribution is simply the conventional normal distribution applied to the logarithms of stock prices. Unfortunately, for the usefulness of the Black-Scholes model, virtually every significant empirical study ever made of the distribution of stock price changes indicates that the actual probability distribution of stock prices deviates materially from the lognormal curve.

Under some circumstances the lognormal assumption can give satisfactory results. For example, the assumption of lognormality provides fairly good results as long as the market price of the stock and the striking price of the option are identical. If, however, the market price and the striking price are materially different, the lognormal assumption can lead to a very poor estimate of the fair value of the call.

Unless it is used with care, the Black-Scholes model will give option values that are, on average, too low; moreover, these values differ significantly from the actual fair value of the option if the striking price and the market price of the stock differ. Widespread use of the Black-Scholes model by institutional investors may have the effect of both depressing and distorting actual option premiums. It is unlikely that all the option traders using the Black-Scholes model have made appropriate corrections for the inherent biases of the Black-Scholes model and for commissions and dividends.

Probably the most important contribution Black and Scholes have made to the literature of options is not their formula but the fact that their equation is based on the construction of an option hedge. They highlight the fact that the investor can completely eliminate systematic or market risk. As any student of portfolio management theory learns early in the course, portfolio diversification permits an investor to reduce exposure to the fortunes or misfortunes of a particular company and its securities. Prior to publication of the two Black and Scholes papers and the creation of listed options, most portfolio management texts argued that it was impossible to eliminate market risk through diversification. These texts argued that, while it might be possible to reduce a stockholder's total risk by buying Polaroid and IBM as well as U.S. Steel and General Motors, the only way to reduce exposure to market risk is to put some of the assets in short-term debt or to invest in less volatile stocks. As long as the portfolio retains any significant exposure to common stocks, its value will probably fluctuate with the trend of the overall market.

Black and Scholes have highlighted the fact that it is possible to eliminate market risk by constructing a hedged position with options. The significance of this point will be easy to understand if the reader will put himself or herself in the place of an institutional portfolio manager who has been looking frantically for a way to insulate investment performance from the vagaries of the market. Options are an answer to this problem.

F. THE GASTINEAU-MADANSKY MODEL

1. General Characteristics of the Model

The development of the Gastineau-Madansky model has drawn heavily on the work of the authors whose formulations were discussed in the preceding sections. In general form, the Gastineau-Madansky model is a probability model. By modifying an assumption here and dropping an equation there, it is possible to reduce the Gastineau-Madansky formulation to the format of any of the probability models, including the Black-Scholes model. In terms of its mathematical relationships, the Gastineau-Madansky model probably is closest to the Samuelson-Merton model.

The fact that there is a family relationship to these other models can be misleading, however. Because it is designed to be used for practical calculation of option values, the Gastineau-Madansky model is substantially more complex than any model discussed in the academic literature. This is not meant as an indictment of any of these formulations. Their creators were not trying to demonstrate a practical technique applicable under all circumstances. They were primarily concerned with the advancement of the theory of options.

The fair value of an option determined by the Gastineau-Madansky model is adjusted for dividends, interest rates, and option commission charges. The model can also be adjusted

Table 7-8. The Gastineau-Madansky Model

$$V_c = a_1 \, e^{a_2 \, r(t - t^*)} \int_{\frac{a_3 S}{P_s}}^{\infty} a_4 (ZP_s - S) \, dQ \, [Z; \, (t^* - t); a_5]$$

V_c = fair value of option

$a_1 \ldots a_5$ = adjustment factors designed to reflect commission charges, dividends, interest rates, taxes, and other variables. Each adjustment factor in this formulation may incorporate part or all of the adjustment for more than one variable. The adjustment factors are frequently complex functions in their own right

r = basic interest rate

t = current date

t^* = maturity date of option or warrant

$\int_{\frac{a_3 S}{P_c}}^{\infty}$ = integral over interval from $\dfrac{a_3 S}{P_s}$ to ∞

∞ = infinity

S = striking or exercise price

P_s = stock price

Z = random variable return per dollar invested in common stock

$dQ \, [Z; \, (t^* - t); a_5]$ = an empirical probability density function of Z over a time period of length $t^* - t$

e = base of natural logarithms = 2.71828

Key Assumptions of the Gastineau-Madansky Model

1. The interest rates at which an investor can borrow and lend money are known and constant through time.
2. Stock price fluctuations conform to the efficient markets model which states that the stock price at any moment reflects all information available to the market participants. The variance rate is proportional to the square of the stock price.
3. The distribution of possible stock prices at the end of any finite interval conforms to an empirical probability function.
4. The variance of the stock price distribution is the same for each period.
5. The effect of dividends and other distributions is reflected in the adjustment factors.
6. The option can be exercised at any time prior to expiration.
7. Commissions and other option transaction costs are reflected in the adjustment factors.
8. The investor is subject to standard margin requirements and borrows at a higher rate than he lends.
9. The short seller can, through option conversion, effectively have the use of some of the proceeds of a short sale. He is unlikely, however, to benefit fully from any short sale the converter must make.
10. The tax rate, if any, is the actual rate paid by each market participant. The tax rate is symmetric in that the tax credit for a loss is computed at the same rate as the tax payment on a gain. Tax rates may differ on each of three types of income: (1) ordinary income, (2) short-term capital gains, (3) long-term capital gains.

for tax rates. A tax-rate adjustment is necessary when the model is used to evaluate option purchases and spread transactions, in particular. One feature, but by no means the only unique feature, of the Gastineau-Madansky model is that it does not use a simple mathematical function to represent the stock price probability distribution. The complex empirical probability distribution gives more useful results than the commonly used lognormal distribution.

One of the most important features of the model is that it is almost completely modular. In most cases an adjustment can be added or removed without affecting the rest of the model. Modularity is important for theoretical as well as for practical reasons. Modularity permits the model to be used to test new ideas and to be improved if the new idea is useful. Furthermore, should any option trading entity adopt an option contract format different from the standard listed or conventional option contract, or should commission rates or margin rules change, the Gastineau-Madansky model can be readily adapted to the new rules. In contrast, many of the classic probability models and, most particularly, the Black-Scholes model, are limited in their flexibility. They are wedded to a particular concept or probability distribution and cannot be readily adapted to a different perception of reality.

Table 7-8 provides an outline of the general form of the Gastineau-Madansky model as it is used to evaluate listed options. The equation in the table is highly simplified, but it should give the reader a feeling for the complexities of adapting a theoretical model for practical application. The formula can be compared with the Samuelson-Merton formulation which, in this simplified version, it most closely resembles. The assumptions should be compared with the Black-Scholes assumptions. If the user is willing to rerun the computer program a few times, several more of these assumptions can be relaxed.

2. What the Gastineau-Madansky Model Tells the Investor

Table 7-9 lists some of the data generated by the Gastineau-Madansky computerized option model for listed options on

Table 7-9. Partial Listing of the Output of the Gastineau-Madansky Computerized Option Model (Date of Analysis: August 12, 1974)

Data	Stock	
	McDonald's	Polaroid
Symbol	MCD	PRD
Expiration month	January	January
Striking price	$50.00	$30.00
Stock price	$41.125	$26.375
Call price	$ 2.75	$ 3.75
Gastineau-Madansky fair value	$ 3.00	$ 2.79
Call price/fair value	.92	1.34
Black-Scholes fair value fully adjusted	$ 2.82	$ 2.72
Neutral hedge ratio (pretax)	2.69	2.11
Net margin required for uncovered writer (30% rate) per share	$ .71	$ .53
Probability option will be exercised	31%	39%
Probability uncovered writer will lose money or buyer will make money	25%	26%
Probability writer of pretax neutral hedge will lose money	36%	24%
Profit parameters pretax neutral hedge	$33.72–59.62	$18.47–40.40
Expected return on equity from a neutral hedge	5.8%	34.9%

NOTES:

1. Stock and option prices are closing prices for the previous Friday.
2. Margin requirements are based on an assumed 30 percent margin rate for uncovered writers and are expressed net of any credit for the premium received by the writer.
3. The profit parameters are simply the prices which bracket the stock price range over which a neutral hedge is profitable.
4. The expected return on equity from a neutral hedge is the probability weighted profit or loss from a neutral hedge divided by the net equity of the investor in the hedge after option premiums received are credited.

McDonald's Corporation and Polaroid. Even a casual examination of these data suggests, under the assumptions incorporated in the model, that the McDonald's option is slightly underpriced and the Polaroid option is substantially overpriced. At the risk of repeating a point, it should be emphasized that the terms overpriced and underpriced do not imply *anything* about the likely direction of stock price movement; they suggest *only* how an option should be used. If an investor is bearish on McDonald's, he might not be interested in buying a call just because it is cheap. Instead, an underpriced call might be reversed to create a put, or the call might be purchased to hedge a short sale. Likewise, a bull on Polaroid might want to write uncovered puts, write straddles against a long position, or set up a bullish hedge. The option evaluation model is a tool to help the investor choose a strategy that is appropriate to his attitude on the stock, the value of the option contract, and his personal risk preferences.

If Table 7-9 is examined carefully, the reader will observe that some of the calculations are based on the fair value of a call option. Others, such as the probability that an option will be exercised or the probability that an uncovered writer will lose money, require direct reference to the probability curve of the stock price distribution. Still others, such as the required margin calculation, are easy enough to obtain without reference to a particular model and are included on the computer run for convenience.

While the amount of data that a computerized model generates can be truly staggering (most of the computations furnished by the computer are not listed on this table), very little of the data need be understood or evaluated to reach an intelligent decision on a *particular* option strategy. In fact, the most important lessons a portfolio manager who uses options must learn are to analyze his assumptions about the underlying stock carefully and to organize the computer output in a format that is relevant to his decision. Usually, organizing the output means disregarding all but a few pertinent numbers.

The variety of possible option strategies is too great to permit one or two examples to be representative of all possible uses of this or any other computerized option model. To illustrate the need to focus on limited data, however, we will study several simple examples in some detail.

On August 1, 1974, an investor considering an option hedge in Monsanto might have checked the market and obtained the following data on stock and option prices:

Stock price		$60.50	
	October $60	January $60	April $60
Option price	$4.50	$6.38	$8.25

The investor decides to use the Gastineau-Madansky computer model to evaluate these options. He examines the historic volatility or stock price variance data on Monsanto. In summary form, the volatility data base looks like this:

Period	Logarithmic Daily Stock Price Variance $\times 10^3$
Lowest quarter	.082
Low quartile	.134
Average volatility	.261
High quartile	.317
Highest quarter	.474

These volatility or variance numbers describe the shape of the probability curve of stock price changes. The higher the number, the greater the average daily stock price change during the period studied.

Although Monsanto had not been volatile immediately prior to August 1974, the overall market had been volatile and the economic outlook was highly uncertain. Because of this uncertainty, the investor tentatively decides to assume a volatility factor of .280 in his evaluation of the options. From the computer he obtains the following information:

	October $60	January $60	April $60
Actual price	$4.50	$6.38	$8.25
Fair value (variance = .280)	$3.81	$5.54	$6.90
Actual price/fair value	1.18	1.15	1.20
Variance at which option price equals fair value	.435	.405	.445

Several important conclusions are readily apparent. First, on the basis of the volatility figure selected, the April option is most overpriced. Second, the market is implicitly assuming, by virtue of the price it assigns to the options, that Monsanto will be almost as volatile over the next 9 months (.445 variance on the April option) as it was during a single quarter (.474) in the period covered by the data base. While the computer cannot promise profitability every time, the Monsanto options appear overpriced, and the April option seems to be most overpriced on the basis of both the ratio of the call price to the fair value of the option and the variance at which the option price equals fair value. Writing these options against a position in the stock appears to be an intelligent investment decision.

In the Monsanto example, the number of shares of stock purchased and the number of options written against the stock position depend on the investor's tax position, his attitude toward risk, the structure of the remainder of his portfolio, and his judgment on the stock. The computer helps organize the data to facilitate the decision. The computer does not manage the portfolio; it simply provides additional input and helps an investor structure his or her thinking. The computer can tell the investor what ratio of options to stock constitutes a neutral hedge at various tax rates. In the case of the Monsanto April $60 call options, the computer tells one that to set up a pretax neutral hedge one needs to sell approximately 1.46 options for each 100 shares of stock one buys. Furthermore, the neutral hedge will be profitable if the stock sells between $48.47 and $85.14 at the end of April 1975. Based on the .280 volatility figure, this neutral hedge should be profitable about 79 percent of the time and the expected annualized pretax return on investment from such a hedge should be about 16 percent. Obviously, the *actual* return will be greater or less than the calculated *expected* return, which is simply a probability-weighted average of possible results.

Another example shows the versatility of the model and how it can be used to divide the decision-making process into manageable segments. Recently brokerage firms generated a sizable volume of commission business by encouraging investors to buy or write options on American Telephone and Telegraph stock and hedge or margin these positions with long or short positions in Telephone warrants. The following brief table compares the prices and the values of the options and warrants as of the close of trading on August 9, 1974. Value figures are calculated by both a modified Black-Scholes formulation (adjusted for dividends) and the Gastineau-Madansky method (also adjusted for dividends).

Option or Warrant	Actual Price	Gastineau-Madansky	Black-Scholes
Oct. $45	$ 1.125	$1.23	$1.32
Jan. $45	2.125	2.10	2.22
Apr. $45	2.75	2.65	2.91
Oct. $50	.25	.23	.21
Jan. $50	.6875	.67	.74
Warrant	1.75	.91	.97
Stock price	43.875		

The most obvious conclusion to be drawn from this table is that, *under a consistent set of assumptions,* the warrant is conspicuously overvalued relative to the options. This apparent overvaluation may or may not represent an arbitrage opportunity for the small investor. A pricing discrepancy of this magnitude rarely occurs without one or more good reasons. In this case, the short interest in the warrants was fairly high and the price of each warrant was low. This combination made the warrants difficult for a short seller to borrow. Furthermore, many investors felt that if these warrants were about to expire unexercised, the company would extend them or offer new warrants in exchange, in spite of the expressed determination of management to let the warrants die. The would-be arbitrageur must estimate the probability and possible cost of a short squeeze or a warrant extension for himself; the computer merely tells how the market has valued these possibilities. The computer quantifies the risk which the market implicitly assumes the warrant short sale involves. The investor can then decide to agree or disagree with "the market's" assumptions.

A further note of caution seems appropriate: The figures in this table are *not* adjusted for commissions. Because the commissions on low-priced securities are quite high, an investor should check commissions carefully. The approximate round-trip commission cost on a hedge transaction involving 5,000 warrants and 50 option contracts would have been $0.20 to $0.25 per underlying share. These commissions would have consumed about one-fourth of the expected profit even though the warrants expired on schedule.

The figures in this brief table suggest that valuations computed using the Gastineau-Madansky model might approximate actual prices more closely than values derived by the Black-Scholes method. As a very broad generalization the Gastineau-Madansky model, because of its more realistic formulation, does give values closer to and more consistent with actual prices when the same variance data are used in both models. We do not wish to imply that this relationship will hold true in every case, however. In fact, the purpose of the model is to uncover instances in which the value of the option is different from its price.

Readers who wish to compare the Gastineau-Madansky and Black-Scholes models more closely may find this simple table useful.

Assumptions:	
Daily stock price variance (log)	$.632 \times 10^{-3}$
Interest rate	10% per annum
Remaining life of option	3 months
Exercise price	$40.
Dividends, commission, and taxes	No adjustment

(1) Stock Price	(2) Gastineau-Madansky Option Value	(3) Black-Scholes Option Value*	(4) Ratio Col. (2) ÷ Col. (3)
$28.	$ 0.22	$ 0.13	1.69
32.	0.70	0.60	1.17
36.	1.76	1.72	1.02
40.	3.72	3.67	1.01
44.	6.59	6.38	1.03
48.	10.12	9.66	1.05
52.	13.99	13.29	1.05

* From Fischer Black's "Fact and Fantasy in the Use of Options" (see Bibliography).

The Gastineau-Madansky model usually gives higher relative valuations, particularly when options are significantly out of the money, than the Black-Scholes model. Both models suggest that in-the-money options are worth more than they generally sold for before the standardization of spread margin requirements in late 1974.

The data that an investor needs in order to make a decision or evaluate an option opportunity will change with the occasion. Though no list would cover every possibility, the following list includes some of the more frequently asked questions:

1. What is the fair value of every available call option on a given underlying stock?

2. Which, if any, of these contracts is attractive to a would-be writer? A would-be buyer? Is there an attractive spread possibility?

3. What is the expected profit in dollars or as a return on investment from a particular strategy?

4. What ratio of options short to shares of stock long constitutes a neutral hedge?

5. What will the probable price of each of these calls be if the stock price rises or falls by a specific amount over the next few weeks? Over the next few months?

6. What is the option market implicitly assuming about the volatility of the underlying stock? Is this assumption consistent with the investor's own expectations? Is this implicit volatility assumption higher or lower than the historical volatility of the stock?

7. How do taxes affect a position?

8. What are other computer models telling their users?

The two tests of any option evaluation system are the realism of the underlying model and the speed and ease with which the investor can get valid answers to questions like these.

APPENDIX A
MARGIN REQUIREMENTS

Margin requirements serve two purposes. First, they protect the investor from his own folly. By limiting an individual's ability to accept risk, margin requirements prevent (or at least delay) his total financial ruin. Second, and most important, they ensure the continuing viability of the market by protecting innocent bystanders from the excesses of speculators who are mindless of the effect their own downfall would have on others. Since the 1930s, the minimum margin requirements set by appropriate regulatory bodies have been adequate to protect the investing public and the brokerage firm carrying the margin account. Option margin rules have usually been stricter than the requirements for other securities.

Apart from disputes stemming from falling stock prices, margin requirements probably cause most of the misunderstandings between investor and broker. Margin requirements for option transactions were particularly troublesome until recently because they depended not only on an individual firm's policies but on its stock exchange affiliations as well. The uniform minimum margin rules illustrated here were adopted at the end of 1974 by the New York Stock Exchange and The Chicago Board Options Exchange. Some firms may adopt stricter "house rules" or impose supplementary requirements for the equity in an account or a customer's net worth.

The purpose of this Appendix is to help the investor understand the effect of option margin rules on his portfolio even if he never actually calculates the required margin on a specific investment. Most published discussions of margin requirements are of no help to the average investor because they do not provide a frame of reference. Few investors really understand the meaning of a 50 percent margin requirement or the statement that an account must be marked to the market. Without more information than is usually provided, it is impossible for the investor who has not worked in a margin department to calculate the margin requirement for a particular transaction. This Appendix will not qualify the reader for a position as a margin clerk, but it should permit him to calculate the required margin for any new option position he may initiate and to determine what kind of stock price behavior would subject him to a margin call.

Rule 1: Long option positions have no loan value; therefore, the option buyer must pay 100 percent of the option premium in cash.

Example: An investor buys a call option at a price of $10.

Cost of option	$10 × 100 shares	= $1,000
Required cash payment	$10 × 100 shares	= $1,000

Rule 2: If he is the covered writer of a call option, the investor need post no additional margin beyond the initial or maintenance margin required to carry the stock or other security convertible into the underlying stock. Also, the investor's account is credited with the option premium received.

Example: An investor writes a covered call option for a premium of $10. The striking price of the option is $100, and the current price of the stock is $95.

Market value of stock position	$95 × 100 shares	= $9,500
Regulation T initial margin requirement on the stock	50% × $9,500	= $4,750

Less: option premium		
received	$10 × 100 shares	= $1,000
Net initial margin required		= $3,750

For margin purposes, the value of the stock underlying a covered writing position cannot exceed the striking price of the option, in this case, $100 per share.

Rule 3: If he is an uncovered writer, the investor must post margin equal to the required margin percentage times the market value of the shares under option less the option premium received, less the amount by which the option is trading out of the money or plus the amount by which the option is in the money. Notwithstanding the result of this calculation, the investor must post a minimum margin of $250 per uncovered option contract written, including the amount of any option premium received.

Example: An investor writes an uncovered listed call option at a price of $10. The striking price of the option is $100, and the current price of the stock is $95.

Market value of shares		
under option	$95 × 100 shares	= $9,500
Basic margin requirement	30% × $9,500	= $2,850
Less: option premium		
received	$10 × 100 shares	= ($1,000)
Less: amount by which op-	($100 − $95)	
tion is out of the money	× 100 shares	= ($ 500)
Net initial margin required		
per contract		= $1,350

The margin percentage is 50 percent for conventional options.

Table A-1 (page 214) illustrates the calculation of initial margin requirements on a call option with a $100 striking price at various stock prices.

Rule 4: Unlike the margin rules applicable to many security positions, the net maintenance margin requirement for an uncovered option writing position is calculated in essentially the same manner as the net initial margin requirement.

Table A-1. Calculation of Initial Margin Requirements for the Writer of an Uncovered Listed Option with a $100 Striking Price

(1) Value of 100 Shares of Stock	(2) 30% of Stock Value	(3) Price of Option Contract	(4) 100 × Striking Price minus Stock Price	(5) Net Required Margin	(6) Margin Advantage over Shorting Stock
$ 6,000	$1,800	$ 100	$4,000	$ 150	$28.50
$ 7,000	$2,100	$ 200	$3,000	$ 50	$34.50
$ 8,000	$2,400	$ 400	$2,000	$ 0	$40.00
$ 9,000	$2,700	$ 800	$1,000	$ 900	$36.00
$10,000	$3,000	$1,300	$ 0	$1,700	$33.00
$11,000	$3,300	$1,800	($1,000)	$2,500	$30.00
$12,000	$3,600	$2,200	($2,000)	$3,400	$26.00
$13,000	$3,900	$3,000	($3,000)	$3,900	$26.00
$14,000	$4,200	$4,000	($4,000)	$4,200	$28.00

KEY TO COLUMNS:

(1) The market value of 100 shares of stock at the time the option is written.

(2) The basic initial margin requirement for writing an uncovered listed option is 30% of the market value of the stock when the position is taken.

(3) This column should be taken only as an indication of a price at which this option contract might sell. The price is rounded for simplicity.

(4) In applying the 30% margin rule to options, 100 times the amount by which the striking price exceeds the stock price is subtracted from the required margin. If the market price exceeds the striking price, the difference is added.

(5) Calculated: (2) − (3) − (4). If the result of this calculation is less than $250 minus the premium received per contract, the writer must still post $250 *less the premium received.*

(6) Stock margin requirements are 50%. The investor should note that *maintenance margin* rules are stricter when applied to options than to short positions.

Example: The market price of a stock underlying the option written in the example for Rule 3 drops to $70 per share.

Market value of shares under option	$70 × 100 shares	= $7,000
Basic margin requirement	30% × $7,000	= $2,100
Less: option premium received originally (*not* the current value of the option)		= ($1,000)
Less: amount by which option is out of the money ($100 − $70) × 100 shares		= ($3,000)

| Net maintenance margin required | $=(\$1{,}900)$ |
| Because this would violate the \$250 per contract minimum, the net required is $250 - \$1,000 premium received | $=(\$\ \ 750)$ |

The reader's attention is called to several features of this calculation. First, because the stock has declined so sharply, the option is unlikely to be exercised. As a consequence of the decline, the uncovered writer can not only withdraw any collateral he posted as margin, he can also withdraw most of the option premium he originally received. (Actually, the writer could have invested the option premium in Treasury bills or substituted other collateral for the portion of the margin contributed by the premium received.) Second, the \$250 minimum margin requirement is reduced by the amount of any unwithdrawn premium received.

Example: The market price of the stock underlying the option written in the example for Rule 3 rises to \$130 per share.

Market value of shares under option	$\$130 \times 100$ shares	$=\$13{,}000$
Basic margin requirement	$30\% \times \$13{,}000$	$=\$\ 3{,}900$
Less: option premium received		$=(\$\ 1{,}000)$
Plus: amount by which option is in the money $(\$130 - \$100) \times 100$ shares		$=\$\ 3{,}000$
Net maintenance margin required		$=\$\ 5{,}900$

The key point to be learned from these maintenance margin examples is that the required maintenance margin moves up and down 30 percent *faster than the value of the underlying shares.* Unless great care is exercised, the uncovered writer runs a high risk of having to meet margin calls.

Rule 5: Calculation of the required margin for puts is similar to the calculation for calls except that a covered put writer is short the underlying stock.

Rule 6: If a straddle writer owns the underlying stock, the call is covered, but he must put up additional margin to collateralize the put side of the transaction. If both sides of the straddle are uncovered, the margin requirement is that of the option requiring the highest margin plus $250 per straddle.

Rule 7: The initial or maintenance margin on a listed option spread is:

A. When the long option position expires before the short option position, the investor must pay 100 percent of the cost of the long option and post margin on the short option according to the rules for uncovered options.

B. When the short option position expires concurrently with or before the long option position, spread margin rules apply.

1. If the striking price of the short option is equal to or greater than the striking price of the long option, the required margin is equal to the premium on the long option less the premium on the short option.

Example: An investor buys a July $100 at $10 and sells an April $100 at $7 on the same underlying stock. He must post ($10 − $7) × 100 shares = $300.

2. If the striking price of the short option is lower than the striking price of the long option, the required margin on the short option is the lesser of the margin required if the options are not treated as a spread, or the difference between the striking prices of the two options.

Example: An investor buys a July $100 at $3 and sells a July $90 at $10.

His net margin requirement is 100 percent of the long position:

$$\$3 \times 100 \text{ shares} = \$\ 300$$

Plus: the difference in striking prices:

$$(\$100 - \$90) \times 100 \text{ shares} = \$1,000$$

Minus: the premium received from the option written:

$$\$10 \times 100 \text{ shares} = (\$1,000)$$

Net margin required per pair of contracts $\quad = \$ \ 300$

There is no further maintenance margin required. Regardless of the behavior of the underlying stock or the option contracts that make up the spread, the short option position does not have to be marked to the market.

Rule 8: When a call is covered by a position in a convertible security, the convertible security must be adequately margined and the investor must also post margin equal to the amount, if any, by which the conversion price exceeds the striking price of the call if conversion requires a cash payment. _____

Example: An investor buys listed warrants at a price of $15 with an exercise price of $105 and sells a July $100 call option on the same underlying common stock at $10.

Initial margin on the warrant position:

$$50\% \times \$15 \times 100 \text{ shares} = \$ \ 750$$

Minus option premium received:

$$\$10 \times 100 \text{ shares} = (\$1,000)$$

Plus amount by which exercise price on warrant
exceeds striking price of call:

$$(\$105 - \$100) \times 100 \text{ shares} = \$ \ 500$$

Net margin required

This example is unusual in that it shows initial margin only. For purposes of maintenance margin _the warrant position has no loan value_ and the net maintenance requirement is $1,000 per hedge in this case.

This summary of the margin rules pertaining specifically to options cannot possibly cover all aspects of the margin requirements. The fine points of margining options with convertible securities and the margin relationship between the rest of an investor's portfolio and his option portfolio are extremely complex subjects and are probably more suitable topics for a book on margin than a book on options. The purpose of this Appendix has been to provide a general explanation of the margin rules. This brief discussion should help the reader understand how margin rules and the possibility of margin calls affect the risk characteristics of his portfolio.

Using this description of option margin rules, the reader may uncover several ways to improve the efficiency and return of his portfolio. For example, an investor may own some marginable securities that can be substituted for the premium received on an option written, permitting him to invest the premium. Alternatively, a credit balance in an option account at one brokerage firm can offset a debit balance in another account if the second account is moved to the firm where the investor does his option trading. An understanding of option margin requirements is one of many ways in which the effective use of options separates a well-managed, controlled-risk portfolio from the typical investor's carelessly handled collection of stocks.

APPENDIX B
CONVERSION

Conversion is the process by which a put is converted or changed into a call or a call into a put. The put-to-call conversion probably accounted for at least 90 percent of all conversions prior to the commencement of trading in listed call options. An active market has sprung up in the conversion of listed call options to conventional puts. The call-to-put transformation is sometimes called reconversion or reversal, though in the case of listed options, the original conversion from put to call may never have taken place.

Conversion is necessary any time a buyer and writer want to trade different *kinds* of options on the same stock. For tax reasons or because they anticipate a rising market, many option writers prefer to write straddles rather than multiple calls. Historically, the demand from option buyers has been largely a demand for calls. These two sets of preferences were responsible for the relatively greater frequency of conversion of puts to calls. For a variety of reasons, some related to the existence of a secondary market in listed calls and others related to the relatively trendless but volatile stock market of the past few years, writers are now more likely to write multiple calls and buyers seem more interested in puts and straddles than in the past. Unless or until trading in listed puts begins, both the buyer and the writer of a put analogous to a listed call will find it necessary to use the conversion process.

Most investors who use options have probably never heard of conversion. Many of those who have feel little need or desire to understand how it works. It is discussed here because any investor who uses puts will be affected by the conversion process at least indirectly. Also, an understanding of conversion will probably increase the reader's overall understanding of options and their contribution to flexibility in risk management.

The process of converting a put into a call begins with the purchase of a put option by a conversion house, usually a New York Stock Exchange member firm. At the time the conversion house purchases the put, it also purchases one round lot of the underlying stock and writes one call which is sold to a call buyer through a put and call broker or an exchange. Both the put and the call have the same striking price, though the striking price is frequently different from the market price of the stock. As a result of this series of transactions, a put has disappeared from the marketplace and an additional call option has been created. A typical effect of the conversion process is that a buyer can purchase two calls when a straddle writer wrote one call and one put.

The investment position of the conversion house is intriguing. The converter enjoys a position that is free of market risk regardless of what happens to the price of the underlying stock between the time the conversion transaction occurs and the expiration date of the options. If the price of the stock declines, the call written by the converter will expire worthless. The converter will then exercise the put by delivering the stock purchased to the writer of the put. If the price of the stock advances, the put will expire worthless and the converter will deliver the 100 shares of stock previously purchased to the buyer of the call. The difference between the price of the put and the price of the call covers the converter's transaction costs and the interest cost of carrying the long position in the stock.

Reversals or reconversions of calls to puts are simply the reverse of the put-to-call conversion process. The converter purchases a call option, sells the underlying stock short, and writes a put. Since puts typically sell at lower prices than calls when the options have the same striking price, the attractiveness of this transaction may seem obscure at first. A reversal or reconversion is only attractive to a brokerage firm which owns or controls shares of the underlying stock that can be borrowed at little or no cost. Selling this borrowed stock short generates a cash balance on which the firm earns interest.

In contrast to the example of conversion from a put into a call, where interest costs are added to commission and other charges to determine the overall cost of the conversion, the buyer of the put should, in effect, be credited with a portion of the interest credit obtained by shorting the underlying shares. A put created by reversal will usually cost slightly more than a similar put originally written as part of a straddle. However, the net cost of the put should still be less than the net cost of a comparable call.

Although the converter receives the difference between the premium he obtains for the call and the premium he pays for the put, this difference is not all profit. There are two major components of the premium difference. The smaller component is a conversion fee which covers floor brokerage costs and transfer taxes on the stock transaction, a commission for the broker who arranges the conversion, and an endorsement fee for the conversion house. The larger component of the premium differential is an interest charge for carrying the stock position. Typically, the interest charge will be based on an interest rate 1 or 2 percent above the broker's call loan rate. Table B-1 gives a fair idea of typical conversion charges for a 6-month option. As the table illustrates, by far the largest component of the cost of conversion is the interest charge.

In general, the converter will receive a consistent return, slightly higher than the return on margin loans to his retail customers. Occasionally, he will receive a small windfall profit because he has written an option that expires so slightly in the money that the buyer does not find exercise profitable. Also, if a call option is exercised prior to expiration, the con-

Table B-1. Cost of Conversion of a Put into a Call

Based on a 100-share transaction in a $50 stock

Conversion fee:	
Transfer taxes	$ 5.00
SEC fee	.10
Floor brokerage	13.20
Broker's spread	40.00
Endorsement fee	6.25
	$64.55
Interest charge at 10% for 6 months:	
$10\% \times \frac{6}{12} \times \$5,000$	$250.00
Total cost of conversion	$314.55
Price obtainable for a call	$600.00
Less: cost of conversion	$314.55
Approximate value in conversion of a put written as part of a straddle	$285.45

verter will own the complementary put option which may have value. Early exercise will also "free up" his capital sooner than expected, increasing his effective yield. If the conversion house has an underutilized floor partner, the floor brokerage commissions provide welcome additional revenue for the firm. Conversion may not be an exciting business as it is usually practiced, but it is consistently profitable.

If the reader ever doubts that conversion terms offered are fair, the formula in Table B-2 should permit an estimate of the converter's fee. The formula works equally well for any striking price/stock price relationship.

Table B-2. A Formula for Put-Call Parity through Conversion*

$$P_c = P_s - S + nrP_s + P_p \pm C$$

Whether C is added or subtracted depends on whether the transaction is initiated by the buyer or the seller of the least marketable option

P_c = price of call
P_p = predicted price of a put with same terms as call
P_s = price of underlying stock
S = striking price of two options
r = implicit interest rate charged by converters
C = conversion fee (see Table B-1 for example of conversion fee calculation)
n = life of options expressed as a fraction of a year

* From a formula in Hans R. Stoll, "The Relationship between Put and Call Option Prices," *The Journal of Finance*, December 1969, pp. 801–824.

APPENDIX C
CALCULATING THE RETURN
FROM OPTION WRITING

Rate of return on investment is a fuzzy concept when it is applied to uncovered option writing. Although the dollar profit is simple enough to compute if the price at which a transaction will be closed out is given, the amount of capital invested (the denominator in the rate-of-return calculation) is not easy to determine.

Calculating the incremental investment required for one investment strategy versus an alternative is ordinarily straightforward. To illustrate, the incremental rate of return on investment from holding a stock for a long-term gain, as in Case 1 from Chapter 5, Section C, is equal to the incremental aftertax profit (or loss) from holding the stock until it goes long-term divided by the net proceeds the investor would have received earlier by selling for a short-term gain. This return can be annualized for comparison with other investments by multiplying it by twelve and dividing the product by the number of months until the gain goes long-term. If the transaction takes place in a margin account and the investor wants to calculate his return on equity, he subtracts aftertax interest costs from the profit (or loss) in the numerator of the fraction and the amount of his borrowings from the denominator.

Writing options complicates this kind of rate-of-return calculation in several respects. The option writer's margin account is credited with cash equal to the net premium from the option he writes. This *reduces* the net cash or equity investment for any investment strategy that involves writing options. *On a cash or equity basis the required investment for writing an option is negative.* Nevertheless, the option writer is required to post margin for the options written. In the margin sense, his incremental investment for writing the option will be the net margin requirement after adjustment for the cash premium he receives. Neither the negative cash investment figure nor the net margin requirement is entirely satisfactory as the denominator in a return-on-investment calculation. This complication is created by the unique cash-flow characteristics of option writing and the margin rules that apply to it.

The choice of whether the denominator in a rate-of-return calculation for a strategy involving option writing should be adjusted by adding the net margin required for writing the option or by subtracting the net option premium is not necessarily a choice between the right way and the wrong way of making the calculation. Either method may be appropriate or not, depending on the investor's overall margin and portfolio risk position. Investors may find the results more meaningful if they assume that the net margin for writing an option is part of the denominator in the rate-of-return computation. Any rational estimate of the fair value of an option will already have credited interest on the premium received by the writer, so only the net margin above this amount will be involved.

A possible refinement to the approach of adding the net required margin to the denominator of the return calculation would be to adjust the calculated return for any interest or profit earned by investing that margin. For example, if a margin deposit is invested in short-term debt, it could earn interest at, say, the 7 percent rate assumed in Chapter 4, Section A. Alternatively, if a cash deposit reduces the investor's debit balance, the interest credit should be at a 9 percent rate, using our example.

To simplify calculations and to clarify explanations, assume that securities deposited as margin would be earning interest or some other return even if they had not been used to meet the margin requirement. The rate of return on net required margin, then, is an approximation of the *incremental* return from a strategy involving option writing. The denominator is a measure of the assets "tied-up" in the investment, but the rate-of-return calculation understates the true return on these assets because the margin collateral included in the denominator is *already invested*. In a sense, these assets are working twice as hard when an option-writing strategy is adopted. Rather than attempt to adjust for this "double duty," the rate of return is expressed as an *incremental return on net margin employed*.

The true expected rate of return on the assets employed in an option-writing strategy will always be higher than indicated by the calculations used in Chapter 4, Section D and Chapter 5, Section C. The difference will be the amount of interest an investor would receive from investing the net option margin requirements for that writing position. A consequence of this approach is that an uncovered option-writing strategy is attractive *if* (a) it shows a positive expected incremental return on net margin required and (b) it modifies the risk structure of his portfolio in a manner the investor deems appropriate.

The principal weakness of simplifying the explanation in this manner is that the investor might consider a transaction less attractive than it really is because the basic return on the margin deposit is not added back. This weakness is at least partly, though only approximately, offset by the fact that investors tend not to adjust their thinking for commissions.

APPENDIX D
AN INDEX OF LISTED
OPTION PREMIUMS

In conversations with investors who are presently using options or are planning to use them, the author is frequently asked why there is no readily available index of the average level of option premiums. The easiest response to this question is simply to dismiss it as being largely irrelevant to a specific option buying or writing decision. Upon reflection, however, it appears that a readily available and easily understood index of listed option premium levels could be useful. If it serves no other purpose, such an index can help investors understand the relative significance of the factors affecting the value of an option contract.

There are a number of obstacles to the creation of a meaningful index of option premium levels. Options are wasting assets—that is, their value declines as time passes if the stock price is approximately unchanged. Any index must take this inevitable decline in the premium over intrinsic value into account. An additional difficulty in the construction of an option premium index arises from the fact that options obtain their value from the underlying common stock. Any index of option premiums based directly on the *price* of a specific option contract or group of option contracts would be extraordinarily sensitive to the level of stock prices and might, as a result, be useless as an indicator of relative premium levels. A further complication in the construction of an index of listed options is that listed options are standardized—that is, the striking price always ends in $5 or $0. Consequently, the market price may differ quite materially from the striking price at the time an option transaction occurs, and no simple relationship between the premium and the stock price can give a meaningful indication of premium levels.

All these difficulties tend to suggest that an option premium index must be developed on a different basis from other indices commonly used in the securities industry. The index proposed here is an indirect measure of the relative level of option premiums.

At slight risk of oversimplification, the major factors affecting option evaluation can be reduced to four. They are (1) time, (2) interest rates, (3) the relationship between the striking price of the option and the market price of the underlying stock, and (4) stock price volatility. In construction of the index, the author is attempting to neutralize the first three variables and let the index measure the market's assessment of the future volatility of the underlying stock. In other words, if time, interest rates, and the relationship of the market price to the striking price can be fixed, the major remaining variable—expected stock price volatility—can be measured by the Gastineau-Madansky option evaluation model. If this measure of expected stock price volatility is then related to historic stock price volatility data, an index can be constructed. The index would simply measure the volatility of the underlying stocks implicitly assumed by the buyers and writers of listed option contracts, *relative* to the volatility of those same stocks in the historic base period.

The base period for construction of the index is the 4-year period from October 1968 to September 1972. The reader may protest that listed stock options were not traded during this period. Actually, the choice of a particular base period has no bearing on the usefulness of the index. The index is a measure of option premium levels relative to the historic volatility of the underlying stocks. A change in the base period would change the level of the index but not the *relative* values of the index over the period for which it was calculated.

An index constructed by using very short-term options could be quite sensitive to changes in sentiment and would tend to be a highly volatile reflection of the mood of the underlying market. While sensitivity is desirable in one sense, it can create problems. The most serious problem in the construction of an index based upon very short-term options is that many of these options sell at very low prices. The principal consequence of the low price is that a small change in the price of the option or the price of the underlying stock can have a material impact on the value of the representation of that stock in the index. This impact can be out of proportion to the significance of the stock or option price change in question. Using options which have lives of between 3 and 6 months minimizes this problem. Just as distortions are eliminated from very short-term option contracts, one also eliminates the impact of option contracts with a life of more than 6 months where tax considerations and extremely inactive markets can distort the relationship between stock prices and option prices. Because options do not expire every month, the index will at times be constructed exclusively of options which have 6 months of life remaining and at other times of options that have 3 months of life remaining. While this fact leads to its own set of possible distortions, it appears to eliminate as many problems as possible while providing an index which can be calculated at the end of any trading day.

Interest rates have a material impact on results only if they change dramatically. Here, the interest rate is considered equal to $1\frac{1}{2}$ percent higher than the 3-month Treasury bill rate on the date the index is calculated.

There has been an attempt to keep the impact of the difference between the market price of the stock and the striking price of the option to a minimum in the construction of the index. Therefore, the option used has the appropriate expiration date with a striking price closest to the market price of the stock.

The index itself is a measure of the relationship between

the volatility of the underlying stock implied by the current level of the option premium and to the historic volatility of the underlying stock. The formula for the index is given by the equation:

$$I = \frac{\sqrt{\Sigma_1^n\, V_i}}{\sqrt{\Sigma_1^n\, V_h}}$$

where I = value of index on particular date

V_i = implied variance calculated by application of Gastineau-Madansky option model to stock price and option premium in question

V_h = historic base period variance of underlying stock price

n = number of stocks and options used in construction of index

The value of the index calculated from this formula for month-end prices of 14 stocks and appropriate options from June 1973 through December 1974 is illustrated in Figure D-1, and Table D-1 lists the stocks used in construction of the index.

What the index shows is that the actual level of listed option

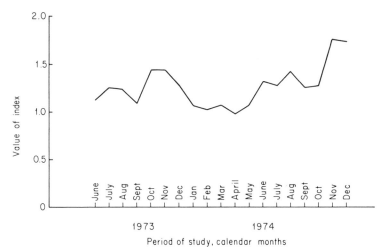

Figure D-1. An index of listed option premium levels (base period stock volatility: October 1978–September 1972 = 1.0).

Table D-1. Stocks Used in Construction of the Index

American Telephone & Telegraph	S. S. Kresge
Atlantic Richfield	McDonald's Corporation
Bethlehem Steel	Polaroid
Eastman Kodak	Texas Instruments
Exxon	Upjohn
Ford Motor	Weyerhaeuser
INA	Xerox

premiums has usually been above the level that might have been predicted on the basis of the historic volatility of the underlying stocks. Though this might imply that listed options were usually overpriced during 1973 and 1974 and that option writers could count on making money with a high degree of reliability, the data are also subject to an alternative interpretation. The higher option premiums, particularly in late 1974, may have been discounting higher volatility for the underlying stocks based on an uncertain outlook for the economy and the stock market. In addition, the actual volatility of most underlying stocks has been significantly greater over the period covered by the index than it was during the base period. The high level of option premiums in late 1974 probably reflects *both* a shortage of option writers *and* a high degree of market uncertainty. Perhaps due to an influx of institutional call writers and growing confidence in the outlook for the market, the index began to drop in early 1975.

APPENDIX E
GLOSSARY

Adjusted striking price or adjusted exercise price: When a dividend is paid on the stock subject to a conventional option or any capital change occurs on the stock subject to either a listed or conventional option, the striking price is adjusted to reflect the change. If necessary, the number of shares subject to option is also changed. For example, if a stock is split three for two and the original striking price of an option was $60, the adjusted striking price is $40 and the option becomes an option on 150 shares of the split stock.

Aggregate exercise price: The exercise price of an option contract multiplied by the number of units of the underlying security covered by the option contract.

Arbitrage: Technically, arbitrage is purchasing a commodity or security in one market for immediate sale in another market. Popular usage has expanded the meaning of the term to include any activity which attempts to buy a relatively underpriced item and sell a relatively overpriced item, expecting to profit when the prices resume a more appropriate relationship. In trading options and other convertible securities, arbitrage techniques can be applied whenever a strategy involves buying one and selling the other of two related securities.

Average price of an option: *See* NORMAL PRICE OF AN OPTION.

Back spread: A spread in which the striking price of the long call option is *greater than* the striking price of the short call option and the remaining life of the long option is *greater than or equal to* the life of the short option. Both options are listed. Also known as a *bearish* spread.

Break out: The process of undoing a conversion or a reversal, re-establishing the option buyer's original position.

Butterfly spread: Although some traders use different definitions, a common butterfly spread is the combination of a front spread and a back spread with the same expiration dates on all options and the same striking price on all options written. For example: long 1 January XRX $80, short 2 January XRX $90, and long 1 January XRX $100. This spread would be most profitable before taxes at an expiration stock price of $90 per share.

Buy-in: When a call is exercised against an option writing account that does not hold sufficient shares of the called stock, the broker will "buy-in" the necessary shares for delivery to the option holder. Also, in short selling, if no stock can be borrowed to continue a short position, the broker will "buy-in" the shares for delivery, forcing the short seller to cover. This type of buy-in occurs in stocks with large short interests and/or small floats.

Call option: An option to buy, ordinarily issued for a period of less than one year. *See* OPTION, TERMS OF OPTION CONTRACT.

Call spread: A spread consisting of a long position and a short position in calls on the same underlying stock.

Capital change: A stock split, stock dividend, merger, or spinoff that affects the number of shares of stock owned by an investor without necessarily affecting their value.

CBOE call: *See* CHICAGO BOARD OPTIONS EXCHANGE, LISTED OPTION, CALL OPTION.

Chicago Board Options Exchange: A registered securities exchange sponsored by the Chicago Board of Trade, set up to trade options which differ from conventional options in a number of respects. (1) The contract terms are standardized. (2) The traditional link between the buyer and the writer is severed because the Options Clearing Corporation is the primary obligor on every option. (3) There is a secondary market for CBOE options. (4) The striking price is not adjusted as a result of payment of ordinary cash dividends on the optioned stock.

Class of options: All listed option contracts of the same type covering the same underlying security, e.g., all listed Texas Instruments call options.

Closing purchase transaction: A transaction in which an option writer terminates his obligation by purchasing an option having the same terms as an option previously written.

Closing sale transaction: A transaction in which the holder of an option liquidates his position by selling an option having the same terms as an option previously purchased.

Collateral: An obligation or security attached to another obligation or security to secure its performance. For example, an option writer may deposit, with his bank or broker, common stock in the company on which an option is written as collateral to guarantee his performance on the option. He may also deposit securities convertible into the underlying stock or unrelated securities with an appropriate collateral value.

Combination option: An option consisting of at least one put and one call. The component options may be exercised or resold separately but they are originally sold as a unit. *See* STRADDLE, STRIP, STRAP, SPREAD.

Commodity option: An option to buy (call) or sell (put) a specific commodity at a given price within a specified time. More widely used in the United Kingdom than in this country due to (1) a hostile regulatory environment (the SEC and state regulatory authorities have tried to stop trading in some commodity options) and (2) the fact that several large firms specializing in these contracts recently went out of business defaulting on their outstanding options.

Conventional option: An option contract negotiated and/or traded off a securities exchange. While the contract is negotiable, it does not usually change hands after the original transaction. The terms of conventional option contracts are not standardized.

Conversion: The process by which a put can be changed to a call and a call to a put. To convert a put to a call, the conversion house buys the put and 100 shares of stock and issues a call. To convert a call to a put, the conversion house buys the call, sells the stock short, and issues a put. *See* REVERSAL, BREAKOUT.

Covered writer: An option writer who owns (or, in the case of a put, is short) the underlying stock which is subject to an option. An investor setting up an option hedge or writing multiple options may be covered with respect to part of his position and uncovered with respect to the rest. *See* OPTION HEDGE, UNCOVERED WRITER.

Day trade: A day trade occurs when a stock or option position is bought and sold during the same trading session.

Down-and-out call: A conventional type call option that expires if the market price of the underlying stock drops below a predetermined expiration price. These options are written by a number of major brokerage firms and sold only to clients able to accept substantial risk.

Econometric model: As applied to options and other convertible securities, a series of mathematical relationships, usually derived by multiple regression analysis or a similar technique. The model is designed to predict the average or normal price of an option or other convertible security when the stock price and other revelant variables are inserted in the formulas that make up the model.

Endorsement: In conventional option transactions a New York Stock Exchange member firm endorses the option contract on behalf of the writer to guarantee his performance on the option. The Options Clearing Corporation performs an analogous function for listed options.

Exercise price: *See* STRIKING PRICE.

Expiration date: The date after which an option is void. The option buyer should check carefully into the time of day by which he must notify his broker to exercise or sell an option. *See* EXTENSION.

Extension: An agreement between the buyer and the writer of a conventional option to lengthen the life of the option beyond the original expiration date. Extensions are not common because both parties have to agree to the extension and to the price to be paid for it. There is no mechanism for extension of listed options.

Fair value of an option: The option value derived by a probability-type option valuation model. The fair value of an option is the price at which both the buyer and the writer of the option should expect to break even, neglecting the effect of commissions. Fair value is an estimate of where an option *should* sell in an efficient market, not where it will sell.

Front spread: A spread in which the striking price of the long call option is *lower than or equal to* the striking price of the short call option and the remaining life of the long option is *greater than or equal to* the life of the short option. Both options are listed. Also known as a *bullish* spread.

Hedging: Using one or more of a variety of techniques to protect an investment position. Hedging usually involves offsetting a long position in one security with a short position in a related security. *See* OPTION WRITING, OPTION HEDGE, REVERSE OPTION HEDGE, SPREAD.

In the money: A term referring to an option which has intrinsic value because the current market price of the stock exceeds the striking price of a call or is below the striking price of a put. For example, a call exercisable at $100 is said to be three points in the money when the stock is selling at $103. *See* OUT OF THE MONEY.

Intrinsic value of an option: The market price of the stock less the striking price of an option. The intrinsic value cannot be less than zero.

Listed option: An option traded on a national securities exchange.

Long option position: The position of the holder or buyer of an option contract.

Margin: The required equity that an investor must deposit to collateralize an investment position.

Mark to the market: In the event that a writer has written options on more shares of a given security than he owns, he will be required to put up more margin if the stock moves against him. The broker will ask for more margin to mark his account to the market.

Match market: A match market occurs when a buyer and a writer for a given option enter the market at about the same time and a put and call broker can bring them together on mutually satisfactory terms. Since the dealer's task is simplified by this common interest and he does not have to look around for one side of the trade, the spread between the price paid by the buyer and the price paid to the writer should be smaller than usual.

Naked option writing: An option writing position collateralized by cash or by securities unrelated to those on which the stock option is written. *See* OPTION HEDGE.

Net margin requirement: The margin required after any option premium received by the investor is deducted.

Neutral hedge: A combination of long and short positions in related securities that is designed to be equally profitable whether the underlying stock goes up slightly or down slightly in price.

Normal price of an option: The option price predicted by an econometric model or similar technique used to estimate typical stock price–option price relationships. The normal price is an estimate based on the assumption that relationships that existed in a prior period are still meaningful. Normal price is a prediction of what an option price will be, not necessarily what it should be. *See* FAIR VALUE OF AN OPTION.

Open interest: The number of listed option contracts outstanding at a particular time. Open interest figures are available on each listed contract.

Opening purchase transaction: A transaction in which an investor becomes the holder or buyer of an option.

Opening sale transaction: A transaction in which an investor becomes the writer or seller of an option.

Option: A stipulated privilege of buying or selling a stated property, security, or commodity at a given price (striking price) within a specified time (in the United States, at any time prior to or on the expiration date). A securities option of the type discussed in this book is a negotiable contract in which the writer, for a certain sum of money, called the option premium, gives the buyer the right to demand within a specified time the purchase or sale by the writer of a specified number of shares of stock at a fixed price, called the striking price. Unless otherwise stated, options are written for units of 100 shares. They are ordinarily issued for periods of less than 1 year. *See* CALL OPTION, PUT OPTION, COMBINATION OPTION, COMMODITY OPTION, TERMS OF OPTION CONTRACT.

Option buyer: The individual or, less frequently, institutional investor who buys options to increase his leverage, hedge the risks in his portfolio, or attain other investment objectives.

Option contract: In conventional options, the actual contract is in bearer form and sets forth the provisions of the contract. It is endorsed or guaranteed by the New York Stock Exchange member firm which holds the option writer's account. Unless the buyer specifically requests a certificate evidencing his ownership of the option, the terms of a listed option are as stated in the prospectus. The buyer's evidence of ownership is his confirmation slip from the executing broker.

Option hedge: A hedged position in which the writer sells more than one call option against each round lot of the optioned stock he owns. The net effect of this position is to maximize the writer's pretax profit when the stock sells at the striking price on the expiration date. The rate of return declines if the shares sell either above or below the striking price. The writer loses money only if the stock rises or falls drastically before the expiration date. Some writers use the terms option hedge and reverse option hedge with opposite meanings to those used in this book. *See* REVERSE OPTION HEDGE, NAKED OPTION WRITING.

Option portfolio: Any portfolio that includes long option positions or collateralizes option writing positions.

Option writer: The individual or institutional investor who sells options collateralized by a portfolio of common stock and other securities.

Optioned stock: The underlying common stock which is the subject of an option contract.

Out of the money: A term referring to an option that has no intrinsic value because the current stock price is below the striking price of a call or above the striking price of a put. For example, a put at $100 when the stock is selling at $105 is said to be five points out of the money. *See* IN THE MONEY.

Premium: Technically, the amount of money an option buyer pays for a conventional put or call or the quoted price of a listed option. Unfortunately, many analysts use the word to designate the amount by which the price of an option exceeds its intrinsic value. For example, if an option to buy XYZ Corporation at $100 is selling at $9 and the stock at $103, the premium is said to be $6. To avoid confusion, the terms *option price* or *premium* are used to designate the market price of an option and *premium over intrinsic value* to designate the amount by which the stock price must rise before the expiration date for the option buyer to break even, neglecting commissions.

Put option: An option to sell, ordinarily issued for a period of less than 1 year. *See* OPTION, TERMS OF OPTION CONTRACT.

Put spread: A spread consisting of a long position and a short position in puts on the same underlying stock.

Pyramiding: Though the term is sometimes used loosely, it generally refers to the practice of using the excess margin or "buying power" generated by a successful speculative operation to increase the commitment to that operation. In options, an example might be the naked writer who writes more options as the decline in the price of the stock frees up some of his margin. Pyramiding is common in commodity futures trading where margin requirements are usually lower than in options.

Rate of return on net margin required: A method of expressing option writing profitability adopted for convenience and clarity. See Appendix C for a detailed explanation.

Ready market: An active option market. Dealer's spreads will be relatively narrow and the prices quoted by various dealers will be practically identical.

Reconversion or Reversal: The process of changing a call into a put. Occasionally used to describe the exchange of a put for a call if the put was originally created by conversion of a call.

Reverse option hedge: A hedged position in which the investor owns more than one call option for each round lot of the optioned stock he is short. This position becomes profitable as the market price of the stock moves away from the striking price of the options *in either direction. See* OPTION HEDGE.

Series of options: All listed option contracts of the same class having the same exercise price and expiration date, e.g., all Texas Instruments July $100 calls.

Short-against-the-box: A short sale of securities when an equal amount is owned in the account but will not be delivered against the sale until a later date. A short-against-the-box is used to defer taxes on profits.

Short option position: The position of the writer or seller of an option contract.

Special options: Special options are conventional options available for sale out of an option dealer's inventory. Some of these are advertised in the newspapers by put and call dealers to stimulate inquiries. These "specials" include some very good buys, but the fact that an option is advertised does not necessarily mean it is a bargain. Unfortunately, many of the most attractive special options will be unavailable on the advertised terms when a buyer calls, either because another caller got through first or because the dealer has changed the price.

Spread: For listed options: The purchase of one option and the sale of another option on the same stock. The investor setting up the spread hopes to profit from a change in the difference between the prices of the two options, or, perhaps, from the different tax treatment accorded the long and short option positions. In the conventional option market: A straddle in which the put side and the call side are written at different striking prices. Typically, the put striking price is below and the call striking price is above the market price of the stock at the time the option is written. The put and call dealer's margin between the option premium paid by the buyer and the premium paid to the writer is also called a spread. *See* CALL SPREAD, PUT SPREAD, BACK SPREAD, FRONT SPREAD, UNMARGINED SPREAD, BUTTERFLY SPREAD.

Straddle: A combination option consisting of one put and one call. Either option is exercisable or salable separately and the striking prices are usually identical.

Strap: A combination option consisting of two calls and one put.

Striking price: The price at which an option is exercisable. While the striking price is set at the time the option contract originates, it is subject to adjustment under certain circumstances. The striking price of a conventional or over-the-counter option is reduced by the value of any cash dividend, right, or warrant issued to holders of the optioned stock, and both the striking price and the number of shares under option are adjusted for stock dividends or splits. Listed options are adjusted for other distributions, but not for ordinary cash dividends.

Strip: A combination option consisting of two puts and one call.

Terms of option contract: The terms of an option contract are defined by the conventions of the market in which it is traded and the terms of the specific contract. A securities option is defined by (1) exercise or striking price; (2) expiration date; (3) security on which the option is written; (4) dividend adjustment, if any; (5) adjustment for splits and other capital changes; (6) quantity of the underlying security that makes up the unit of trading.

Type of option: The classification of an option as a put, a call, or a combination option.

Uncovered writer: A writer who does not own the underlying stock which is the subject of an option. *See* COVERED WRITER, NAKED OPTION WRITING.

Underlying stock: *See* OPTIONED STOCK.

Unmargined spread: A spread in which, for one of the following several reasons, the short option is margined as a "naked" option rather than as part of a spread: (1) the long option may expire before the short option; (2) the difference between the striking prices of the two options in a back spread may be so great that the margin rules for a "naked" option are more favorable than those for a back spread; and (3) one or both of the options may be unlisted.

Up and out put: This is a conventional-type put option that expires if the market price of the underlying stock rises above a predetermined expiration price. These options are written by a number of major brokerage firms and sold only to clients able to accept substantial risk.

Volume or size buyer: A buyer who wants to buy a large number of options on a single stock.

Volume or size writer: A writer who is willing to sell a large number of options on a single stock.

Warrant: An option to purchase securities at a given price and time, or at a series of prices and times outlined in the warrant agreement. A warrant differs from a call option in that it is ordinarily issued for a period in excess of 1 year and is usually issued by the corporation whose securities it represents the right to purchase. Warrants are issued alone or in connection with the sale of other securities, as part of a merger or recapitalization agreement and, occasionally, to facilitate divestiture of the securities of another corporation. Ordinarily, exercise of a warrant increases the number of shares of stock outstanding, whereas a call is an option on shares already outstanding.

Whipsaw: A sharp price movement quickly followed by a sharp reversal.

Work-out market: A market in which any quote an option dealer may furnish is subject to his ability to find the other side of the trade. Frequently, these markets are thin and the option dealer is not willing to commit his own capital to the option except at a prohibitive markup. Prices quoted by different dealers may vary greatly in a work-out market.

APPENDIX F
ANNOTATED BIBLIOGRAPHY

This listing is an attempt to catalog most of the important books and articles on options and related subjects which might be of interest to the reader who wishes to explore a particular topic in depth. With a few exceptions, articles originally published in academic journals are not listed separately if they are reprinted in one of the volumes of readings, such as those edited by Cootner and Lorie. Papers and books which the author found to be of minimal value are omitted. Aside from important journal articles which have not been reprinted in a form readily available to the average investor, the author has tried to list only material which the reader can obtain through a bookseller or local library. If a reader is interested in undertaking a comprehensive survey of option literature, most of the material not listed here is mentioned in one or more of the articles and books which are listed.

Alverson, Lyle: *How to Write Puts and Calls*, New York, Exposition Press, 1968.

   While he covers some of the same material as the Asens' book (see below), Alverson's book is much less comprehensive.

Asen, Robert, and R. Scott Asen: *How to Make Money Selling Stock Options*, West Nyack, N.Y., Parker Publishing Company, 1970.

   This book is written almost exclusively from the viewpoint of the option writer. While the text tends to drag at times, the explanations of complex topics are clear and comprehensive. Margin requirements are more complex today than when this book was written, but the Asens' explanation of the application of margin rules to basic conventional option transactions is unusually clear. An excellent feature of this book is the chapter on taxes, which goes well beyond the basic rules. Except for minor changes resulting from the IRS rulings on CBOE options, this tax material is both current and accurate.

Black, Fischer: "Fact and Fantasy in the Use of Options," *Financial Analysts Journal*, July–August 1975.

   This is an excellent analysis of the risk characteristics of various option and stock positions. In this article Black goes a long way toward shattering much of the conventional wisdom concerning the risks of option trading. Must reading for the serious investor.

Black, Fischer, and Myron Scholes: "The Pricing of Options and Corporate Liabilities," *The Journal of Political Economy*, May/June 1973, pp. 637–654.

   The basic article in which Black and Scholes derive their option valuation model. The article has some useful comments on alternate models as well.

Black, Fischer, and Myron Scholes: "The Valuation of Option Contracts and a Test of Market Efficiency," *The Journal of Finance*, May 1972, pp. 399–417.

   In this article Black and Scholes test their model against actual conventional option transactions. During the period studied, they concluded that options on highly volatile stocks tended to be underpriced while options on less volatile stocks tended to be overpriced. They found that transaction costs in the conventional option market largely eliminate any chance for consistently superior profitability.

Boness, A. James: "Elements of a Theory of Stock-Option Value," *The Journal of Political Economy*, April 1964, pp. 163–175.

A clear explanation of a general probability model. Somewhat technical.

Brealey, Richard A.: *An Introduction to Risk and Return from Common Stocks*, Cambridge, Mass., M.I.T. Press, 1969.

Brealey, Richard A.: *Security Prices in a Competitive Market*, Cambridge, Mass., M.I.T. Press, 1971.

These two books provide an excellent nontechnical introduction to the literature of portfolio theory and stock price behavior. The second book has an excellent review of various studies on option writing and buying results. Brealey concludes that transaction costs in the conventional option market are so high that in the long run only the put and call broker will make a profit. The bibliographies are excellent.

Buskirk, Richard H., and Benjamin R. Howe: *Preplanning a Profitable Call Writing Program*, Larchmont, N.Y., Investors Intelligence, 1970.

This book, devoted exclusively to option writing, falls between the Alverson and Asen books in both complexity and overall quality.

Chen, Andrew H. Y.: "A Model of Warrant Pricing in a Dynamic Market," *Journal of Finance*, December 1970, pp. 1041–1059.

One of the better probability-based option and warrant valuation models. Slightly easier reading than most, but still fairly technical.

Chicago Board Options Exchange: *Constitution and Rules*, Chicago, 1973.

This document is an invaluable and essential source of information on the rules for trading and holding listed option positions. The discussion of floor procedures should help the investor get better executions.

Cloonan, James B.: *Stock Options: The Application of Decision Theory to Basic and Advanced Strategies*, Chicago, Quantitative Decision Systems, Inc., 1973.

This book is a hodge-podge of explanatory material on basic option terminology and strategies and the author's ideas for what is, in essence, filter-rule trading of stocks and options. Cloonan proposes that the investor cover and uncover an option writing position as the stock price moves up and down. Any trader who feels that such an approach will give superior results should read Chapter 16 of Cootner's book. (See reference below.)

Cootner, Paul, ed.: *The Random Character of Stock Market Prices,* Cambridge, Mass., M.I.T. Press, 1964.

An excellent collection of academic journal articles and doctoral thesis extracts on the subject of the probability distribution of stock prices. Any serious student of options will find this book invaluable. An interesting feature of this book is that so much of the work on stock price fluctuations has been done in connection with the development of option pricing models. Unfortunately, most of the material is highly technical and an ability to deal with complex mathematical formulations is essential.

Cunnion, John D.: *How to Get Maximum Leverage from Puts and Calls,* Larchmont, N.Y., Business Reports, Inc., 1966.

This is one of the better basic books on conventional options.

Dadekian, Zaven A.: *The Strategy of Puts and Calls,* New York, Charles Scribner's Sons, 1968.

This introductory book on option writing is much less comprehensive than the Asens' book in its treatment of taxes, margin, and other technical topics. Dadekian does, however, stress the importance of stock price volatility as a factor in option pricing. His calculations of return on investment are seriously misleading, but the decision process he advocates is more rational than that suggested by most basic option books. Unfortunately, his techniques are not very helpful in analyzing listed options.

Fama, Eugene F.: "Efficient Capital Markets: A Review of Theory and Empirical Work," *The Journal of Finance,* May 1970, pp. 383–423.

An outstanding review of the literature on the efficient markets model and the random walk hypothesis.

Fama, Eugene F., and Marshall E. Blume: "Filter Rules and Stock-Market Trading," *Journal of Business,* January 1966, pp. 226–241.

An excellent discussion of filter rules and similar mechanical trading techniques. In spite of articles like this one, mechanical rules continue to attract attention. If one is ever tempted by seemingly good results from a mechanical technique, the reader should study this paper carefully.

Fama, Eugene F., and Merton H. Miller: *The Theory of Finance,* New York, Holt, Rinehart and Winston, 1972.

A standard textbook that covers not only portfolio and capital market theory but a number of topics of particular interest to advanced students of options. The bibliographic references at the end of each chapter will be particularly helpful to the reader wishing to pursue a specific topic in depth.

Filer, Herbert: *Understanding Put and Call Options,* New York, Popular Library, 1966.

This is the book many brokerage firms use to explain conventional put and call options to registered representatives and customers. Filer does an excellent job of explaining the conventional option market clearly and accurately. In addition to definitions of the basic terms in the option vocabulary, Filer provides brief illustrations of various strategies that can be employed using options and a summary of the income tax treatment of option transactions.

Giguère, Guynemer: "Warrants, A Mathematical Method of Evaluation," *The Analysts Journal,* November 1958, pp. 17–25.

This is one of the earliest attempts to develop a simple formula to relate the value of an option or warrant to the stock price.

Granger, Clive W. J., and Oskar Morgenstern: *Predictability of Stock Market Prices,* Lexington, Mass., D. C. Heath, 1970.

Probably the most comprehensive single book on the predictability of stock price behavior. Granger and Morgenstern review the major studies of stock price behavior and test the random walk hypothesis and various technical trading rules. Unfortunately, most of the book is highly technical.

Gross, Leroy: *The Stockbroker's Guide to Put and Call Option Strategies,* New York, New York Institute of Finance, 1974.

As the title implies, Gross focuses on ways the registered representative can keep clients happy. While his explanation of the mechanics of option trading on the CBOE is excellent, much of the trading advice Gross offers is of doubtful value.

Kassouf, Sheen T.: "An Econometric Model for Option Price with Implications for Investor's Expectations and Audacity," *Econometrica,* October 1969, pp. 685–694.

A good summary of Kassouf's doctoral thesis.

Kassouf, Sheen T.: *Evaluation of Convertible Securities,* New York, Analytical Publishers Co., 1969.

A slightly more technical version of the material available in Thorp and Kassouf's *Beat the Market.*

Kassouf, Sheen T.: *A Theory and an Econometric Model for Common Stock Purchase Warrants,* New York, Analytical Publishers Co., 1965.

A reprint of Kassouf's doctoral dissertation, this short book provides detailed background information on the construction of the Kassouf model for anyone wishing to apply the Kassouf approach to options.

Lefèvre, Edwin: *Reminiscences of a Stock Operator,* New York, Pocket Books, 1968.

This fictionalized biography of Jesse Livermore provides an excellent account of the activities of the "bucket shops" which provided investors with optionlike contracts prior to the passage of strict securities legislation.

Lorie, James, and Richard Brealey, eds.: *Modern Developments in Investment Management,* New York, Praeger Publishers, 1972.

While relatively few of the articles reprinted in this volume pertain directly to options, much of this material will help readers integrate their understanding of options with other aspects of investment and capital market theory. This volume is the only place the author has seen Shelton's original articles reprinted.

Mackay, Charles: *Extraordinary Popular Delusions and the Madness of Crowds*, New York, The Noonday Press, 1969.

This reprint of Mackay's classic provides an excellent description of the Dutch tulipomania.

Malkiel, Burton G., and Richard E. Quandt: *Strategies and Rational Decisions in the Securities Options Market*, Cambridge, Mass., M.I.T. Press, 1969.

Malkiel and Quandt's introductory chapter discusses the historical background of options and the organization of the modern option market (pre-CBOE). In addition, this chapter provides a theoretical framework for the rational evaluation of options. While this theoretical framework is far from comprehensive and is not in a form useful to the investor, it should help the reader appreciate the inadequacies of "back of an envelope" option evaluation techniques. Chapter 2 outlines and graphically illustrates the wide variety of strategies available to the option writer or buyer, and provides a quick summary of the tax treatment of each of these strategies. The remainder of the book is more technical and deals primarily with utility theory and the application of utility theory to option transactions.

Merton, Robert C.: "Theory of Rational Option Pricing," *The Bell Journal of Economics and Management Science*, Spring 1973, pp. 141–183.

A comprehensive review of option valuation formulations based on the stock price probability approach. The discussion is rather technical, but many nonmathematically oriented readers will find it possible to follow much of Merton's argument. Merton's bibliography is quite extensive.

Miller, Jarrott T.: *The Long and the Short of Hedging*, Chicago, Henry Regnery Company, 1973.

The virtue of this book is that it contains a fairly comprehensive discussion of the margin rules as they apply to certain arbitrage-type operations. Unfortunately, the discussion of margin rules does not extend to options.

Noddings, Thomas C.: *The Dow Jones-Irwin Guide to Convertible Securities*, Homewood, Ill., Dow Jones-Irwin, 1973.

Though it covers much of the same material as the Thorp-Kassouf and Prendergast books, this work has little that is unique to recommend it. Some of the material on evaluation of convertible securities is misleading.

Noddings, Thomas C., and Earl Zazove: *CBOE Call Options: Your Daily Guide to Portfolio Strategy*, Homewood, Ill., Dow Jones-Irwin, 1975.

Because this is a "how to do it" book, the question at issue is how well the Noddings-Zazove approach "does it." In contrast to most such books, this one focuses on option evaluation. Unfortunately, the graphic evaluation system these authors present is oversimplified and is based on what they assert is normal value rather than fair value. Based on an analysis of the curves they provide, it appears that they markedly overvalue out-of-the-money calls and undervalue in-the-money calls. Though actual market prices show some tendency to reflect this same pattern, the distortions in the Noddings-Zazove graphs are probably due to misuse of the unadjusted Kassouf equation, not to any empirical study of actual prices. Other important failings of the Noddings-Zazove approach are that the authors ignore the effect of interest rates completely, that they do not adequately adjust for dividends, and that they use an inappropriate measure of stock price volatility. The edition reviewed had outdated margin data and incorrect and incomplete commission information. The book's loose-leaf format allows for updates and corrections; but the price ($75 including quarterly updates for one year) seems high, even with this service.

Options Clearing Corporation: *Prospectus*, Chicago, 1975.

Essential reading.

Practicing Law Institute: *Option Trading*, Corporate Law and Practice, Course Handbook Series, no. 146, New York, 1974.

Contains reprints of many important regulatory documents. The general reader will find the study prepared for the Chicago Board of Trade by Robert R. Nathan Associates of greatest interest. This study examined the public policy aspects of option trading in preparation for the Board of Trade's application to start the CBOE.

Prendergast, S. L.: *Uncommon Profits Through Stock Purchase Warrants*, Homewood, Ill., Dow Jones-Irwin, 1973.

Prendergast is a cofounder of a leading warrant and option advisory service, and his understanding of the techniques of warrant and option hedging is excellent. The reader who has read and thoroughly mastered *Beat the Market* should proceed to the Prendergast book. The material covered is slightly more difficult, and the strategies discussed are occasionally more complex. The basic evaluation technique, however, is identical. Prendergast (and presumably his advisory service, C&P Research, Inc.) uses the Kassouf model for the evaluation of warrants.

Press, S. James: "A Compound Events Model for Security Prices," *The Journal of Business,* July 1967, pp. 317–335.

One of the better discussions of the probability distribution of stock market prices. This article plus those cited in Press's bibliography will tell the reader much about stock price probability distributions.

Reinach, Anthony: *The Nature of Puts and Calls*, New York, Bookmailer, 1961.

This is one of the better books focusing on the over-the-counter option market. Unfortunately, even the conventional option business has changed since 1961.

Rosen, Lawrence R.: *How to Trade Put and Call Options*, Homewood, Ill., Dow Jones-Irwin, 1974.

The material in this book would have made an excellent 40-page pamphlet for free distribution by a brokerage house. Unfortunately, the basic "pamphlet" is fattened with a variety of extraneous forms and newspaper clippings, apparently in an attempt to justify the $9.95 price tag. Save your money.

Samuelson, Paul A.: "Mathematics of Speculative Price," *SIAM Review*, January 1973.

An excellent, though rather technical, summary of the literature on option value and stock price fluctuations. The bibliography is unusually comprehensive.

Samuelson, Paul, and R. C. Merton: "A Complete Model of Warrant Pricing That Maximizes Utility," *Industrial Management Review*, Winter 1969, pp. 17–46.

This is one of the most comprehensive recent adaptations of the classic probability model. Unfortunately, the work of Black and

Scholes makes some of the features of this utility model unnecessary. The article is highly technical.

Sarnoff, Paul: *Puts and Calls: The Complete Guide,* New York, Hawthorne Books, Inc., 1968.

Sarnoff does a good job of explaining how the conventional put and call market operates. Specific examples illustrate his points and make the text quite readable. Unfortunately, Sarnoff's flair for examples does not extend to his discussion of margin requirements which is not particularly readable or complete. Sarnoff's discussion of taxes is misleading and should be omitted entirely. Apart from Appendix B and the article by Stoll cited below, Sarnoff's chapter on conversion techniques is one of the few generally available discussions of conversion.

Sharpe, William F.: "Risk, Market Sensitivity and Diversification," *Financial Analysts Journal,* January/February 1972, pp. 74–79.

A brief, clear explanation of the impossibility of diversifying away market risk without options.

Shelton, John P.: "The Relation of the Price of a Warrant to the Price of Its Associated Stock," *Financial Analysts Journal,* May/June, pp. 143–151 and July/August, pp. 88–99, 1967.

The original article describing the Shelton model. Not highly technical.

Stoll, Hans R.: "The Relationship between Put and Call Option Prices," *The Journal of Finance,* December 1969, pp. 801–824.

A slightly technical discussion of the economics of conversion.

Thorp, Edward O., and Sheen T. Kassouf: *Beat the Market, A Scientific Stock Market System,* New York, Random House, 1967.

Chapters 4 and 6 of *Beat the Market* provide one of the best discussions of the basic principles of hedging to be found anywhere. Chapter 8 discusses reverse hedging with warrants. The warrant hedge and the reverse warrant hedge are analogous to the option hedge and the reverse option hedge. Chapter 9 discusses the things that can go wrong in hedging. Chapter 10 extends the basic principles of warrant valuation to the evaluation of other convertible securities, principally convertible bonds. There are brief discussions of convertible preferred stocks and call options. Chapter 13 is one of the most interesting chapters in the book. It discusses the difficulty of persuading investors to engage in hedging activities. The excellent publicity generated by the Chicago Board Options Exchange and the weak markets of the past several years probably make hedging easier to sell to a skeptical public than it has ever been in the past. While there are several option and warrant evaluation techniques that give more useful results than the Kassouf econometric model, this book is a classic and should be read by any serious student of options and hedging.

U.S. Securities and Exchange Commission: *Report on Put and Call Options,* August 1961.

This document is relatively scarce and somewhat out of date, but even today it is the only comprehensive empirical study of the conventional option market. Copies may be obtained by writing directly to the SEC.

Wellemeyer, Marilyn, ed.: "The Values in Options," *Fortune,* November 1973, pp. 89–96.

An excellent description of the Black-Scholes model and some of the things investors are doing with it.

Zieg, Kermit C., Jr.: *The Profitability of Stock Options,* Larchmont, N.Y., Investor's Intelligence, 1970.

This book describes what is probably the most extensive study ever made of the profitability of conventional stock option transactions. Zieg concludes that option buyers, particularly straddle buyers, appear to have an edge over writers. Like all other examinations of option profitability, this one is highly dependent on the time period it covers. In the terminology I have used in the chapters on option evaluation, options were undervalued relative to the magnitude of stock price fluctuations during the period Zieg studied.

The following items were not available in time to be included in the alphabetical listing:

Ansbacher, Max G.: *The New Options Market,* New York, Walker and Company, 1975

This is a basic book describing most major option strategies, tax treatment of option transactions, and margin requirements. Ansbacher's style is quite readable, although he sometimes achieves clarity by oversimplifying. After examining his unequivocal arguments against the purchase of call options, one is left with the feeling that he does not fully understand the mechanism of stock price change and the determinants of option value.

Gallagher, Michael C.: "Option Trading Markets Offer Unique Tax Savings Opportunities for Investors," *The Journal of Taxation*, May 1975, pp. 258–260.

An excellent review of the basic option tax rules for individuals and institutions. The material on institutional taxation is particularly good.

McMillan, L. G.: *How to Make Money with Stock Options*, Hicksville, N.Y., Exposition Press, 1975.

The best features of this book are the author's discussion of CBOE trading and floor procedures and his suggestions for order entry. While much of the basic explanatory material is good, there are numerous factual errors. Many of the errors are due to changes in the rules for margining and exercising listed options. McMillan relies too heavily on some inaccurate rules of thumb in his evaluation of specific option contracts.

Mayo, Herbert B.: *Using the Leverage in Warrants and Calls to Build a Successful Investment Program*, Larchmont, N.Y., Investor's Intelligence, 1974.

While the approach is different, readers will find little material in this book that was not covered in Thorp and Kassouf's *Beat the Market* and Prendergast's *Uncommon Profits through Stock Purchase Warrants*. The section on listed call options is very brief; it stresses the similarity between options and warrants.

Miller, Jarrott T.: *Options Trading*, Chicago, Henry Regnery Company, 1975.

There is little material in this book that the reader cannot get from CBOE or brokerage house publications. Miller's trading advice and option selection approach are questionable. His stories about the use and misuse of options by Jay Gould, Jesse Livermore, Russell Sage, and their contemporaries are the best feature of the book.

Robert R. Nathan Associates: *Review of Initial Trading Experience at the Chicago Board Options Exchange*, December 1974.

This is the first comprehensive study of listed option trading activity. Unfortunately, several key questions were left unanswered. For example, the report concludes that option trading may slightly reduce the overall volatility of the underlying stock. Although they may accept this conclusion as generally valid, many observers believe that stocks with listed options are *more* volatile during the week or two preceding and following an expiration date. This hypothesis is so widely accepted that testing it would seem to be almost mandatory. A careful examination of the impact of option trading on the short interest in the underlying stock would also have been desirable. The report has an excellent appendix written by Myron Scholes.

Pihlblad, Leslie H.: *On Options*, New York, Pershing & Co., 1975.

This small pamphlet, written by the Chairman of the Board of the Options Clearing Corporation, is by far the best basic explanation of listed options yet published. Available from Pershing & Co., 120 Broadway, New York. Price $5.00.

INDEX